THE ETHICS OF AUTOBIOGRAPHY

Replacing the Subject in Modern Spain

THE ETHICS OF AUTOBIOGRAPHY

Replacing the Subject in Modern Spain

Angel G. Loureiro

VANDERBILT UNIVERSITY PRESS
Nashville

04 03 02 01 00   5 4 3 2 1

Publication of this book was supported by a subvention from the Program for Cultural Cooperation between Spain's Ministry of Education and Culture and United States Universities.

Library of Congress Cataloging-in-Publication Data

Loureiro, Angel G.
  The ethics of autobiography : replacing the subject in modern Spain / Angel G. Loureiro.— 1st ed.
      p. cm.
Includes bibliographical references and index.
  ISBN 0-8265-1349-2 (alk. paper) — ISBN 0-8265-1350-6 (pbk. : alk. paper)
  1. Spanish prose literature—20th century—History and criticism. 2. Spanish prose literature—19th century—History and criticism. 3. Autobiography.
4. Authors, Spanish—Biography—History and criticism 5. Authors, Exiled—Spain—Biography—History and criticism. 6. Biography as a literary form. 7. Self in literature. I. Title.
  PQ6137 .L68 1999
  868'.60809492—dc21   99-050475

Para Ilia

CONTENTS

ACKNOWLEDGMENTS

This book would not have been possible without the invaluable contributions of many friends. My deepest gratitude to Harold Boudreau, Jeanne Brownlow, Alice Clemente, and Christopher Maurer for their generous help, indefatigable support, and cherished friendship. Profound thanks to Antonio Carreño, Luis Fernández Cifuentes, and Gonzalo Sobejano for their unfailing support throughout the years. I owe a special debt to José María Rodríguez García, whose transatlantic messages offered much needed support in many a moment of doubt. I also wish to express my gratitude to Randolph Pope for our fruitful discussions about autobiography. Bill Adams of Vanderbilt University Press improved this book considerably, thanks to his meticulous editing and sound advice, for which I am most grateful.

Research for this book was possible thanks to a faculty research grant from the University of Massachusetts and to a travel grant from the Program for Cultural Cooperation between Spain's Ministry of Culture and the United States Universities. I wish to express my appreciation for their support.

PREFACE

I became interested in autobiography, for reasons that eluded me for a long time, more than ten years ago. Having decided to write a book on autobiography in modern Spain, I began to explore the numerous approaches to the genre that flourished through the eighties and early nineties. Soon, however, my enthusiasm gave way to considerable confusion and even anxiety and discouragement, on account of my dissatisfaction with the limitations I perceived in all approaches and my own glaring inability to produce a type of reading that could do justice to the complexities of the genre. Paul de Man's demolishing critique of the cognitive illusions of autobiography, and his ensuing radical questioning of the genre, appeared to me as an especially insurmountable objection.

De Man presented two challenges to a conception of autobiography as cognitive representation of the past. In "Autobiography as De-Facement" he argued that prosopopeia, the figure that gives "face" and voice to a dead or absent entity, is the fundamental figure at play in autobiography. However, de Man contended, tropes are always privative, and prosopopeia in particular simultaneously gives face to the past of the autobiographer and disfigures it: an autobiographer can have access only to a "shape" of the past that is determined not by the past itself but by the figure at work in shaping it. Furthermore, in the last chapter of *Allegories of Reading* de Man argued that in a paradigmatic work such as Rousseau's *Confessions* there is a conflict between two contrary types of rhetoric, a rhetoric of self-knowledge and a rhetoric of excuses. In other words, autobiographers do not simply attempt to represent the past but also do things with/in their personal writings, thus undermining the idea of autobiography as representation. Under the spell of de Man's pieces I remained dazed and despairing for a long time. Although I admired the analyses of autobiography, especially some authored by feminists scholars, that foregrounded the discourses put into play by autobiographers, such political/discursive approaches seemed to leave unexplained some important dimensions of the genre. I was thus at an impasse for a long time.

And then there was Levinas. The elation I felt when I began to get acquainted with his work is something I had never felt before in my life. In Emmanuel Levinas's conception of ethics I found an splendid formulation of issues that I had been struggling to articulate in connection with autobiography. And yet I found in Levinas much more than a way out of my autobiographical confusion, because he spelled out some ideas, intuitions, and feelings that had been with me forever, that had been a fundamental part of my upbringing and formed also the core of my most personal beliefs. Could it be that my childhood in a peasant village in Galicia, Spain, had a commonality of experiences with a shtetl in Galicia, Poland (or in Levinas's native Lithuania for that matter)? Whether it did or not, it was unquestionable that a strand of postmetaphysical thinking, Levinas's proposal that ethics constitutes the primary bearings of the subject, connected seamlessly with some of my defining childhood experiences and explained some of my most deeply rooted beliefs. More important, it offered a luminous rejoinder to rhetorical and discursive explorations of autobiography.

As I am finishing this manuscript we seem to be going through some type of ethical turn. Certainly the volume of recent publications on ethics seems to support that assertion. It is now the end of 1998, and in just the last few weeks three books by Levinas himself and three others on his work have been published; journals such as *Philosophy and Literature* and *PMLA* have recently devoted special issues to ethics; and a good number of books and articles on that same topic keep appearing as I write. Judging by what has happened to other recent critical trends, I doubt that this one is going to last for very long. Perhaps this attention to ethics is after all nothing more than the latest way to feed the frantic urge for theoretical novelty that seems to be the norm in the last few years; however, another, and arguably more weighty, reason for the ethical turn is the perceived exhaustion and shortcomings of politics as an overarching critical explanation. Viewed in this way, ethics would work as a corrective and a supplement to an inordinate emphasis on the explanatory power of the political. Politics permeates everything, and it would be foolish to deny its importance; but it would be even more foolish to pretend that politics explains everything.

When I was writing this book I was convinced that my enthrallment with Levinas was most untimely and went against the prevailing critical winds. The fact that we are now experiencing an undoubtedly brief and not universally accepted focus on the ethical does not change anything. And I am convinced that after a fleeting flare-up of interest, Levinas will return to the realm of the unfashionable and the inopportune. My "encounter" with Levinas, however, was as inevitable as it was fateful. It was not a choice at all, in the same way that one cannot choose one's parents or the place and time of one's birth. Levinas was imposed on me by my own life and beliefs, not by any consideration of fashion or prestige (or the lack of it). This is not to say that I agree with all he has written or that I consider ethics to be sufficient for an explanation of autobiography.

Stressing its dissimilarity to morality, Levinas defines ethics as the domain of the other. As such, he argues, ethics antecedes ontology and politics. Accordingly, for Levinas the self is not an autonomous, self-positing entity, but it originates as a response to, and thus as a responsibility toward, the other. This responsibility that initially constitutes the subject is the core of the ethical domain. By proposing that the other antecedes the subject, Levinas deposes the subject from its position of centrality; however, the beauty of his conception of ethics is that this displacement of the subject in no way entails a diminishment of its obligations or capabilities. As Levinas argues, although deposed, the subject is a singularity because nobody can respond for it. Nobody can take the place of another; nobody can take responsibility for/away from any of us. The subject is thus both decentered and unique. My book's subtitle, "Replacing the Subject," alludes to the ethical re-placement that I propose for both the subject *of* autobiography and the subject *in* autobiography.

Thus Levinasian ethics opened up for me the possibility of answering de Man's powerful objections to autobiography as failed cognitive enterprise (autobiography is *both* an attempt at cognitive self-reconstruction *and* a performative act, and those two operations are not contrary to each other), while simultaneously elucidating dimensions of personal writing that a discursive analysis left unexplained. In other words, as I try to show in the first chapter, the discursive/political, rhetorical, and ethical dimensions of the genre are inextricably linked. In my view the ethical manifests itself in autobiography in a variety of performative operations and forms of address that are inherent to the genre. I further propose that the subject's final constitution through political interpellation, or access to the symbolic, or whatever we choose to call it, grounds itself on the ethical but also displaces it. And yet the political never supersedes the ethical but enters into complex interplays with it.

I would like to insist on the fact that Levinasian ethics should in no way be confused with morality or with the customary use of the word *ethics*. As far as rhetoric is concerned, as I explain in the first chapter, I am dealing exclusively with the figures of prosopopeia and apostrophe. However, I do not use those figures strictly in their contemporary definitions; instead I go back to Quintilian's definitions, not for the sake of restoring the "original" meanings of those figures, but simply because they have a richness of signification in Quintilian that, although lost in contemporary usages, can nonetheless be very useful for an examination of autobiography. A word on the relationships between cognition, ethics and rhetoric also seems necessary. Since it gives "face" to an absence (the past of the autobiographer), prosopopeia is, in a way, de Man's terminology for what a different school of thought would call the discursive strategies of self-cognition displayed by autobiographers. Thus, when I talk about discursive strategies, I am talking about prosopopeia and thus about rhetoric, although I usually will not mention any of those terms. Any autobiographical statement is a response to an other that demands that one explain oneself. By displaying this responsibility, autobiography shows its ethical nature. But how does such an ethical dimension, such an inexcusable need to respond to the other, manifest itself in autobiography if not primarily as an explicit or implicit apostrophe? Therefore, when I speak of ethics, I am already speaking of apostrophic strategies, and thus again of rhetoric (apostrophe, I will argue, involves not two parties but three). Prosopopeia's primary, "forgotten" meaning has nothing to do with giving "face," but points instead to structures of address and response to the other that not only make it complementary to apostrophe, but also place prosopopeia, in this peculiar sense, in the terrain of the ethical.

In the Levinasian sense ethical responsibility has two basic meanings. Primarily it means that the subject originates as a response to the call of the other. While this can sound highly abstract and speculative at first sight, it reveals itself in a myriad of very concrete, common manifestations. Who does not live in a continuous, usually internal, running dialogue with others, in a perennial justification of the most minute deeds and words, in a back-and-forth dialogue, in a need to explain and clarify, to answer and object, that takes place even in the

minds of those living in the most absolute loneliness or the most iso-
lated conditions? Christianity had the sagacity to institutionalize and
deepen this unavoidable responsibility as confession, and it is not by
chance that the two most prominent examples of the autobiographical
canon bear the title of "confession." In a way all autobiographies are
confessions in that they render accounts to an other that, although
invisible, unacknowledged, or even negated, leaves its unquestionable
imprint in any autobiography. No other genre's thematics and strategies are so dependent on, and determined by, its addressees. In its second sense (tightly linked to the first), ethical responsibility implies
that one cannot remain unmoved before the plea of the other: compassion, solidarity, generosity, and sacrifice would be some of the manifestations of this inescapable need to respond to the other's suffering
(this dimension will be more prominent in the chapters on León and
Semprún). There is no humanity without this double responsibility,
without this ethical foundation that, as Levinas observes, does not
originate in any pragmatic covenant but, on the contrary, precedes any
social contract.

Put simply this book examines the interactions between the ethical
and the political in self-writing. More specifically it explores the complex interplays among political conditions, cognitive strategies, rhetorical procedures, and ethical manifestations in four of the most
fascinating autobiographies written in nineteenth- and twentieth-century Spain, those by Joseph Blanco White (1775–1841), María Teresa
León (1904–1988), Juan Goytisolo (1931–), and Jorge Semprún
(1923–). Those authors' lives are closely linked to, and were disrupted by, some of the most crucial events in Spain's tortuous road to
modernity and democracy. All four writers went to live in exile for
political reasons.

Each of the analytical chapters (except the one on Semprún) goes
through three stages. They all begin with a fairly descriptive section
whose aim is to offer some basic information to those readers not familiar with the authors or the texts discussed. Thus in the first pages of
each chapter I run the risk of belaboring what for some readers will be
obvious or already well known, but it is a risk I have decided to take.
At this first level I usually offer a paraphrase of the texts in question,
which begins to outline some of the self-cognitive strategies that are
examined in more depth in the following segment. The final section of
each chapter engages the varied manifestations of the ethical in each

text and their interplay with the cognitive strategies foregrounded in the previous stage of analysis.

The book concludes with a disquisition on the puzzling dearth of a more questioning autobiographical tradition in Spain. The dramatic vicissitudes of modern Spanish history must have forced many individuals to reassess their identities and should have motivated them to produce compelling personal writings. A considerable number of autobiographical works have been published in Spain in the last two centuries, yet only a small number of them veer from a safe memoiristic pattern. Models such as Rousseau's *Confessions* were readily available, but they were imitated only at the most superficial level. However, the scarcity of compelling personal writings in Spain cannot be attributed simply, as Ortega y Gasset and others have done, to some sort of Spanish "character" that is not inclined to confess.

It is pertinent at this point to explain how I selected the texts to be examined. I did not follow any specific criteria, other than my predilection for autobiographical texts that take risks in their examination of the self and its writing. Only after I had made the selection did I realize that the four writers I had chosen were voluntary or involuntary exiles. My selection of autobiographies of exiles was thus largely unconscious, but its results might have a bearing on an explanation of the weak tradition of autobiographical writing in Spain, the conclusion being that, by and large, only in exile have Spanish writers seemed inclined to probe the self. However, my selection of texts, and thus my conclusions about the connections between exile and autobiography, might be vitiated by another stunning discovery I made when the book was well in progress. I find the realization stunning because it now seems so obvious to me that I wonder why I did not come to it much earlier. Obviously my interest in Spanish autobiography, and my inclination for personal writings of Spanish exiles did come, without a doubt, from my own self-exilic condition.

In 1979 I left Spain with great relief—not simply because my brand-new degree in philosophy offered no future to speak of, nor because I found the political atmosphere, Left and Right, asphyxiating and intolerant. Perhaps it was just a case of wanderlust. I think, however, that I simply sensed that there had to be a place that could offer more than the limited possibilities my homeland could offer me. Offer what? Call it hope, or the chance to develop my capabilities or simply to waste them, but not for lack of opportunities. I was looking for a place where

I could begin to feel some sense of worth, that my life was not a waste: a sense of empowerment, whose denial to less privileged people in Spain had for me much more dramatic consequences than any lack of political freedom or basic democratic rights. Perhaps away from home I could make sense of the alienation I felt there. This leads me to confess another belated realization, another admission of stunning blindness: only recently I realized that my longtime indifference to the history of Spain was a result of my deep-seated belief that it had nothing to do with me.

I left Spain in 1979 and none too soon. Away from it I achieved the right to call it mine, to accept or reject it. Away from home I had access to dimensions of my self that I know would never have manifested themselves had I remained there. I am not implying that being away from Spain has facilitated a better or truer knowledge of myself, as Blanco White and Goytisolo seem to believe to be their case. Self-imposed exile has offered the joyous and jolting possibility of accessing, or perhaps fabricating, more complex spaces of subjectivity, even though the obscurities, as we all should know, will always, thankfully, remain.

Thus I was drawn to Spanish autobiography, and to autobiographies of exiles in particular, for obvious reasons. I never had any doubt that I wanted to write the book in English, but again the motives for such decision were unclear to me for a long while. Once I began to write I realized that the choice of language was inextricably linked with the topic of the inquiry. I do not think I could write the same book in Spanish despite the fact that it would be a much easier task to use my native language. I certainly would not say to Spanish interlocutors the things that I have written in this preface: I would be tongue-tied in Spanish. It is not so much a matter of the language itself, but of the strikingly different addressees each language offers. Even if no native speaker of English were to read this book, the situation would not change. Writing in English offers certain forms and themes of communication that I would be very reluctant to use were I to write the book in Spanish. A similar reason explains why only in exile could the authors examined in the book write their autobiographies the way that they did. With their deterritorialization they also parted with the encumbrances any homeland imposes on those who live in it. In the cases at hand, in exile they found addressees for their autobiographical "saying" who were more receptive but also much more rigorous. And autobiographers always take more risks when they reckon with an exacting and inexhaustible addressee. By writing in English, therefore, I find myself mimicking once again the subject under consideration, because if my interest in autobiographies of Spanish exiles originated in a shared condition with their authors, the decision to write the book in English was imposed on me by the laws of a genre that is deeply marked by its addressees. By writing a book on texts where I see myself reflected in many ways, I am not so much attempting to find clues or consolation as I am giving myself to an obscure, imprecise addressee whose unremitting demands cannot be refused. There is no self without an other who listens constantly, even in the midst of the deepest silence or the greatest solitude. There is no self without an other whose entreaties to speak can never go unheeded.

THE **ETHICS** OF **AUTOBIOGRAPHY**

Replacing the Subject in
Modern Spain

BEFORE REFERENCE
The Ethics of Autobiography

1

A momentous shift in contemporary theory of autobiography occurred with the replacement of a conception of autobiography as reproduction of a life with the idea of autobiography as a performative act, as the creation or re-creation of the self at the time of writing. This shift is already perceptible in George Gusdorf's pioneering article, where he writes that autobiography "effects a true creation of self by the self." As a result, Gusdorf continues, we have access to a "new and more profound sense of truth as an expression of inmost being."[1] The rejection of autobiographical truth as external and verifiable, and its replacement with a new and elusive concept of truth as internal and created, brings with it, however, a new set of problems, the first one being that as an act of self-creation autobiography is transformed into a rhetorical artifact. Gusdorf called for a critique that would view autobiographical narratives "as the symbol, as it were, or the parable of a consciousness in quest of its own truth" (44), and other rhetorical terms such as *metaphor, allegory,* and *symbol* unavoidably creep up in connection with issues of reference and cognition in critical assessments of autobiography as an act of self-creation.[2] One of the most elaborate considerations of autobiography in this vein is the one offered by Paul John Eakin, who argues that autobiography is a type of self-invention at the moment of writing that parallels the individual's access to identity at the moment of acquisition of language: "the writing of autobiography," argues Eakin, "emerges as a symbolic analogue of the initial coming together of the individual and language that marks the origin of self-awareness."[3] However, like all critics who see autobiographical cognition as a rhetorical operation, Eakin leaves unexplained the unfathomable meaning of that "symbolic analogue."

Another response to the predicaments brought about by the displacement of emphasis to the present of writing consists in appealing to the sanctioning powers of the reader, a role stressed by Elizabeth

Bruss, who argues that autobiography works as an illocutionary act, and by Philippe Lejeune, whose theories on self-writing have many concomitances with those of Bruss.[4] Although in a substantially different way than in Bruss's and Lejeune's theories, the reader also performs a fundamental role in feminist theories, as is well known. The numerous and important contributions made through feminist approaches to autobiography center mainly on the discursive construction of identity and referentiality and on issues of reading and reception.[5] In *A Poetics of Women's Autobiography*, one of the strongest efforts to delineate a distinctive female autobiography, Sidonie Smith foregrounds the familiar shift to the present of writing, arguing that autobiography is an act of interpretation of a past that is not fixed and thus is never fully recoverable. Undoubtedly one of the great contributions of feminist theory to an understanding of autobiography resides in its relentless exploration of the varied and conflictive discourses that come into play in the construction of female subjectivities, an issue that Smith stresses insistently.[6] Effecting the usual conjunction of autobiographical cognition with rhetoricity, Sidonie Smith equates the "cultural scripts of signification" used as patterns for women's self-representation with "interpretative figures (tropes, myths, metaphors, to suggest alternative phrasings)" (47). In the end, like Eakin and all proponents of a rhetorics of autobiographical reference, Smith is impelled to characterize autobiographical cognition as a fiction, asserting, for instance, that female scripts are "fictions that bind her."[7] Obviously one could argue whether *fiction,* even in the special sense in which those critics use the term, is the most appropriate term to characterize autobiographical cognition. But instead of engaging in a terminological discussion, it is much more productive to call attention to another issue that, although inextricably linked to the peculiar nature of autobiographical fictional constructs, has received scant attention in contemporary theory at large (and not only in autobiographical criticism). It is widely customary today to talk about discursive constructions, but little has been written about the *attachments* of the subjects to the discourses that shape them as subjects. Such dearth of attention is at odds with the radical importance of the issue.

The historization of subjectivity (promoted by Foucault more than anyone else) has led to exhaustive, detailed analysis of the discourses that participate in the construction of subjectivities in different cultures and historical moments. However, those analyses rarely go beyond a more or less elaborate unveiling and description of discourses, rarely entering in a consideration of how and why subjects embrace the discourses that constitute them. An examination of the nature of attachments to discourses could start by asking some basic questions: what makes the subject receptive to certain discourses and not others? As a matter of fact, what in the constitution of the subject impels it to embrace any discourse at all? And what is the nature of such attachments? How can those attachments be broken, so that the subject can effect changes by discarding some discourses and embracing others? To call such attachments fierce, and even irrational, is warranted by the tremendous difficulties implied in effecting profound changes in personal outlooks and forms of life. The challenges involved in fighting racism, sexism, or discrimination of any sort, for instance, clearly indicate that it is not simply a matter of the cogency or the commonsense of certain ideas, nor simply a matter of rational discussion and exchange. Even more, changes that seem to take place at a conscious level are frequently belied by unconscious tendencies that betray them and attest to the ingrained nature of certain beliefs and attitudes. If deep-seated assumptions, ideas, biases, and prejudices are so difficult to dislodge, it is due to the nature of the attachment of the subject to those ideas. Actually it is not even appropriate to speak of the subject and the discourses it subscribes to as different entities, such is the nature of their intimate connection, since the subject is unthinkable outside of its discursive construction. If autobiographical self-understanding is a fiction, it is certainly a most powerful one. Only an ethical consideration of the subject can begin to explain the subject's passionate attachments to certain discourses.[8]

Another important issue brought to the fore by feminist theorizations of autobiography is the relational nature of identity. Usually following the well-known theories of Nancy Chodorow and Sheila Rowbothan, critics such as Susan Stanford Friedman and others set out to prove that such relationality is a feature unique to female identities, an idea that has not gone uncontested.[9] In her exploration of female Latin American *testimonios,* Doris Sommer proposes a conception of the relationality of autobiographical identity that is both more suggestive and less problematic than the one just mentioned. Sommer shows that the identity of the speaker in the *testimonios* is an intricate representational affair involving tensions between the speaker's metonymic relation with the community and the metaphoric relation with her own identity. But more relevant than this new twist on the rhetorics of self-knowledge is her foregrounding in testimonial literature of the speaker's interpellation, which seeks the political complicity of a hearer/reader who is nonetheless kept at an unbridgeable distance from the speaker due to the impossibility of a total identification between them.[10] Although this interpellative connection has a fundamental role in *testimonios,* it is not necessarily limited to them. On the contrary, the issue of address in autobiography is of paramount importance for an understanding of the complexities of self-writing. In this regard, special attention needs to be given to the role that the figure of apostrophe plays not only in the formal configuration of autobiography but also in the determination of its thematics.

From this brief consideration of some significant contributions to the study of autobiography, one can conclude that an interpretation of autobiography has to address the tight links between issues involving referentiality, rhetoricity, discursivity, and address. Neither a true expression of the writing subject nor a mere textual construction deprived of any referential power, autobiography might be best apprehended not as re-production of a life but as an act that is at once discursive, intertextual, rhetorical, ethical, and political.[11] In the end it could be said that all autobiographies are actually heterographies, pervaded as they are by different guises and disguises of the other. In order to go beyond a complacent, unexacting conception of referentiality and to escape the apparent quagmire of a disfiguring rhetoricity, autobiographical studies should counterbalance their concern with cognition with an attention to the multiple ramifications of an ethical conception of the self as an entity that originates as a response to the other's address.

From Epistemology to Ethics

The relentless contemporary scrutiny of the subject has led to its deposition or decenterment from a privileged location. Self-identity, consciousness, intention, autonomy, property, personality, absolute origin, substance, or substratum—the traditional characteristics of the subject, which Derrida summarizes in the subject's presence to itself—have undergone a relentless scrutiny that has brought about a resituation or reformulation of the subject.[12] As a consequence the subject is now viewed by many not as an immutable substance but as a changeable entity, not as an origin but as an effect. The deconstruction of the subject in no way implies a denial of its existence, as Derrida clarifies with little patience for those who are too quick to make such pronouncement; it simply means that the subject has to be rethought, and therefore even the word *subject* has to be replaced by a new term that might reflect more adequately its resituation. In this way Derrida prefers to talk of "effects of subjectivity," and not of the "subject."[13] With a similar vocabulary Foucault speaks about processes of subjectivation; the Greeks, according to Foucault, invented the subject "but only as a derivative or the product of a 'subjectivation,'" as a fold, "*a relation which force has with itself, a power to affect itself, an affect of self on self.*"[14] This conception of the subject as effect or "passion" has enormous consequences since, as is already intimated in Foucault's Spinozian language of "affectus," it involves a momentous displacement of the subject's terrain from epistemology to ethics, a shift that characterizes the thought of the final Foucault. Before being obscured by the injunction to know oneself, argues Foucault, the Greek subject consisted in a self-formation through technologies of the self, a cultivation of the self through modes of behavior, practices and procedures that constituted what Foucault called an aesthetics of existence, which he understands as the creation of ways of existing, of the relation one ought to have with oneself: in other words a self-constitution as ethical subject through what Foucault calls the care of the self.[15] This ethical redefinition of the subject carries a decisive repercussion for a reconsideration of autobiography since, according to Foucault, the literature of the self has to be understood in the context of the Greek practices of the self, and therefore it is incorrect to consider autobiography a modern European product. Far from beginning in modern Europe, alleges Foucault, the literature of the self was "one of the first uses of writing."[16] With the shift from orality to writing, already in the Hellenistic period, "[t]aking care of oneself became linked to constant writing activity. The self is something to write about, a theme or object (subject) of writing activity. That is not a modern trait born of the Reformation or of romanticism; it is one of the most ancient Western traditions."[17]

Viewing the subject not as a substance capable of self-presence, but as an effect of processes of subjectivation, promotes a displacement of the problematics of autobiography from epistemological concerns to ethical cares. And yet the work of the self on itself, the care of the self proposed by Foucault, offers a limited understanding of the subject in ethical terms. We need a more sweeping understanding of ethics than Foucault's, without, on the other hand, neglecting his contribution. Another French thinker, Levinas, who has placed ethics as the center-piece of his conception of the subject, offers a formulation that, while having some points of contact with Foucault's, differs from it in many respects and, above all, is much more comprehensive.[18] Like Foucault, Deleuze, and many others, Levinas distinguishes between morality, which dictates civic rules and governs "the social interchanges between citizens in a society," and ethics, which cannot legislate or prescribe rules of conduct.[19] For Levinas, the "I" is not an originating, auton-omous self-consciousness; on the contrary it begins in an ethical rela-tionship with the other. Ethics is for Levinas *prima philosophia;* he also calls it metaphysics, in opposition and prior to ontology—the thinking of being, which he qualifies as the main Western philosophical tradi-tion—as well as to epistemology, which apprehends the other through the objectification proper to knowledge: "Ethics is not a moment of being; it is otherwise and better than being, the very possibility of the beyond."[20] In opposition to ontological formulations of the self, for Levinas the constitution of the self begins in its relation with the other, in an "ethical intrigue prior to knowledge."[21] The other is absolute exteriority, and the originary, constituting relationship of the self with the other takes place in the nonspace of this unbridgeable, radical sep-aration. The relationship between self and other admits neither repre-sentation nor apprehension through any type of knowledge, be it ontological or epistemological, since "[t]here is in knowledge, in the final account, an impossibility of escaping the self."[22] Since the non-phenomenal other cannot be apprehended as an object, it follows that I cannot speak of the other as a theme or an object; on the contrary, as Derrida states, "I *must* only speak to the other," and for this reason speech raises up in the vocative, not in the attributive.[23] In sum, "[t]he disproportion between the Other and the self is precisely moral con-sciousness. Moral consciousness is not an experience of values, but an access to external being: external being is, *par excellence,* the Other. Moral consciousness is thus not a modality of psychological con-sciousness, but its condition."[24]

The self does not begin as a self-positing consciousness, but as an address from the other that calls for a response: the self constitutes itself only as a response to, and responsibility for, the other that cannot be an attribute of selfhood because this ethical responsibility precedes the self. The inescapable need to answer that call inaugurates a responsibility for the other that constitutes the fundamental structure of subjectivity. Thus the self does not begin with a self-positing but, on the contrary, with a deposition and a subjection that strip the subject "of every identical quiddity," while at the same time endowing it with an irreplaceable uniqueness, with a singularity that comes from the undeclinable obligation to respond to "an absolutely heteronomous call." It follows then that the subject is first of all an exposure to the call of the other in an asymmetrical—because nonreciprocal—relationship that befalls prior to time, in an immemorial duration that is irrecuperable in the synchronic gatherings of history or memory. The ensuing, inexcusable responsibility of the self for the other manifests itself as what Levinas calls "a saying prior to anything said." The saying would be the structure of address, so to speak, that antecedes and institutes the possibility of any possible linguistic exchange, of any thematic conversation between the self and the other, of anything at all being said. The saying, therefore, is "an 'otherwise than being' which turns into a 'for the other.'" The identity of the self comes to it from the outside, and in self-consciousness, therefore, there is not self-presence but a disjunction of identity, a diachrony that is beyond the recuperative powers of memory.[25] Levinas summarizes with magnificent if dense precision this de-position or defection of identity: "The subjectivity of a subject is vulnerability, exposure to affection, sensibility, a passivity more passive still than any passivity, an irrecuperable time, an unassemblable diachrony of patience, an exposedness always to be exposed the more, an exposure to expressing, and thus to saying, thus to giving."[26]

Levinas warns repeatedly against assuming that the responsibility for the other proceeds from biological brotherhood, from a preexistent freedom of the subject, or from an inaugural contract with the other; on the contrary, that responsibility for the other comes before the legal and obliges beyond it; furthermore it is neither a property of the subject nor a natural tendency.[27] On the other hand, Levinas is also careful to point that the predisposition to being affected that constitutes the self as an "irreplaceable hostage" of the other or as a subjection,[28] far from being concealed in an inaccessible domain, manifests itself daily "in the empirical event of obligation to another, as the impossibility of indifference . . . before the misfortunes and faults of a neighbour, the unexceptionable responsibility for him."[29] Close attention needs to be given to that "exposure to affection" constitutive of the subject as defection, defect, and deficit, but in order fully to do so, one will have to respond to Levinas, to think perhaps otherwise than he does.[30]

From Ethics to Politics

For all their urgency and rigor, Levinas's formulations represent only a first step in any consideration of the subject's heteronomous relationship with the other, since they revolve primarily only around the ethical, originary dimension of selfhood. The call that grounds the self on an infinite difference with, and deference to, the other explains the unequal duality of self and other in the ethical origination of the subject. Levinas distinguishes between ethics and morals, but he concentrates his speculations almost exclusively on the former and hardly addresses in his works the possible affinities and discords, contacts and disconnections, between foundational ethics and the realm of everyday, sociopolitical morality. Derrida argues that Levinas's thought indulges in a nonviolent language "which would do without the verb *to be,* that is, without predication," a language of pure adoration of the other, which uproots the subject from history: "It is evident that to separate the original possibility of speech—as non-violence and gift—from the violence necessary in historical actuality is to prop up thought by means of transhistoricity. Which Levinas does explicitly. . . . For Levinas, the origin of meaning is nonhistory, is 'beyond history.'"[31] A number of questions, therefore, are left unanswered in the self's dislodgement from history provoked by Levinas's ethical proposition. Although the other's priority opens up the possibility of time and the infinite responsibility of the self toward the other, history will not be possible without the self's violence to the other, whether in the form of the subject's forgetfulness of its ethical debt in the everyday moral sphere or in its objectification of the other in the attempt to know or dominate it.

While Levinas denounces the violence proper to knowledge and ontology, he rarely addresses the forces involved in the personal and the political, the social and the historic. But for all his reluctance to broach the political, Levinas insinuates a possible direction of research when he suggests that "because there are more than two people in the world, we invariably pass from the ethical perspective of alterity to the ontological perspective of totality. . . . As soon as there are three, the ethical relationship with the other becomes political and enters into the totalizing discourse of ontology. We can never completely escape from the language of ontology and politics."[32] The call of the nonsimultaneous, untotalizable other originates language as vocative and selfhood as responsibility for the other, but the appearance of the "third" takes us beyond the ethical and into the political, which, in contrast with the responsibility and debt that characterize the former, could be characterized as violence to the other, the need for justice, the prevalence of reason, the illusion of (self)knowledge, the objectification of the world and the other in ontology and epistemology, and the oblivion of responsibility: in sum, all human philosophical, epistemological, and political beliefs and fabrications. The third party is another neighbor, but it is also other than the other, argues Levinas. This will produce two simultaneous, interrelated consequences: the apparition of self-consciousness and the need for justice. Consciousness and self-consciousness cannot appear in the relation between the self and the other because the responsibility for the other antecedes all questions; however, the apparition of a third party that will be an other for the other dislocates the one-on-one relationship between the self and the other and converts the self into an other for the other, i.e., into a self-consciousness; and thus "I am approached as an other by the others, that is, 'for myself.'"[33] Also, being another neighbor, the third party will make justice necessary or, in other words, will effect the need for the contemporaneous comparison between the others, the need to adjudicate between them. Levinas adamantly denies that this justice has anything to do with the legality that regulates societies: "That would be a justification of the State delivered over to its own necessities."[34] It should be clear therefore that justice for Levinas is merely the need to compare and evaluate—to judge—provoked by the apparition of the third party. In this way the neighbor becomes visible, and we have synchronicity, coexistence, assembling, logos, essence, representation, cognition, thematization, and therefore intentionality and the intellect, consciousness, and self-consciousness.[35]

Freud seems to offer a brief glimpse of a similar ethical foundation of the subject. In Borch-Jacobsen's opinion in both Freud and Lacan one finds a narcissistic conception of subjectivity that sees the subject as the subject of a (self)representation that preexists and underlies all representations, including the representation of the subject's own desire, its splittings, and the unconscious itself. However, he argues that in *Totem and Taboo* Freud insinuates an intriguing "*ethical* 'beyond'

of the subject" in the myth that tells of the primordial crime committed by the members of the tribe who try to appropriate the narcissistic
autonomy of the other (the Father) by murdering and devouring it.
This violent incorporation fails, however, because after the murder of
their father the sons are left with nothing but guilt, since death, "the
absolute Master" "sets the absolute limit on identification." Although
this failed assimilation prevents the foundation of the subject as
complete self-presence, it results nevertheless in its constitution as
guilt/debt to the other. This myth narrates an alternative ethical foundation of the subject—promptly discarded by Freud—that appears to
go one step further than Levinas's conception because, by reaching
beyond the subject's pure reverence for the other in the domain of the
ethical prepolitical, it moves into, and tries to account for, the social
realm of violence and guilt. With this fleeting incursion into a possible
ethical grounding of the subject, Freud deposes the subject from the
narcissistic self-determination that in modern times has its beginning
in Descartes's positing of the subject as an autorepresenting cogito and
reaches its culminating point in Husserl's egology, centered around
intentional subjectivity.[36]

Like Levinas, many influential contemporary thinkers posit a two-
step configuration of the subject in which a preliminary self-reflection
creates a fundamental configuration for the subsequent effects of
sociopolitical forces. A case in point is Lacan's foundation of the subject on an initial duality that is later transformed into a triadic structure. As manifested in the mirror stage, Lacan's imaginary recalls
Levinas's primary alterity of the self, and Lacan's psychoanalytic symbolic, sustained by the Oedipal triangle, resembles the Levinasian triad
that underlies the social and moral realms. Those similarities, however, should not mask the fundamental differences between Levinas and
thinkers of Hegelian lineage such as Sartre and Lacan, for whom the
foundational alterity of the subject leads to an emphasis on fictionality, misrecognition, lack, shame, and deceit in their constructions of
identity, while Levinas, positing a similar originary alterity of the self,
stresses notions of deference, debt, and responsibility toward the
other.[37] While Lacan's ego of the imaginary is later followed by the self
of the symbolic, Deleuze and Guattari postulate a primary subject of
enunciation that is then doubled up by a subject of the statement; and
Foucault in his turn theorizes the constitution of the subject as a folding of the outside, which later on is subjected to the domain of

sociopolitical energies. In contrast with those thinkers, Levinas's disquisitions about the self revolve almost exclusively around the first stage, which he sees as the site of the ethical. In clear contrast with Lacan, Levinas insists on the affective character of the primordial encounter between the self and the other, while, as Mikkel Borch-Jacobsen shows convincingly, in his formulation of the mirror stage Lacan purposely eschews an evident affective identification of the ego in favor of its specular objectification because only by doing so could he theorize an otherwise unrepresentable "affection."[38] That specular objectification betrays the visual nature of Lacanian—and, in general, Western—thought, while, as Martin Jay demonstrates, Levinas, proceeding from a Jewish tradition that mistrusts visual representation, bases his stance toward the world in the senses of hearing and touching.[39] Lacan, then, postulates an imaginary stage that gives the ego a constitutive fictionality that will later facilitate the settlement of the symbolic; but his freezing the other's originary affect on the ego into a specular object and his lopsided insistence on lack and mistrust in his explanation of the symbolic make it impossible for him to offer a satisfactory formulation of certain aspects of the human world, such as moral consciousness, friendship, sacrifice, generosity, and responsibility. However, Levinas's explanation of the originary alterity of the self makes sense of those positive manifestations, while at the same time positing a space of freedom and thus leaving room for the occurrence of the objectification of the other, evil, and deceit. At any rate the basic assumption, shared by some of the most distinguished contemporary thinkers, of the need for a preliminary self-affection that sets the stage for a sociopolitical imprint offers grounds for a productive analysis of autobiographical writing that, instead of overtly or covertly viewing it as a cognitive operation, explores instead the manifestations in self-writing of the ethical as originary premise of the self, while at the same time paying attention to the complex relationship between the ethical and the sociopolitical.

As with Levinas's, Foucault's work is marked by a profound distrust of what passes as truthful self-knowledge and by a deep preoccupation for the ethical dimension of the subject, although their answers differ markedly. We have seen that the final Foucault gives preeminence to an ethical consideration of the subject. Levinas and Foucault are joined in their ethical concerns by Deleuze and Guattari, who link their philosophy with an old if somewhat overlooked tradition. Labeling their thinking, as well as Foucault's, "Cosmos philosophy," Deleuze and Guattari assert that their thinking proceeds in terms of forces and intensities, in contrast with the emphasis on form, matter, essence, and properties that characterizes the traditional cogitations of philosophy. Following a Spinozian line, for Deleuze and Guattari an ethology or true ethics studies what a body can do, "what its affects are," what intensities, whether coming from the inside or the outside, affect an individual, "augmenting or diminishing its power to act."[40] Consequently for them consciousness is not self-presence but self-affection, not a property but a passion, a result of affects whose power comes not from the interiority of the individual but from the exteriority of social forces. Adhering to "the hatred of interiority, the externality of forces and relations" privileged by Lucretius, Hume, Spinoza, Nietzsche, and other of their lineage,[41] what is important for Deleuze and Guattari is not interiority or the determination of the individual in terms of forms and substances, but the exteriority of forces. This thinking is obviously very close to Foucault's understanding of power as "a way of acting upon an acting subject or acting subjects by virtue of their acting or being capable of action," a definition that is especially enlightening for its emphasis on affection and resistance.[42] Power is not a one-way street going from the source of power to a passive subject; on the contrary, there is no power without the ability to react, without the obstinacy and sedition of the subject, without the possibility to respond and react to the injunctions of power, and, Foucault argues, without the one over whom power is exercised being "recognized and maintained to the very end as a person who acts."[43] With a similar emphasis on affection and resistance, Deleuze and Guattari contend that the individual is conformed by the power to be affected by, and to react to, what they call "collective assemblages of enunciation" (a concept very similar to what Foucault calls "discourses"), from where all enunciation necessarily comes: "There is no individual enunciation. There is not even a subject of enunciation;" rather, all enunciation is social, all discourse is indirect.[44] The collective assemblages of enunciation, as organizations of power, constitute therefore points or processes of subjectification, and for Deleuze and Guattari several important consequences follow from here. In the first place, for them the subject is a multiplicity in a state of constant transformation; it is not a being, but a becoming that results from the affects it encounters at the point of subjectification in the collective assemblage where it is produced as an effectuation of affects. Second, dichotomies such as authentic self and alienated self (or, at a more general level, science and ideology) are false, idealistic choices. In this way there are no true social relations and no true self, only collective assemblages that are constantly changing, as are also the subjects created through them. The dream of finding, or liberating, a true self is just one more collective statement that affects individuals, a way in which they are branded by the affecting power of that idea. Finally, speaking of Foucault, Deleuze argues that since all discourse is indirect, speaking for oneself, speaking in one's own name is "not of course a matter of everyone finding their moment of truth in memoirs or psychoanalysis; it's not just a matter of speaking in the first person. But of identifying the impersonal physical and mental forces you confront and fight as soon as you try to do something. . . . Being itself is in this sense political."[45]

Autobiographers necessarily write through the mediation of scientific, philosophical, psychological, historical, political, sexual, moral, religious, linguistic, and literary discourses, to name just a few, in which they believe or which have currency in their time, as well as in the context of practices and institutions that allow them to speak.[46] It could be affirmed that those ingrained credences/currencies constitute the real unconscious, which therefore would be located not in the dark dungeons of interiority but, on the contrary, in the great (social) outdoors. Their not being visible helps disguise those discourses as the most personal and passionate of possessions, adding a further belief, a new truth, to the writer's presumed properties. But it should also be clear that no single discourse can be privileged in the unveiling of the multiplicities that conjoin to form the subject nor should any of the discourses be deemed fictional. There is no alienated self in the idealistic sense that presumes the possibility of a final liberation or a reencounter, delivery, or discovery of one's true self, although, by the same token, the self is always alienated, but only in the sense of being always other, with this primordial alterity in no way entailing a promise of self-presence. As Deleuze says, referring to Foucault, history "doesn't fix our identity, but disperses it into our essential otherness."[47] By dreaming of finding a true self in autobiography, some critics blind themselves to the other, to the absolute alterity of the self. Still, what is a flaw in an interpreter of autobiography is by no means a fiction at the hands of an autobiographer. It has been quite common for autobiographers to envision their lives both as a process of liberation from false or forcefully imposed self-images and as a (re)encounter with what they believe to be their true identities, but our skepticism concerning this model of life as a journey in search of one's truth does not imply that this pattern is a fiction for the writer, since its truth does not reside in its intrinsic verity but in its conforming value, in its capacity to produce a self-understanding perceived by the writer to be accurate. And that is the only truth we can expect from autobiography: the writer's belief in his or her truth, but not truth as adequation to past experience. In other words, discourses are not floating fictions that writers or critics can discard at will. Discourses become beliefs and desires, impress themselves upon flesh and mind, produce corporeal and incorporeal transformations on account of our passional constitution. The subject can neither transcend discourses nor is it the helpless victim of smothering ideology; and, importantly, while discourses are not disposable disguises, the discursive can never contain the Real, for it will always exceed all attempts to represent it. In other words, and this is a crucial characteristic of self-writing, autobiographical representation will always bear the marks of the disruptions produced by a Real that refuses to be contained.

While for Levinas ethics is "prima philosophia" and thus antecedes ontology, for Deleuze and Guattari "politics precedes being."[48] And if Levinas pays attention fundamentally to the relation between self and other that antecedes justice and politics, Deleuze and Guattari, professing like Levinas adherence to an ethology, focus relentlessly on the political. Therefore one has to focus on the affecting power that the collective assemblages of enunciation (the sociopolitical) have over the self; but conversely one will also have to extricate from the manifestations of the political subject the traces left by the primary form of affection that brand the self as responsibility for the other. In other words, one will have to complement Levinas's emphasis on the ethical prepolitical with the conforming power of the social discourses; but by the same token unless one accepts a reduction of the subject to a passive result of political forces, the last resort is to go back again to Levinas in order to rescue from the "said" the primary ethical gesture of the "saying" that underlines language as code and sociopolitical discourse. The subject is neither purely political nor purely ethical, but for the political to be able to affect and conform the subject, there has to be a preceding predisposition to being affected: not a substance, but only a structure of affection, the underlying initial mark of the other on the self.

Consequently, although if can be said with Deleuze and Guattari that the collective assemblages of enunciation speak for a self that does not have a proper voice, it has to be affirmed as well that the self could not be a mouthpiece for those assemblages unless it had a previous order to speak, to respond to the other, as manifested through what Levinas calls the saying. In this respect the Levinasian distinction between the said and the saying proves considerably enlightening. Stating that the saying "is to respond to another," Levinas argues that when the responsibility for the other—the pure signification of saying—falls into being, ethics gives way to ontology and the preontological saying becomes language as a code. Truth and error have meaning only in this order of being and essences, of intentionality and consciousness, and although the thematization of the saying is absolutely necessary for a world and a social self to appear, Levinas indicates that the said has to be reduced to the saying if one wants to show "the signification proper to the saying on the hither side of the thematization of the said," the ethical antecedent of ontology, the core of responsibility for the other that precedes objectification and the synchronicity of memory and knowledge. Levinas cautions against believing that this reduction to the saying involves the replacement of one ontology with another, the passage from a world of appearances to a more real world, because truth and error do not pertain to saying. He equates the saying with "the power to say," whose signifyingness, forgotten in ontology but preceding it, is not "in the service of being," since its significations are forgotten in ontology and precede it.[49] While the said is "an act commencing in a conquering and voluntary ego," in the saying the subject declines its sovereignty,[50] exposes itself to the other before anything is said and prior to any experience,[51] signifies to the other with a signification different from that borne by language. In sum, "[s]aying is communication, to be sure, but as a condition for all communication, as exposure. Communication is not reducible to the phenomenon of truth."[52] However, the saying will always leave a trace on the themes articulated through the said, thus making it hesitate between an order of entities and truth and an always already order of alterity, difference, debt, and responsibility: what is thought is limited to the parameters of "essence and reminiscence (that is, to synchronic time and representation),"[53] and truth will always bear the mark of a response to alterity that as such escapes the order of being and truth. Truth is always traversed by debt/guilt.

The Rhetoric of Autobiography

The displacement, promoted by some critics and referred to at the beginning, from an understanding of autobiography purported as reproduction of a life to autobiography as an act of self-creation at the moment of writing bears consideration. Autobiographies try to portray with words a past experience, but that representation can be accomplished only through the mediation of established discourses or assemblages of enunciation that make an autobiography intelligible. It would be erroneous to measure that reproduction from the point of view of truth as correspondence, since such representation is always going to be aleatory and provisional and will always fall short of its presumed goal of faithfully representing the past. Or to put it in another way, at the level of the said, identity is not merely expressed or designated in autobiography, it does not exist prior to its textual verbalization. But this does not imply that identity is merely linguistic or textual; it indicates only that, as manifested in an autobiographical text, identity is created or constructed at the moment of writing, resorting to a number of collectively shared discourses.

There is another, concomitant, level of manifestation of identity in autobiography that is tied to the moment of writing considered not as said but as saying. This second aspect of the verbal in autobiography takes identity as a gesture that refounds the ethical dimension that antecedes and originates the subject as a response to the call of the other. At this level language functions as vocative and not as predicative, evincing a fundamental structure of address—of saying—that underlies all autobiographical linguistic acts at the level of the said. In autobiography the role of this structure of address goes well beyond functioning as a mere frame for the autobiographical discourse, and an examination of its complex structure will show the constitutional role that language as vocative and the subject as response to the other play in the textual proclamation of identity. An exploration of this issue leads to the role of rhetoric in autobiography and, in particular, to the framing and foundational function of apostrophe. At this level autobiography goes beyond its restorative pretensions to embark instead upon an interaction with the world that orients the writing of the self toward the future.[54]

A consideration of autobiography as ethical/political/discursive phenomenon can clarify the conundrum of referentiality and its nagging sequels—especially the rhetorical and performative dimensions of autobiography—that haunt all considerations of it as a representation-al genre. Paul de Man, who, more than anyone else, has implacably dismantled many naive assumptions about autobiography, wonders, rhetorically, concerning its presumed mimesis: "does the referent determine the figure [mimesis], or is it the other way round: is the illusion of reference not a correlation of the structure of the figure, that is to say no longer clearly and simply a referent at all but something more akin to a fiction which then, however, in its own turn, acquires a degree of referential productivity?"[55] De Man's probing question hits the mark, but his answer misses the point, for the simple reason that much more is at stake in autobiography than the tropological, specular structure of (self)knowledge. In the same way that he chastises those who, like Lejeune, are eager to move from speculation to resolution, from epistemological to legal authority, de Man can be blamed for stopping his inquiry at the moment of pure negativity afforded by his unveiling of tropological structures behind all (self)understanding and for refusing to go beyond a consideration of the presumedly cognitive aspects of autobiography. While one cannot ignore his perceptive debunking of mimesis as a figure that supposedly, and naturally, emanates from, and copies, reality—being instead an artifact that surreptitiously produces and (mis)represents reference—his charge that autobiographical reference is simply a fiction needs clarification. Thus de Man's pertinent question, far from being a dead end, calls for a rejoinder and for a new, different inquiry. Moving beyond a mere denunciation of mimesis as akin to fiction we must also move beyond the domain of cognition and ask how mimesis produces referentiality while at the same time it tries to perform a disappearance act, to turn invisible and give autobiographies the appearance of a natural, transparent adequation between life and language.[56]

It is necessary to distinguish a triple temporal dimension of autobiographical mimesis, depending on whether mimesis is connected with the past, the present, or the future. As commonly used, mimesis would reproduce the past of the writer. De Man is right when he criticizes this cognitive misuse of mimesis, and he is also correct when he argues that mimesis produces, and not merely reproduces, reference. By pointing to the referential productivity of mimesis, de Man exposes the temporal connection of mimesis with the present (of writing) and not simply with the narrated past. Unable to overcome the specular structure of linguistic self-understanding, autobiography's restoration of the past is undermined by the workings of rhetoric at the moment of writing, since, according to de Man, "[l]anguage, as trope, is always privative," because when it gives "figure" to reality, it simultaneously disfigures it. This affirmation is followed by a widely quoted, lapidary condemnation: "As soon as we understand the rhetorical function of prosopopeia as positing voice or face by means of language, we also understand that what we are deprived of is not life but the shape and the sense of a world accessible only in the privative way of understanding. Death is a displaced name for a linguistic predicament, and the restoration of mortality by autobiography (the prosopopeia of the voice and the name) deprives and disfigures to the precise extent that it restores. Autobiography veils a defacement of the mind of which it is itself the cause."[57] As the figure that gives voice and face to the absent or the dead, prosopopeia is for de Man the dominant trope of autobiography. And by showing that prosopopeia simultaneously figures and disfigures the past of the autobiographical self; by bringing attention, in short, to the inescapable and depriving rhetoricity that underlies and undermines the very possibility of autobiography, de Man undoes its cognitive pretensions.[58]

De Man's apparent abolition of autobiography's restorative dreams seems fitting in an essay devoted to epitaphs, but there is more than meets the eye both in his premise as well as in his conclusion. His obliteration of autobiography is indisputable only if we persevere in claiming reproductive rights for the genre, if we insist on considering autobiography fundamentally as a cognitive operation. While it is true that many critics cannot renounce viewing autobiography as primarily epistemological, they are matched in their obstinacy by de Man's refusal to move beyond the impediments faced by cognition, which, on the other hand, are not limited to rhetoric's privative undertaking. Actually, what de Man perceives as limitations constitute in fact autobiography's conditions of possibility. "Real" mimesis would be unbearable, since it would eliminate the distinction between language and reality and would produce the collapse of all temporal distinctions. Instead of remaining puzzled before the spectacle of the specular, as de Man does, one should examine the productive workings of mimesis not as re-presentation but *as a desire and belief in representation* that, as such, is not a re-creation but a discursive creation of reality. This allows us to go beyond a consideration of autobiography as restoration of life and into an inquiry concerning prosopopeia—and its mimetic production—not as a distorting rhetorical figure but as an effect of discursive practices that produce a sense of autobiographical reality. The strength of prosopopeia lies not in its presumed restorational powers but, on the contrary, on its being referentially productive, because what the set of discourses and practices involved in mimesis produce is not a fiction—a falsity or an illusion, as de Man would have it— but a constructed sense of reality that will be shared but also necessarily contested and contradicted. "Mimicry is a very bad concept, since it relays on binary logic to describe phenomena of an entirely different nature," write Deleuze and Guattari, who, rejecting the conception of the book as image of the world propose, instead, exploring the mutual interaction between them.[59] In this context it is indispensable to remember Laclau and Mouffe's insistence on "the *material* character of every discursive structure," a principle that makes possible the overcoming of the dichotomy between a presumed objective, material reality existing outside discourse and discourse considered as "the pure expression of thought."[60] Viewed as a set of discursive practices, autobiographical mimesis should no longer be considered as an attempt to restore an objective past or as a purely rhetorical structure. There is no objective reality outside discourse; on the contrary, discursive practices construct reality; and, as forms of relationship between entities (as Laclau and Mouffe define them), rhetorical figures perform a fundamental role in that constitution of reality. If the text always resists a mimetic reading, it is due not to a suspension between figurality and referentiality, as de Man argues, but to the fact that mimesis is discursive and, as such, is always insufficient and contestable.[61] This does not mean that there is nothing outside of discourses. It that were the case, discourses would be either totally arbitrary or, even worse, stifling necessities. In order for them to be constitutive forces, discourses need what Laclau and Mouffe call a "field of discursivity," a surplus of meaning that prevents any discourse from attaining a final, totalitarian suture of reality (111). Similarly, autobiographical mimesis can function as a productive figure because there is a past life that language can refer to, can point to, but not reproduce or saturate, since life will always exceed any discourse that tries to encompass it. Put differently, although there is life outside discourse, it has no meaning outside autobiographical constructions. *Life has no meaning;* autobiographical texts do. Or, better still, autobiographies provide life with a form and a semblance of sense, construct a meaning through the indispensable mediation of always

inadequate, refutable discourses. In the same way that Lacan's symbolic would not make any sense were it not for the existence of an
unreachable Real, autobiographical mimesis—as productive figure—
could not even be thought without that recalcitrant referent constituted by a life.

A life can only be told, then, through collective discourses, otherwise neither life nor personal writing would have any meaning. And
yet every life is singular, unrepeatable, unique, and therefore ultimately unrepresentable. This singularity brings the ethical to bear upon the
discursive in autobiography. As discursive performance, autobiography
moves within a thematic domain that must be unoriginal if it wants to
be meaningful; but, as saying, autobiography is an ethical act, and for
this reason the subject constituted *through* the discourses that integrate
the autobiographical text is also constituted *in* the autobiographical act
as a response and a legacy to the other. While the discourses that com-
pose an autobiography can be questioned and, with enough temporal
perspective, ultimately show their conventional nature, the ethical
structure of address inherent to autobiography as saying guarantees
that autobiography is never a fiction, no matter how distorted the narrative can be or how wrong or naive the writer's assumptions are about
the nature of language and the restorative efficacy of the autobiographical enterprise. At any rate the writer's illusion about referentially should not become the critic's delusion. The past cannot be
reproduced by means of language, but the constitutive alterity of the
subject requires that it respond to the other, and in autobiographical
writing that response cannot be measured in terms of truth or mimetic restoration because as ethical gesture it remains outside the domain
of thematics and epistemology.

Autobiography is then ultimately a performative act and not a cognitive operation. A central obsession in De Man's work is precisely the
discord of contrary rhetorics in texts that purportedly foreground an
epistemological dimension. De Man brings attention to the disruption
caused in Rousseau's *Confessions* by the contrary presence of parts
dominated by a cognitive rhetoric and other parts that are not referential but work instead like speech acts (excuses in the case of the
Confessions). This interference or lack of convergence between a cognitive rhetoric and a performative one produces a "systematic undoing
. . . of understanding" that, according to De Man, "threatens the autobiographical subject not as the loss of something that once was present

and that it once possessed, but as a radical estrangement between the meaning and the performance of any text."[62] The dispossessive, disfiguring role of prosopopeia and the disruption of autobiography's epistemological illusion by its performative dimension are complementary dangers that share a concern about cognition, for both deflate the naive delusion that clings to the idea that autobiographies are primarily cognitive texts. But the conflict between the referential and the performative can be formulated only if one maintains a restrictive understanding of autobiography as fundamentally referential. Thus, in a way that is inherent to de Man's deconstruction, he is unable to leave the same terrain that he disrupts; and, again typically, he is content with stopping his deconstructive undoing at a moment of perplexity and pure negativity.[63] It suffices to shift the discussion from epistemological concerns to discursive determinations to escape the pitfalls of rhetoric; similarly a complementary displacement from a consideration of autobiography as a cognitive text to a conception that sees it fundamentally as an ethical response to the other renders moot de Man's conjecture about the disjunction between the cognitive and performative dimensions of autobiography since the epistemological concerns would now be subsumed under the ethical cares. On the other hand, one can no longer understand the autobiographical act as an epistemological operation, as a creation at the moment of writing of a self which is truer than the lived self, because that would entail a return to the dispossessed terrain of the cognitive and its privative rhetorical operations. This leads to a theoretical conclusion that will constitute the central assumption in the critical examination of the personal writings discussed in this book: autobiographical mimesis is necessarily and inextricably discursive, rhetorical, and ethical. As such, it is limited but also limiting: it is limited because it cannot conceivably reproduce a life; it is limiting because a life can be meaningfully apprehended only through the mediation of discourses whose restorative powers are always exceeded by a past that must be unsuturable and undecidable if there is to be any freedom and any history.

If a rightful comprehension of the constitutional role of prosopopeia deprives autobiography of its long-lasting epistemological illusions, a further consideration of this figure discloses new venues for the ethical understanding of self-writing. Two aspects in particular warrant attention: a return to the classical definition of prosopopeia, which stresses aspects that appear as secondary in the prevalent characterization of that figure in modern times, and an examination of its close ties with apostrophe, a figure that plays a fundamental structural role in autobiography. Quintilian calls prosopopeia "fictio personae" (9.2.29)—generally translated as "impersonation" or "personification"—and his definition consists of two clearly differentiated parts, the primary one operating as follows: "By this means we display the inner thoughts of our adversaries as though they were talking with themselves . . . ; or without sacrifice of credibility we may introduce conversations between ourselves and others, or of others among themselves, and put words of advice, reproach, complaint, praise or pity into the mouths of appropriate persons."[64] These features of prosopopeia, gathered in classical rhetoric under the rubric of "sermocinatio" or "ethopoeia,"[65] receive scant attention in modern definitions of prosopopeia, such as Hugh Blair's or Fontanier's, and are equally absent from contemporary formulations and uses of that figure, such as de Man's and Riffaterre's. Quintilian continues his characterization of prosopopeia with a secondary understanding of that figure: "Nay, we are even allowed in this form of speech to bring down the gods from heaven and raise the dead, while cities also and peoples find a voice" (9.2.31). While "ethopoeia" is reserved for the imitation or figuration of the speech of natural (or real, or live) people,[66] according to its second acceptation prosopopeia gives face or voice to irrational things—to dead, fantastic, imaginary, or absent people or to collectivities (fatherland, city, etc.) or even abstract entities (Justice, etc.).[67] Contemporary interpreters of prosopopeia such as de Man concentrate, and pounce, on the restorative powers of that figure, on its hypothetical power to give face and voice to an absent entity, leaving aside the dialogical dimension given preeminence in Quintilian's primary definition of that figure; in that way those critics emphasize the cognitive aspects of the figure at the expense of its ethicopolitical dimension. However, in its primordial sense prosopopeia does not attempt the phantasmatic re-presentation of an absence but dramatizes instead the relational dimension of the self, its conflictive dialogical structure. This power to represent the adversarial and other-directed makeup of consciousness is what makes prosopopeia such an apt figure for autobiography, provided that one understands that type of writing as an ethical, other-directed discursive enterprise and not as an impossible, and unavoidably disfiguring, epistemological restoration. It is worth noting that most of Quintilian's examples, even those taken from literary sources, always refer back to a more or less clearly defined judicial setting, a facet that maintains its pertinence in an ethical examination of autobiography. As representation of the voice(s) of alterity, prosopopeia is both the perfect emblem and the best tool for the writing of autobiography.

In the judicial setting (and the autobiographical act very often, perhaps always, mimics that site), prosopopeia appears quite frequently, usually by necessity, in the company of another rhetorical figure, apostrophe, that plays a prominent role in the ethicodiscursive workings of autobiography. As defined by Quintilian, who deals with it immediately following his treatment of prosopopeia, thus acknowledging their proximity and frequent joint use, apostrophe "consists in the diversion of our address from the judge,"[68] directing the speech instead to another addressee, whose attitude can range from friendly to unsympathetic. Structurally, then, judiciary apostrophe involves three poles, the speaker occupying one of them, while the other two correspond to different potential interlocutors. A similar structural triad is present in autobiography, one corollary of this suggestion being that apostrophe complements and dramatizes the work of prosopopeia. While the latter enables a dialogical presentation of the self, frequently that exposition does not foreground explicitly the ethical structure of address and the social triad of justice that shape the self. In autobiographical writings apostrophe dramatizes prosopopeia's workings in two ways: at the ethical level by foregrounding very explicitly prosopopeia's dialogical dimension, by bringing into the open the self's alterity, its fundamental makeup as response to, and responsibility for, the other; and at the sociopolitical level by unequivocally displaying the triangular configuration of the adjudication of truth/justice, exhibiting in this way that autobiographical truth is not a matter of correspondence with the past, but an issue pertaining to the present and the future that as such will always remain unsettled since the prevalence of those temporal dimensions imposes, and demonstrates, that autobiographical truth is played out over a terrain of undecidability. And far from undermining the autobiographical enterprise, such undecidability defines and sustains it.[69]

Even in an extreme case such as St. Augustine's *Confessions,* it is not enough that the other (in this case no less than God) whom Augustine addresses knows: despite God's knowledge of every detail of his life, Augustine still has to tell, has to respond for himself in telling, and this responsibility makes autobiography exceed the mere cognitive re-presentation and displays again its ethical composition.[70] Not a life's details, but the autobiographer "saying" them, constitutes the fundamental aspect of autobiography, provided that one understands that such "saying" is both a response and a legacy to the other.[71] It is in this regard that besides dramatizing prosopopeia, apostrophe indispensably complements it by disclosing that while as said autobiography deals primarily with the past, as saying it is not simply concerned with the present but also looks toward the future. Derrida talks about the "testamentary structure" of any text in general, and of autobiography in particular: "The ear of the other says me to me and constitutes the *autos* of my autobiography. When, much later, the other will have perceived with a keen-enough ear what I will have addressed or destined to him or her, then my signature will have taken place."[72] By signing an autobiographical text, an author performs a very complex operation which appears, and in most case pretends, to be cognitive but that in reality is an ethicopolitical gesture that entails a double responsibility: in the first place, by signing, the self is responding for itself before the other; and in the second not only the signature responds to the other's injunction to speak, but that same logic of alterity implies that the signed text is also a legacy to an other that not simply receives it but has to cosign it and thus take responsibility for it. Autobiography comes from the other and is for the other.[73]

The other-addressed, future-directed quality of autobiography shows not only in the saying, but also obviously in the said as a discursive borrowing (in order to bequeath, the self has first to borrow) that makes the self intelligible to itself and also understandable— readable—to the others. But above all it often manifests itself through the presence of textual addressees, always present in autobiography, either implicitly or, in many occasions, even explicitly. It is in this foregrounding of addressees that apostrophe shows its defining role in autobiography. Already St. Augustine devotes considerable space in his *Confessions* to the respective importance of the two main addressees of his life's narrative, God and the readers, as well as to the relationship between them. To the implicit question of why he confesses to God when he knows everything, St. Augustine explicitly adds: "Why, then, does it matter to me whether men should hear what I have to confess . . . ?"[74] Not surprisingly, also in Rousseau's *Confessions* the addressees perform an indispensable structural role. Despite Rousseau's protestations to the contrary, his *Confessions* was conceived as an apology since it was written primarily as an answer to his enemies.[75] Obsessed with schemes, treason, and deceit ("the ceiling under which I live has eyes, the walls that encircle me have ears, surrounded by spies and malevolent and vigilant watchers, anxious and distraught I hastily throw on to the paper some interrupted words which I barely have time to reread"),[76] Rousseau not only writes his life as an answer to the others, but he also passes the responsibility of its interpretation to the reader. He acknowledges that he does not attempt to tell the truth of his life but only to present facts without worrying about omissions or mistakes, his goal being not to offer the external story of his life but to present the history of his soul (*Confessions* 234) so that it becomes transparent to the reader, who is ultimately responsible for the interpretation of his autobiography: "It is up to him to assemble these elements and to define the being made up of them; the result ought to be his work, and if he is deceived then, all the error will be of his making."[77]

The failure of the *Confessions* as apologetic text exacerbated Rousseau's fears, and this in turn led him to write a new autobiographical work that in his opinion would display perfect objectivity. With this goal in mind, he structured *Rousseau Judge of Jean-Jacques* as a three-poled dialogue between a Frenchman (an emblem for his enemies), Rousseau (an impartial double), and Jean-Jacques (who represents the intimate, authentic Rousseau). Motivated by "the readers' incredible blindness" to discern the purpose of his *Confessions,* Rousseau feels the need "to say how, if I were someone else, I would view a man such as myself."[78] In view of the other's injustice, of its blindness and delirious judgement that "freely disfigures and defames" (6), Rousseau feels obliged to take its place, to attempt to become other than himself in order to enunciate the truth about himself. Rousseau's narrative stratagem results in the dramatization of apostrophe's judicial setting. In the *Confessions,* Rousseau invokes the supposedly impartial readers as the ultimate judges of his narrative's truth, but in reality he aims to convince his enemies: already there is the triad of the apostrophic configuration, since Rousseau is addressing directly the reader/judge, but indirectly his enemies: the path to autobiographical truth proceeds by indirection. When the reception of *Confessions* brings home the realization that the readers are not the honest judges he thought they were, Rousseau creates a new autobiographical response, *Rousseau Judge of Jean-Jacques,* which he structures, now explicitly, around a new triangle (Jean-Jacques, Rousseau, the French). This work dramatizes openly the apostrophic roles involved in the *Confessions,* since the direct and supposedly honest addressee of the latter now becomes the character Rousseau, while the figure of his enemies, implicit addressee of the *Confessions,* is now personified manifestly in "the French." Widely considered as the first and paradigmatic manifestations of modern autobiography, Rousseau's texts display in an ostensible manner the triangulation proposed in this examination of autobiography as the fundamental structure of self-writing. The fact that Rousseau utilizes the apostrophic triad with the avowed purpose of reaching an ultimate, inner truth should not divert one from the truly fundamental parameters involved in his ploy. Rousseau is aware, albeit perhaps only indirectly, that his dogged pursuit of the truth will never come to an end, and consequently he resorts once again to the final assurance of God's honest judgement (*Rousseau Judge of Jean-Jacques* 7). Rousseau thematizes his plea in terms of truth and deception, but in this process he reveals the unequivocal and inescapable ethical dimensions of autobiography since any self-reflection involves a duplication of the self that unavoidably passes through the other, and consequently the search for inner truth becomes an endless exercise in indirection.[79] And in both Rousseau's and Augustine's confessions, God's role, as objective and nonduplicitous other, is to bring closure to the infinite play of truth provoked jointly by the inescapable undecidability of autobiographical reference and by the necessary invocation of the other implicit in the signature of any autobiographical self-reflection. For Augustine and Rousseau, God acts as a supplement that would stop the autobiographical (ethical) machine. Ultimately, however, and despite the fact that the recourse to a just, all-knowing God should make any autobiographical narrative totally uncalled for, both Augustine and Rousseau still feel compelled to write their lives, which suggests that the other-directed ethical saying of truth, and not epistemological truth itself, constitutes the authentic concern and vocation of autobiography.[80]

Both the apostrophic triad and the preeminence of autobiography's ethical import are in evidence in "Circumfession," Derrida's autobiographical text. A play with the meanings of circumcision and confession, Derrida's title encloses also the circumvention through the others involved in autobiographical apostrophe. The apostrophic circumvention is evident in the following quotation, in which Derrida triangulates his narrating self with the reader and with his dying, partially amnesiac mother: "the admission I owe the reader, in truth that I owe my mother herself for the reader will have understood that I am writing *for* my mother, perhaps even for a dead woman," although, he elaborates, "if I were here writing for my mother, it would be for a living mother who does not recognize her son, and I am periphrasing here for whomever no longer recognizes me." And the ethical fundamentation of self-writing as responsibility, which Derrida seems to reduce to the search for pardon, is also explicitly foregrounded: ". . . the *essential* truth of avowal having . . . nothing to do with truth, but consisting . . . in asked-for pardon, in a request rather, asked of religion as of literature, *before* the one and the other which have a right only to this time, for pardoning, pardon, for nothing."[81] The tripolar configuration of apostrophe can be very clearly delimited in the forensic scene but in the case of autobiography the situation can be much more complicated since there are multiple and constantly changing combinations, many figures that can occupy the addressees' positions. In some Spanish autobiographies (Blanco White's in particular) the "author" writes the text as a letter addressed to a friend but destined in reality for a number of third parties; in some other cases the narrating self addresses primarily its former self and only indirectly speaks to the reader (the structure in Goytisolo's writings). The possibilities are numerous, but at any rate they all evince the imperative ethical mediation of the other in any form of self-reflection.

In sum, this analysis of Spanish autobiography will focus on the ethical, discursive, and figural dimensions of self-constitution in writing, as well as on their interrelationships. In each case examined herein, multiple, heterogeneous, and oftentimes conflictive discourses emplot autobiographers' lives, discourses that, although contingent, weave lives that in no way are to be seen as fictions, falsities, or fabrications.[82] It is in this regard that one can fully evaluate the significance of the ethical for the discursive configuration of the subject. As already evidenced, many contemporary thinkers (Foucault, Deleuze and Guattari, Lacan, Levinas) theorize the constitution of the subject positing an initial phase of self-affection that works as a matrix for the second stage (sociopolitical, collective, symbolic) of the subject's composition. The discourses that structure the subject in that second phase could not operate were it not for the affective disposition previously created, and it is here that one finds Levinas's formulations much more convincing

than those of the other thinkers mentioned above. While Foucault and
Deleuze and Guattari are not altogether clear when formulating the
connections between the two phases and while Lacan eschews the
affective in favor of an specular identification, Levinas foregrounds the
affective imprint of the other in the constitution of the self as debt and
responsibility. Although the subject is not initiated, as Lacan specu-
lates, as a fiction that would constrain its life toward a phantasmatics,
its primary alterity converts it nevertheless into an incompletion that
needs, indeed must, respond to the other. In this way the grounds are
set for the self to hear the commanding voice of the collective or the
sociopolitical order and to attach itself passionately to them to the point
of viewing them as the subject's own nature or substance, while at the
same time the very makeup of power, as Foucault argues, endows the
self with the freedom to heed not, resist, or disobey those impositions.
One further advantage of Levinas's formulation is his (and Derrida's)
insistence on how the constitutional alterity of the deposed subject converts it into a singularity, since nobody can take its place and respond
for it. In this way the subject can be simultaneously a construction and
a unique singularity. However, this double constitution of the subject
precludes to see it as a fiction, to argue that because it is a construction
the subject's true identity resides somewhere else, or to assume the subject is free to change subject positions at will. The current, unexamined
credence in a will and/or a reason with seemingly no bounds has to be
tempered with Deleuze and Guattari's view of the will and reason as just
forces among many others and with Laclau's observation that power
simultaneously makes freedom possible and limits it: "the condition of
possibility of something is also its condition of impossibility. . . . a totally free society—from which power would have been eliminated—and
one which would be entirely unfree are equivalent concepts."[83]

The autobiographical subject, then, can disclose itself only through
communal discourses that are historical but also coercive, and so the
subject necessarily believes that those discourses offer an accurate representation of its past. Criticism of autobiography should only examine that belief in truth—and not truth as correspondence or as hidden
elsewhere—its concomitant desire for (self)knowledge, and the implications of that belief and such desire. In this regard there are three
interrelated aspects in autobiography that counteract the subject's cognitive illusion: the inability of any set of discourses to contain fully or
saturate the life being told, the irruptions and interruptions of what

one could call chaos or trauma, and the emergence of the ethical in the form of address to the other. In the same way that history and the subject would not be possible without a leeway or disarrangement within their otherwise unavoidable structural determinations—a leeway that allows for the possibility of change, agency, and a certain amount of self-determination—a life could not be written without the constriction of communal discourses and without simultaneously the freedom occasioned by the inadequacy of discourses to represent fully an always already never fully representable past. This discursive limitation results not only from the temporal deferment between a life's past and the time of writing, but also from the imperative need for memory to be imperfect. As the Borgian character "Funes el memorioso" proves, an impeccable memory endowed with the ability of total recall would be just another form of madness.

The impossibility to attain a discursive saturation of the past can be discerned in the various ways in which autobiography's narrative tissue appears disrupted: fragmentation, narrative hesitations, multiple and potentially conflictive explanations and perspectives, fissures in the teleological design, ruptures that prevent the narrative from attaining a coherent closure, etc. In general those disruptions occur when the autobiographer strives to represent the irruption of chance, crisis, traumas, epiphanies of self-consciousness, an immersion in darkness, an unexpected confrontation with death, an exposure to (self)destruction, a shaken sense of selfhood, or simply perhaps when the self endeavors to explain the right to be: in other words all the reasons that make certain autobiographies more compelling than others. In some cases what a writer believed to be an accurate representation of an state or an experience is actually reducible to the narrativization of a figure that for the writer passes as true self-knowledge. Most often, but not always, this happens with psychological formulations that become outmoded with time: consequently obsolete psychology betrays the rhetorical structure of beliefs, but this in no way involves a new devaluation of rhetoric, but just the opposite, a revalorization of its inescapable role in structuring our modes of thinking. At any rate the presence in autobiography of heterogeneous and conflicting discourses, as well as its narrative disruptions, evinces an intrinsic instability in autobiography that, already implicit and perceivable in its classical manifestations, is frequently foregrounded by many contemporary autobiographers in the form of metafictional self-reflection and is often thematized through aleatory forms of emplotment (*Roland Barthes by Roland Barthes* is a case in point in this regard). In the extreme this authorial irony can become parody or pastiche. The recalcitrance of the referent makes autobiography into an approximate representation from the point of view of cognition, but far from eradicating the genre, such recalcitrance reveals that, more than a restoration, autobiography is a singular act of self-creation as response, responsibility, and promise (of truth). As such that act is dialogical, addressed to the other, and therefore intrinsically contestable and always incomplete. One could say, therefore, that autobiography's performative rhetoric does not undermine—as de Man argues—but actually supersedes autobiography's cognitive pretensions, since if autobiography always fails as cognitive enterprise, it is bailed out by its consideration as a performative, other-directed, ethical act: although autobiography will never achieve a representation of truth, it will nevertheless always present the self's will to know.

In his memoir *A Sort of Life,* Graham Greene writes that his motive to record the past is "a desire to reduce a chaos of experience to some sort of order."[84] But can chaos be conquered? As previously noted, Levinas explains the need for the other and the ethical as a way to exorcise what he calls the *il y a* and Blanchot denominates *disaster,* which, explains Levinas, "signifies neither death nor an accident, but as a piece of being which would be detached from its fixity of being, from its reference to a star, from all cosmological existence, a *dis-aster . . .* [a] maddening, obsessive situation" from which there is no escape.[85] As ethical endeavor, as response and legacy to the other, autobiography could ultimately be a struggle to make sense of a dislocation, the always provisional conjuration of the disaster, an attempt to hush the rumblings of the *il y a.*

BLANCO WHITE
Decolonizing the Affects

2

On a first approximation, the idea of the Enlightenment could serve as a provisional, basic structure for Blanco White's autobiographical writings. As Kant characterizes it, the Enlightenment is the coming of age of human beings: they dare at last to use their understanding without the tutelage of others. Kant suggests that the motto of the Enlightenment should be the Horatian "Sapere aude," which he interprets as "Have the courage to use your own reason." He argues that the established powers strive to maintain a state of subjugation, and he believes that freedom is the only requirement for the arrival of the Enlightenment. Commenting on Kant's text, Foucault states with precision that "Enlightenment is defined by a modification of the preexisting relation linking will, authority, and the use of reason."[1]

Blanco White structures all his autobiographical writings as a conflict between coercive institutions that perpetuate an oppressive, damaging system and the individual's struggle to attain freedom to act, think, and exchange ideas. As a process of shedding immaturity, the Enlightenment provides the basic figure and the primary set of discourses that allow Blanco White to give form to feelings and phenomena whose existence (and representation) are negated by the system that he combats. He perceives his life as a war against religious institutions (aided and abetted by the political establishment) whose stakes are the governance of minds and bodies. In his numerous autobiographical writings, Blanco obsessively represents different variations on that basic pattern, doggedly insisting that the Catholic Church's primary means of controlling individuals resides in the exacerbation of feelings at the expense of reason. Through mischievous practices—such as spiritual exercises, confession, and liturgical pageantry, which work on the faculty of the imagination—Catholicism cultivates the affects of its followers, inciting them to surrender mind and body to pastoral control, to relinquish their freedom to act and their ability to know both the world and themselves. Blanco views his life as a deliverance from the pernicious effects of Catholicism, as a reeducation of his feelings (by submitting them to the command of reason), and as a progressive access to a deeper understanding both of the nefarious workings of religious institutions and of the true spirit of Christianity. In his autobiographical narratives he tells the story of the life imposed on him by the church. Underneath that official story, however, he reconstructs an alternative account whose events he retraces in episodes and struggles that escaped his comprehension when he was living them but that later he can retrospectively thread together into a teleological narrative of liberation. In that narrative he progressively and inexorably dares to move from the disorder of feelings to the order of reason; from the control of intolerant Christian institutions to the liberating spirit of Christianity; from religious superstition to enlightening knowledge; from the darkness of an incomprehensible life to the clarity of self-knowledge. At each step of this ordeal, Blanco White faces moral quandaries that command that he sacrifice family and friendships in the name of truth. Not surprisingly, he ends up by portraying himself as a martyr of truth.

José Blanco White, born in Seville in 1775 to parents of Irish origin (Blanco is the repetition, in Spanish, of his Irish surname), was an apostate in the modern sense of a person who abandons a religious faith or a cause. In 1799 he became a Catholic priest. Blanco left Seville for Madrid in 1805 to escape the life of dissimulation that his dwindling faith imposed on him, but also, it seems, to break his attachment to a married woman. Although there are few references to his stay in Madrid, his own intimations and other indirect sources indicate that he indulged in a life of pleasure, purposely ignoring the restrictions inherent to Catholic priesthood. In the summer of 1808 (a few weeks after the French invasion of Madrid), he returned to Seville, without knowing that in Madrid he had just conceived a son with a sick woman he had helped and who later died in 1816. In 1809, during the Spanish War of Independence against the French and after a long period of religious crisis, Blanco White decided to leave for England, where he already knew distinguished dignitaries such as Lord Holland and where through the years he established an impressive net of intellectual relationships that included Samuel Taylor Coleridge, John Stuart Mill, and Cardinal Newman, among other notables. When in 1812 he found out about his son's existence, he promptly began to help supporting him and later brought him to England; although he did not acknowledge his paternity immediately, he always showed great concern about his son's education and well-being (Ferdinand White later joined the British army). Blanco White became an Anglican in 1812 and was appointed a fellow at Oxford's Oriel College in 1826, where he lived until 1832, when he moved to Dublin to live with the family of Archbishop Richard Whately, who had been one of his strongest supporters at Oriel. His unhappiness with Anglican dogmatism impelled him to leave the Church of England at the end of 1834, and he promptly became a Unitarian, settling down in Liverpool at the beginning of 1835. From the time of his arrival in England until his death there in 1841, he dedicated himself almost obsessively to combating religious dogmatism, first in Catholicism and later in the Anglican Church, which he accused of a religious intolerance as pernicious as the papists'. Menéndez Pelayo, who condemned Blanco White to his pantheon of Spanish heterodoxes, wrote that he "pasó sus trabajos [sic] e infelices días, como nave sin piloto en ruda tempestad, entre continuas apostasías y cambios de frente"(spent his troubled and unhappy days, like a rudderless ship in a harsh storm, between continuous apostasies and changes of mind).[2]

While this analysis will concentrate on Blanco's *The Life of the Rev. Joseph Blanco White,* his longest autobiographical effort, it will also pay attention to his other personal writings, especially to *The Examination of Blanco by White.* Besides keeping a commonplace book as well as a student diary, in which he mainly recorded his progress in different fields of study, Blanco White kept a journal almost from the moment of his arrival in England until the very year of his death. In the entry for October 4, 1812, he already announces his decision to write the story of his life, which will have the goal to explain how Catholicism pushed him into the "madness" of atheism.[3] In a note that he added later to that entry, he states that he accomplished his objective in *Letters from Spain.* Little did he know that autobiographical writing would be a lifelong obsession. In all, he wrote six works that are either autobiographical in their entirety or include a short history of his life (usually in an introductory chapter). They are:

> *The Examination of Blanco by White* (1818–1819)
>
> *Letters from Spain* (1922)
>
> "Despedida del autor de las *Variedades* a los Hispano-Americanos" (1825)

Practical and Internal Evidence against Catholicism (1825)

The Poor Man's Preservative against Popery (1825)

*The Life of the Rev. Joseph Blanco White, Written by Himself;
with Portions of His Correspondence* (1845)

Born to Be a Rebel

In his programmatic books (*Letters from Spain, Practical and Internal
Evidence against Catholicism,* and *The Poor Man's Preservative against
Popery*), Blanco White makes an unidimensional presentation of his
life, using it to exhibit the corroding, demoralizing, and destructive
effect that religious institutions, with the connivance of the state, can
have over individuals.[4] Because he professes to speak of himself "only
to shew the state of my country" (*Letters from Spain* 73) and moved by
"a sincere desire of being useful to others" (58), Blanco uses his case to
depict only the misery, dissimulation, and even depravity that the
Catholic religion can cause and to demonstrate that such effects can be
"an insuperable obstacle to the improvement of the mind." In refusing
to explore more personal and darker realms of experience, Blanco
remarks that he does not possess "the cynical habits of mind which
would enable me, like Rousseau, to expose my heart naked to the gaze
of the world . . ." (58). The *Letters from Spain,* after all, had clearly educational and political objectives, and Blanco sees himself not as an individual but as representative of a group. As such, he speaks in sweeping
generalities, while simultaneously beginning to essay trends and topics
that he will develop with greater depth in *The Life of the Rev. Joseph
Blanco White.* The Enlightenment structure, however, is already fully
present in this work, and the Spanish priest describes himself as being
free after escaping from his "early bondage" through the power of reason, whose guidance he vows never to relinquish (64). Striking a note
that will resonate through all his future autobiographical works, he
writes in *Letters from Spain* that "probably as a compensation for a too
soft and yielding heart," nature has granted him "an understanding
which was born a rebel" (82).

In "Despedida del autor de las *Variedades* a los Hispano-Americanos"
(Farewell to the Spanish-Americans from the Author of *Variedades*), he
offers a similar self-portrait, but, tailoring it to his specific Spanish
American readers who had just waged a war of independence against
the oppressive Spaniards, he represents himself as a "criatura racional"

(rational creature) oppressed by "the double tyranny of the Inquisition and the Ecclesiastical laws" (306).[5] His scathing, polemical attacks against Catholicism, *Practical and Internal Evidence against Catholicism* (1825), and a new version of the same book, which he adapted for the lower classes, *The Poor Man's Preservative against Popery* (1825), start with autobiographical chapters. Blanco conceived *Practical and Internal Evidence* as a presentation "of the moral and intellectual state of Spain" (36), in which the history of Blanco's mind—which he also calls a "moral dissection" of himself—functions as representative of the state of much of Spanish clergy (22).[6] In both works Blanco presents his life, as in *Letters from Spain,* in abstract terms, more as an example of the mental and spiritual damage that Catholic practices can produce than as the narrative of his personal vicissitudes.

The *Examination of Blanco by White* (1818–1819), written earlier, has a very different slant. In contrast with his approach in the more politically minded *Letters from Spain,* in *The Examination of Blanco by White* he has no qualms about disclosing private affairs.[7] In this document Blanco seems haunted by two obsessions: his struggles with his erotic inclinations during his life in Spain, and his fall into atheism in the years before leaving for England. In contrast with the rest of his autobiographical texts, *The Examination of Blanco by White* stands out for its disjunction between discourses and experience. The discourses used by Blanco seem unable to explain and justify feelings and events—in particular those related to his sexual urges and his atheism—that resist the explanations he essays. Hence Blanco's obsessive return to those topics and his endless string of interpretations and justifications.

As noted, in 1812 Blanco had already prepared his life script's main guideline, in a journal entry where he writes that when he was "an open Atheist," in his last years in Spain, it was not due to evil or malignancy, but because "Catholicism had worked me into that madness, as I shall explain in my Memoirs" (*The Life of the Rev. Joseph Blanco White* I, 242). Blanco had left himself open to criticism for boasting openly about his atheism immediately after his arrival in England, convinced as he was "that men, *enlightened* as the English, could only regard religion as political engine. . . . I did not expect to find a sincere Christian among educated Englishmen" (*Practical and Internal Evidence* 25). He soon became aware that in England, where religion was highly respected and the Anglican Church had intimate links with the government, his boasting was a serious blunder, and at least his first autobiographical works can be seen as a response to his critics as well as an attempt to explain to himself his former atheism, a state that, in his new social environment, had become a moral mystery to him. On the other hand, news of his libidinal looseness in Madrid had followed him to England, and in *The Examination of Blanco by White* and other works he attempts to respond to such innuendo and to justify his amorous behavior to others and, overwhelmed again by a moral quandary, also to himself.

The Examination of Blanco by White is a treatise on the moral miseducation of a Catholic priest. Blanco writes that the church has led him both to dissipation (22) and to atheism and that for at least ten years the church's lack of "soberness of thought" made him unable to believe in any moral cause or universal order.[8] In his new English setting, which clearly helped shape his views at the time of writing, both are seen as defects that make him an immoral being, regardless of his beliefs or doubts.[9] Blanco tries to counteract that striking realization adducing his innate sense of morality, but that does nothing to diminish his puzzlement: "My dislike of every thing grossly immoral was, I may say, born with me. Yet I have to blush at the recollection of the orgies in which I used to join, and which were always preceded and followed by a feeling of unhappiness" (23).[10] In his later autobiographical works, Blanco's insistence on his natural and inborn sense of moral duty and on his "innate love of truth" (*Letters from Spain* 83)—qualities he then merges with the rational and the divine—grow stronger, supplying the main ground for his final thoughts about religion and morality.

In 1818–1819, however, he had not yet been able to work out a satisfactory explanation based on any natural characteristics of his being, and therefore he was forced to grope unsuccessfully in search of an explanation. In its absence he resorts to different types of justifications: the nefarious role of celibacy imposed on Catholic priests—in opposition to the domestic government of pleasures that the Protestant system allows (22), or the noxious state of a society where "the power of the Church of Rome is supported by the sword of the Magistrate" (21). It could be said that Blanco fails in his first autobiographical attempt because the church's strictures and his family's restrictions prevented him from knowing himself. Consequently in *The Examination of Blanco by White* the story of his life consists of a series of battles to control his youthful erotic impulses and to accommodate himself to the standards and role of priesthood. There are constant minidramas played at this level: his visits to temptation-filled Cadiz, his flirtatious relationships with several women and, of course, his "dissolute" life in Madrid. Blanco will spend most of his life in England trying repeatedly to assert his right to know himself and to rewrite his life according to that constantly hard-won knowledge.

As for politics, they play a very limited role in Blanco's plotting of his life—surprisingly for someone who had been for four years (1810–1814) editor of a political, antiestablishment journal, *El Español*. Contemporary historical events serve in *The Examination of Blanco by White* only as a diffuse background to Blanco's moral dilemmas and do not offer him any hermeneutical role for the story of his life. A crucial event such as the French invasion of Spain is treated in *The Examination of Blanco by White* as little more than an opportunity for him to be freed of his misery, though it could well have represented on a grand scale the central struggle in his life script: the struggle between enlightened freedom and religious and political absolutism. In this respect in *The Life of the Rev. Joseph Blanco White* Blanco alludes to being criticized by people such as the Hollands, who thought he should have remained in Spain to fight for its freedom and modernization; and he also will mention the general incredulity he met among his English acquaintances as to religion being the only cause of his fleeing to England. Perhaps as a response to critics such as the Hollands, in *The Life of the Rev. Joseph Blanco White* Spanish politics plays a more prominent explanatory role in the direction and dilemmas of his existence, but its relevance still is fairly minor—and limited mainly to the years of the French invasion and to his first years in England—compared to his life-long obsession with religion. After he stopped editing *El Español* (1814), Spanish politics virtually disappeared from his life.[11] Besides, he rarely participated in British politics, and when he got involved in it, as he did when he wrote *Practical and Internal Evidence against Catholicism* (1825) opposing Catholic emancipation (the admission of Catholics into the British parliament) or when, reversing his position regarding emancipation, he voted for Peel in 1829, religious reasons were always first and foremost. This primacy of religion led him to ignore some troubling dimensions of the political restrictions imposed on British Catholics since, as Martin Murphy argues, Blanco "was totally ignorant—culpably ignorant—of the politics of Emancipation and took his stand on abstract principle."[12] When he later lived in Dublin and saw firsthand the oppression of Catholics, he bitterly regretted having written *Practical and Internal Evidence,* realizing the support it had provided to Ireland's subjugation.[13]

The Examination of Blanco by White already gives considerable weight to the role of the struggle for reason and enlightenment as well as to the role of Providence as the glue that holds together, and gives a semblance of meaning to, the most foolish and meaningless episodes of his life. He uses this model to a greater extent in *The Life of the Rev. Joseph Blanco White.* However, in 1818 eroticism, atheism, and religious zeal were areas of wilderness and reticence for which Blanco had not yet found a satisfactory explanation. At the time he wrote *The Examination of Blanco by White,* he was unable to bridge the gap between senseless experience and explanatory discourse, between incomprehensible behavior and enlightened rules, and such disadjustment appears in his manuscript as bafflement and as unresolved hesitation between justificatory discourses. He found an easy and ready-made solution in *Letters from Spain,* whose intent and potential readership called for a denunciation of the damaging influence of the Catholic Church. It is the Spanish priest, portrayed in a fairly abstract way, who makes that denunciation. Excessively personal details would be inappropriate in that type of work, and Blanco is spared the embarrassment of not being able to offer a rational explanation for crucial aspects and moments of his story. When, several years later, he wrote *The Life of the Rev. Joseph Blanco White,* he tightened his autobiographical discourse with an incontestable teleology that not only explains past experiences but also serves as guide for his later deportment.

Life Imitates Autobiography

The Life of the Rev. Joseph Blanco White appeared posthumously, as intended, in 1845, and in it Blanco tells his story twice, the first time in "Narrative of the Events of His Life," an account of his life's "external events" in the words of his editor Thom (1: 234, note), and the second time in a significantly different way, in "A Sketch of His Mind in England." One could say that there is a third autobiography, composed of the selection of his letters and journal entries, but since that is a partial selection of autobiographical documents made by the editor, one cannot lend it full credit as a personal narrative, although that information does complement and refine the accounts that he personally wrote and arranged as a sustained autobiography.[14] But surely his lengthy and crucial statement, "Letter to the Rev. John Hamilton Thom" (*The Life of the Rev. Joseph Blanco White* 3: 125–161), written in August 1839, is yet another autobiographical narration, one which displays from the perspective of his final faith and ideas a view of the events that led to his definitive rupture with orthodoxy.

In *The Life of the Rev. Joseph Blanco White*, Blanco finally finds a way to narrate the events of his life as a seamless unit whose meaning becomes fully transparent to him.[15] At this point his philosophy seems to allow him to catch up with feelings and experiences that in his first autobiographical narratives were either omitted (as happened in *Letters from Spain* with his erotic struggles) or resisted a satisfactory, enlightened explanation. The "Narrative of the Events of His Life" spans his life in Spain and England until 1826 (the year he was elected a fellow at Oriel College), and he wrote it between 1830 and 1832, a period of intense doubts and increasing realization that the Church of England was as orthodox, popish, and intolerant as the Catholic establishment.[16] He began "A Sketch of His Mind in England" at the end of 1834, when he decided to break with the Anglican Church and was about to embrace the Unitarian faith, as his journal entries show (see *The Life of the Rev. Joseph Blanco White* 3: 45–86).[17] Ostensibly, the sketch's objective was to present the story of his religious ideas under such evolutionary light that it made it appear inexorable that he embrace a new faith, Unitarianism. With "A Sketch of His Mind in England," complemented with "Letter to . . . Thom," he not only offers his final philosophical and religious statement, but he also redefines his past, literally to "make into events" what had been mere flow of unformed experience, inexplicable actions, or senseless aberrations. In other words his final ideas furnish a clear discursive network that brings sense to the aspects of his life that showed reticence in his previous autobiographical formulations, and they also provide a distinct teleological thread to his life.[18] Even more, in 1834, the year he began "A Sketch of His Mind in England," his newly gained freedom from Anglican orthodoxy actually shaped—forced out of the darkness of the past—feelings and attitudes that, once unmasked, convert recalcitrant past experiences into crucial events. Blanco retrospectively granted a prominent role to his discovery that, even after his breach with Catholicism, he unknowingly maintained many of the feelings and ideas seared into his mind by that church. Thus his life now appeared to him not simply as divided into clear-cut Catholicism and after, but as a rupture followed by a long purgation of the insidiously latent remnants of popish tenets and affects, a purification that, once accomplished, led him to a second break with the religious establishment, and it allowed him finally to attain the ability to know himself and to act accordingly. In this way his final narrative is simultaneously the story of a double liberation: a retrospective shedding of light that literally unveils a new past, and the foundation of a program for present and future moral action. In other words Blanco's final reconstruction of his life is not a reproduction of his past but a re-presentation of it, an act of recreation that not only rediscovers the past but also illuminates the future. In the remaining seven years of his life, he will strive to adjust his life to the script delineated in the sketch: at least in this case, life imitates autobiography.

In the account of his life in Spain, Blanco narrates the past as two parallel stories, and while the first story features the traps and snares of institutions and their consequences for individuals, the other story assembles episodes marked by his personal resistance to suffocating institutional impositions and the gradual emergence of truth. From the frictions and clashes between the two stories emerges a drama of carnal quandaries, religious ruptures, and soul-wrenching separations from family and fatherland. It could also be said that Blanco's life narrates the substitution of a new set of discourses and practices for the oppressive ones favored by the church. That change of discourses became necessary for Blanco when he increasingly discovered a disjunction between his feelings and desires and a reality that he perceived not only as burdensome and oppressive but also as unyielding and thus unable to accommodate his gradually-uncovered truer and freer self. That double story develops around a main axis or figure, (religious) enlightenment, and Blanco's drama takes place in three sites where his personal truth gradually imposes itself against stifling dogma: his mind, his body, and his family (and, later, in England, the community of his friends). In different but interrelated ways, on each of those fronts Blanco wages a painful struggle whose stakes are the form and future of his mind, body, friendships, and filial relations.

Blanco's account of his life in Spain centers mainly around his moral and religious education. It presents the painful and intermittent story of his personal acquisition of knowledge despite the instruction of the church and of the official institutions of learning. In this narrative

Blanco contraposes the story of his "official" education with another story, one which strings together the more informal but much more significant episodes of learning through influential friends such as Mármol and Arjona, who give him access to previously unknown realms of knowledge. A similar effect was produced on him by authors and books that, discovered haphazardly, profoundly affected the development of his mind: Fénelon's *Telemachus,* which he read at the age of eight and which revealed to him that a non-Catholic world could still be a world of moral beauty; *Don Quijote,* which he had to read behind his father's back—his father felt even that book was dangerous; and, above all, the works of the Benedictine Feijoo, who introduced him to Baconian philosophy and whose ideas he daringly used to dispute with the friar who taught him scholastic logic at the Dominican school he was attending at the time. Echoing Feijoo, Blanco presents that dispute as a watershed event in the development of his mind: "A great love of knowledge, and an equally great hatred of *established* errors, were suddenly developed in my mind, at the period of my quarrel with the Dominican" (*The Life of the Rev. Joseph Blanco White* 1: 14). When Feijoo states in the "Prologue to the Reader" of his *Teatro crítico universal* that he is going to deal with all sorts of common errors, he adds that he will purposely leave aside any consideration of religious ideas.[19] Continuing Feijoo's work with a vengeance, Blanco devotes himself almost exclusively to the errors of religion.[20]

However, this neat account of chance encounters with influential friends and books becomes a story only after the fact when, much later, during his exile in England, Blanco projects a retrospective glance over his past, and he "figures" a teleological tale that brings into relief experiences that only in this retelling really become events, which he now threads together with seemingly predestined necessity. By thus creating events and constructing a story, Blanco is able not only to make sense of the past, but also to explain his changes of faith and his present position, and in this way he can respond to the charges of religious volubility, since his intellectual counterhistory makes his acts of apostasy appear as inevitable.[21] In other words, in Blanco's hands, autobiography is not merely a reproduction of the past, but a conscientious effort of self-reconstruction that fully justifies his temporary atheism and his changes of faith and, even more important, commands that he act in a certain way, that he sacrifice friends and family to the truth discovered and supported by his autobiographical exploration.

A Sentimental Reeducation

If the narrative of his education accounts for the development of his mind, another crucial narrative, involving Catholic practices, takes place in, and affects, both mind and body. This narrative of Catholic cruelties does not possess the synchronic logic of the story of his intellectual education but functions more like spiraling variations on the same nightmare. However, this account is the story of another kind of education, one that does not deal with books, ideas, and reason, but with feelings, desires, and the imagination. Spiritual exercises, confession, self-flagellation, mandatory readings, and forms of meditation: to these Blanco White devotes his most expressive pages, insisting almost with relish on the different ways Catholicism abuses flesh and fancy with the purpose of bringing the believers into subjection to its rules and into compliance with its tenets. Blanco's peerless fifteen-page description of the spiritual exercises—"a masterpiece of church machinery" (*The Life of the Rev. Joseph Blanco White* 1: 35)—revolves insistently around the ways its director effectively worked on the imagination of the attendants during the ten days the exercises lasted. The director, writes Blanco, recalling one session, unfolded a gradual scale of terrors to "agitate and subdue the mind" (1: 40), displaying great ingenuity to strike the imagination with wily stratagems (like, for instance, a vivid description of the damned howling in eternal fire) that allow him to manipulate the feelings of the attendants to the point of leading them to break into "convulsive cries" and pleas for mercy and general confession. The goal of the exercises, Blanco argues, was to create a state of mind "which renders the mental faculties powerless, and reduces the moral being to the weakness of infancy," a characterization that is exactly the opposite of Kant's depiction of the Enlightenment. Blanco recognizes the powerful effects that this "mystical discipline" had over "my mind and feelings" but counteracts that influence by finding within himself a secret source of resistance to that education; like everyone else, he cannot avoid the tears and sobs at the height of the emotional tension created by the exercises but, at the same time, he writes, "my natural taste recoiled from that mixture of animal affection . . . with spiritual matters." The exercises attempted to induce the need for general confession, and confession, Blanco writes, "is one of the most mischievous practices of the Romanist Church" because of its minute attention to every fault and because it confers on another total authority over the conscience of the confessed. It is noteworthy, however, that of the two main characteristics of confession, self-examination and confession to another, Blanco actually rejects only the latter, the submission of the self to the authority of the confessor, not the detailed exploration of one's conscience. He sees confession as a practice that could have destroyed "the quick moral perception which God had naturally given to my mind. . . . Free, however, from that debasing practice, my conscience assumed the rule, and, independently of hopes and fears, it clearly blamed what was clearly wrong, and, as it were, learnt to act by virtue of its natural supremacy."[22]

In the same way that in the account of his intellectual education Blanco constructs a posteriori a history of his alternative instruction, in the case of his condemnation of Catholic practices, he counterbalances the church's manipulation of the imagination with a resisting and inborn moral feeling and a vigilant and unbending rational faculty. In this way Blanco can denounce the church's excesses, explain the formation in him of an early and unhealthy remorse that he attributes to the practice of confession, and set the grounds for his positing the unarguable reality of what he will later call "conscientious reason" as an inherent, natural faculty that is the dwelling place of both a sense of the divine and an unerring moral feeling. Once again, Blanco's autobiography becomes simultaneously a document of self-exploration, a performance in self-defense, an act of religious propaganda, and a program for religious and moral action. In other words, in Blanco's autobiographical enterprise it is impossible to separate the past from the present or the future, to disentangle the cognoscitive, the performative and the prospective (memory, understanding, will). However, Blanco makes clear that not everybody has the strength or the possibility to resist the church's noxious education of the feelings and the flesh, and, as he had already done in *The Examination of Blanco by White,* he again remembers the women in his family (his mother and two sisters), whose "ardent female character" made them easy prey for the church's insidious work on the affects. Blanco sees himself in Spain under the spell of his mother's affection, and in his moments of religious doubt before and after becoming a priest, he describes her hovering constantly over him, crying (1: 50, 51), or even refusing to talk to him to avoid having to denounce him to the Inquisition (1: 157, note). The nuns (his two sisters died in convents) are for him the exemplary victims of Catholic superstition: shut off for life at an early age, victims of cruelty and constant disease, they spend their internment ridden by the fears typical of morbid consciences (1: 67). The death of his oldest sister and the appearance in the younger one of "hysteric symptoms" that were for Blanco the sure sign of her future commitment to a convent provoked in him "a moral and intellectual storm . . . which would at once sweep away all the religious impressions so industriously . . . inculcated on my mind." All this made his life in Spain intolerable, pushed him to the conclusion that Christianity was not true (1: 111), and led him into atheism.

Blanco and Victorian Autobiography

In her interpretation of Newman's *Apologia*, Linda H. Peterson argues that Victorian autobiographers are indebted to the tradition of spiritual autobiography, whose exemplary narrative of conversion is Bunyan's *Pilgrim's Progress*. In her opinion Victorian autobiography follows the basic structure of spiritual autobiography, whose narratives typically portray life as a series of stages or passages: a period of bondage or sin, an act of conversion or flight, an interval of confusion or wandering in the wilderness, and finally access to peace in the promised land. Peterson shows that Newman professed great admiration for Thomas Scott's *The Force of Truth* (1779), a narrative of his conversion from Socianism to Evangelism that follows the pattern of spiritual autobiography although it rejects its typical episodes of enthusiasm (visions, dreams, revelations, etc.) and violent conversions.[23] In his book, "literally a debate among theological texts," Scott follows the tradition of spiritual autobiography in so far as he "organizes his account in terms of books read and doctrines derived." Peterson characterizes spiritual autobiography (and, by extension a whole strand of Victorian autobiography) as a narrative of "textual encounters."[24]

This succinct description of the characteristics shared by spiritual and Victorian autobiography also sheds light on the overall configuration of Blanco's autobiographical accounts. When he felt the necessity to write the story of his life—and, it will be remembered, he was already toying with that idea in 1812—Blanco could not resort to a Spanish autobiographical tradition. That tradition barely existed, and, besides, in no way could it offer him a model for anti-Catholic tribulations. Although the idea of enlightenment provided him with a broad lay pattern, Blanco needed to account for very particular religious phenomena, and therefore he required a more specific model for his narrative of conversion (the need for models was imposed also by modern autobiography's incipient character as a genre). No doubt he found a convenient prototype in the tradition of spiritual autobiography. Like Newman, he had no use for that genre's enthusiasm, but there he could find not only an overall shape for his account but also a way to normalize his period of atheism as spiritual autobiography's typical interval of errancy in search of the promised land. This tradition offered him both a way to explain/write his temporary abandonment of the Christian path and a means of allaying his long-lasting and unsettling remorse in that respect.[25] In Blanco's case autobiography as representation and as therapeutics are indistinguishable.

St. Augustine's *Confessions* must have loomed large in Blanco's writing also, but he could not explicitly accept a model of Catholic conversion. Peterson suggests that Newman passes from the model of intertextual debate of spiritual autobiography (the first two chapters of *Apologia* are dominated by textual encounters) to the pattern set in the *Confessions* by Augustine who, after the narrative of his conversion (books 1–10), shifts to a theological exposition (books 10–13). Newman would follow this Augustinian pattern in moving from a presentation of the sources of his beliefs in "History of My Religious Opinions" to an exposition of his theological principles in "Position of My Mind since 1845."[26] In *The Life of the Rev. Joseph Blanco White,* Blanco follows a similar pattern: an exposition of his religious ideas ("A Sketch of His Mind in England") follows the narrative of his life. Whether he followed the Augustinian model or not, the sketch was for Blanco the logical culmination of the narrative of the external events of his life. For him external events are important only insofar as they can explain his mental evolution.

Jonathan Loesberg proposes that Victorian autobiography "transforms philosophy into literature" and that writers of the period, unsatisfied with the flaws of philosophy, turn "to autobiography to substantiate through narrative description what cannot be substantiated through philosophical discourse." If one sees autobiography as "an empirical defense of a philosophy," Loesberg argues, then one can understand that a work such as Newman's *Apologia* "is very much the autobiography of a philosophy," and as such it "centers on issues that may not seem autobiographical: the relationship between faith and reason, the status of historical development, and . . . the ways in which self-conscious reason can support instinctive intuition."[27] Although Loesberg's thesis is very suggestive—and it may be correct in Newman's case—it seems doubtful that Blanco's preeminent foregrounding and discussion of his religious ideas sprang from skepticism about philosophy. His attention to those issues at the expense of biography originated simply in his conviction that his mind was the true protagonist of his life. For him autobiography had nothing to do with memoirs: it was not a history of his life but the development of his religious philosophy. Only in this sense can one call *The Life of the Rev. Joseph Blanco White* the autobiography of a philosophy. Besides, one should never lose sight in Blanco's writings of his pastoral penchant, which gives his quest for self-knowledge a performative, indoctrinating dimension. His autobiographies try to give a pattern not only to his past but also to the future, both his own and that of others.

Decolonizing the Affects

In the narrative of his life Blanco stressed his influential encounters with books and authors. In "A Sketch of His Mind in England" his basic procedure is to reread himself, scouring the entries of the journal he had kept almost since his arrival in England, in search of a coherent story line for his religious views.[28] The sketch strives to bring order and continuity, for himself and for his readers, to the detours and discontinuities, changes and slippages in his religious positions: his atheism in Spain; his rediscovery of Christianity in England; his joining the Anglican Church, which in retrospect he interprets as a relapse into abstract, theological habits of mind; and finally his rupture with that church and his insistence that he has discovered the "original spirit" of Christianity. Because the story of his religious conflicts and credences is enmeshed with his affects, he will also have to narrativize the pull of his theological and social attachments. He will also have to recount decisions he made, so that reason could rule unimpeded and he could live fully according to the imperative conclusions of his understanding.[29]

Blanco brings coherence to this tangle of pathos and theology by constructing the history of his mind and his body as a process of Catholic colonization of the affects and the intellect. This is balanced with a counterstory of the organic, progressive process of purification in which he casts off a lifetime accretion of feelings and fidelities. The sketch narrates the double diseducation of his mind and of his feelings, organized in two very different but tightly related stories that he constructs primarily by culling entries from his journal between 1812 and

1823 and by rethreading them in an account of his current beliefs that his infirmity forced him to interrupt. The first of these stories chronicles his changing conception of Christianity (which revolves around his interpretation of the Bible), while the second narrates the role played by both his affects and his social attachments in preventing him over the years from accepting the conclusions of his understanding.

The first story has a simple but emotionally tortuous plot. Subjecting the Scriptures to modern hermeneutics, he stresses their historical origins, pointing accordingly to their inherent limitations as human and linguistic creations and debunking the widely accepted theory of their divinely inspired origins and their revelatory nature.[30] This demystification of the Scriptures takes place as a long, convoluted process that Blanco details minutely, but which is reduced here to an elementary outline, because the story of his prolonged resistance to accepting the results of his hermeneutical inquiry is more revealing. Blanco attributes that resistance to "strong and deep-rooted affections:" "Affections alone, . . . prevented for a long time my deliberate and open adoption of principles which, the moment the influence of these affections was checked, became to me plain and almost self-evident truths" ("Letter to . . . Thom," *The Life of the Rev. Joseph Blanco White* 3: 136). And thus the story of his mind does not pit him against institutional religion but is instead an internal contest between what he calls "the natural freedom of my understanding" and his early religious habits— theological thinking and "morbid devotional feelings" (1: 314, 340).[31] He describes these two powers as acting side by side, ignoring each other until their collision becomes inevitable. But early habits, which he calls "mental slavery," do not disappear simply by acknowledging their existence: "conviction has no chance against old prejudice till the new habit . . . shall have destroyed the old" (1: 363).[32] Ultimately, then, his true story is that of the trials and tribulations of reason in its long and painful road toward supremacy over the imagination. Describing himself as being "haunted by reason" (1: 345), Blanco details his sixteen-year resistance to accepting the intimations of his reason. In retrospect he realizes that, while in 1818 his understanding was already in conformity with the spirit of Unitarianism, it was not until 1834 that he fully accepted his reason's dictates and finally joined that denomination (1: 347).

In order to explain the painful but inescapable way in which he reached that point, Blanco scours the record of his past as set forth in his journal and ransacks his mind at the time of writing to retrace the manifestations in his life of past and present forms of religious enthusiasm or superstition. Obsessively exploring the territory of religious feelings, theological tenets, and familial and social attachments, Blanco retraces the struggle he endured to decolonize his affects, to release them from the insidious and enduring governance of the church. In other words, the narrative(s) of his life may be characterized as an account of his discovery of the proper management of the imaginary, a reeducation of the affects that allows reason to prevail and thus makes it possible for him to accept the full consequences of his hermeneutical analysis of the Scriptures. In Blanco's view the enduring hold of the church over people rests primarily on two bases: the theological tenet of the Catholic Church's infallibility (the Protestants replace this with the theory of the Bible's inspiration); and the emotional impact of its devotional practices, which aim to create morbid, unthinking enthusiasm (see *The Life of the Rev. Joseph Blanco White* 1: 280).[33] Both foundations of institutional religion prey on the affects, and the sketch narrates how the theological and emotional habits instilled by his Catholic education survived his rejection of that faith and came insidiously back to life the moment he again embraced Christianity and became an Anglican (*The Life of the Rev. Joseph Blanco White* I, 245). As account of his double purification, "A Sketch of His Mind in England" chronicles his arduous liberation from any vestige of orthodoxy and the painful process of his deliverance from the grip of enthusiastic affects.

His Catholic habits were not the only hindrance to his reason. Blanco presents a complementary struggle between another manifestation of the affects (the attachments to family and friends) and the moral/hermeneutical dictates of his reason. As expected, reason will also prevail on this front, commanding Blanco time and again throughout his life to sever the affective ties that hamper the development of his mind. He faced that type of decision for the first time when he was forced to decide between his family and the free expression of his religious ideas, and that event is only the first in a series that becomes a subtext in Blanco's life: his break with Newman and other friends at Oriel; his separation from the Christies (1: 391), whose Evangelical enthusiasm he sees as contagious; and finally his refusal to live with Archbishop Whately's family in Dublin, when he perceives that remaining with them hinders the full, honest expression of his religious conclusions. He faces this last dilemma after writing to a certain Rev. Armstrong, a Unitarian he tried to bring back to the church, from whom he receives a demolishing answer that makes Blanco aware of his self-deception: "In my private meditations I had never given distinct utterance to, I had not embodied the state of my own thoughts; everything had been resolved into feeling; but the moment that a written discussion obliged me to express my ideas distinctly, I could not hesitate a moment as to my conduct. I instantly determined to tear myself from my friends. I knew well that great sufferings awaited me; but alas! they have exceeded my conception" (3: 141–42).

This episode of 1834, recounted in Blanco's 1839 "Letter to . . . Thom," will bring closure to Blanco's arduous process of enlightenment.[34] One might say that the story of his life reaches an end before his death. For finally he has been able to break all the attachments that made him cling to beliefs he no longer sustained, and he can find a final formulation of his ideas in which nature, self, and divinity become inextricably fused. Refusing to view the Bible as an oracle of God, Blanco sees true religion, once it has been freed from its institutional encumbrances and manipulations,[35] as a state of mind and an external conduct that arises from the original relation between God and "his rational creature Man." Conflating Christian and Stoic formulations, he finds this idea in St. Paul's assertion that we carry a deity within us, a statement he sees confirmed in Seneca's famous dictum, "Sacer intra nos Spiritus sedet" (3: 152; a sacred spirit dwells within us), and in the more detailed development by Marcus Aurelius to which he enthusiastically subscribes: "Nothing can be more wretched than the man who moves in a perpetual whirl after knowledge, who will . . . undermine the earth in search of it . . . ; forgetting all the while that it is sufficient for us to keep inseparably near to that one Deity who dwells within us, devoting ourselves sincerely to his worship. Now, that worship consists in keeping oneself pure from passion, from rashness of conduct . . ."[36] Blanco found a contemporary and practical formulation of those Christian and Stoic ideas in Kant's enlightened conception of religion as "the acknowledgment of all our duties as divine commands," and he replaced religion with a "purely spiritual religion of the conscience" (3: 154), "whose worship consists in the cultivation of our intellectual nature, that faculty which is capable of knowing and delighting in *truth*," not only logical truth but also moral truth or practical reason (3: 155), which Blanco also calls "conscientious reason" to distinguish it

from mere reason (1: 405).[37] Blanco's various formulations of his life
may therefore be seen as exemplary narrations of the "civilization" of
the feelings (which he considers a primigenial, and primitive, form of
human response) or as the subjugation of the faculty that is responsible for them, the imagination, to the power of conscientious reason.

The result of reason's double struggle against theological affects and
social attachments was never in doubt for Blanco, who sees his life as
being driven ineluctably by an organic process of development: "nothing whatever remains but what has grown from the root. Any one qualified for that sort of observation will be able to trace my present
features of mind to the original lineaments of its embryo. My first act
of mental emancipation in Spain was only the rough sketch of the now
finished drawing" ("Sunday letters" to Thom [1836]; *The Life of the
Rev. Joseph Blanco White* 3: 400).[38] And yet this story of the unveiling
of true Christianity has a final wrinkle: it requires an ultimate sacrifice
imposed by the asynchrony between the development of Christianity
and the evolution of Blanco's mind. Blanco believes that the history of
Christianity and his personal history follow the same pattern, but
while Christianity as institutional establishment is still far from recu-
perating its original spirit, Blanco (and sects such as the Unitarians) are
ahead in the process of such restoration. This asynchrony between parallel but not perfectly coincidental evolutions is ultimately responsible
for Blanco's tragedy, and in his arduous process of enlightenment he
portrays himself successively in the roles of victim (of the Catholic
Church), witness (first to Catholic manipulations and later to Anglican
orthodoxy), and lastly martyr. In this way the final intellectual and
moral triumph of reason brings a somewhat paradoxical consequence
for someone who strove all his life to separate reason and imagination,
mind and body. In his diary entry for July 19, 1839, after remembering
that Whately had said "that in me he had seen a martyr to truth" (3:
142), "[i]n a fit of agony" Blanco wrote: "I am at the stage of that martyrdom when the flame, which has not been able to extinguish life by
suffocation, subsides, and the burning coals melt the limbs."[39] At
this point, and during the last years of his life, Blanco meticulously
chronicles in his diary the painful progress of a physical malaise—
whose onset he traces back to his strenuous work for *El Español*
(1810–1814)—that gradually undermined his strength to the point of
preventing him from getting up from his bed for stretches of several
months. In the last years of his life he conflates his physical hardships

and his spiritual agonies to such a point that it becomes increasingly more difficult to separate them, as is the case with his self-depiction as a martyr at the stake.

Governing the Body

This leads to a history of Blanco's body—yet one more story in Blanco's life—which comprises three main stages, or chapters. As noted, in Blanco's view Catholicism stresses the need to master the body through ascetic practices that despise and punish it, such as permanent enclosure (the nunneries), self-flagellation, or the constant surveillance and control of erotic impulses, which in the case of priests led to the institution of celibacy. This story, narrated by Blanco in the Spanish chapters of *The Life of the Rev. Joseph Blanco White,* is more the story of the Catholic body than of Blanco's body. But in *The Examination of Blanco by White,* written years earlier, he presents a more personalized narrative of the body, one in which it is primarily the seat of uncontrollable erotic impulses that Blanco is at pains to fit into a meaningful narrative. The reason for that failure to explain the body resides in the fact that Blanco has not been able yet to move away from the Catholic imagining of the body. This conception fills with guilt his gropings for freedom and hinders his intelligibility of that process. Once again, it would be later in England that the story of his body would evolve, simultaneously with his reshaping of his mind.

The second important chapter in the story of his body takes place around the years (end of 1815 through the beginning of 1817) that he spent living with the Hollands as tutor to their son. In his journal, and later in retrospect, he traces the convolutions of his diseased body and his melancholy mind in an attempt now to relate, now to disentangle, their respective manifestations. In any case his body and his mind are intertwined and his observation of them is accompanied by a constant "government of [his] thoughts" in order to control "his disorder of the imagination and feelings," which he also relates to being punished for his previous sins. During his time with the Hollands, he leads an ascetic life, not by bodily mortification, but by monastic devotions and meditations designed to subdue his understanding (1: 294, 296, 293).

With his embrace of Unitarianism, his body changes again, and he writes its final chapter. During the last years of his life, the body is no longer the seed of unsettling and uncontrollable erotic impulses, nor is it a part of him obscurely but tightly tied to his bouts of melancholy. In its final avatar the body is still primarily the seed of passions and the seat of disease, but as such it is also the palaestra where reason endures its final ordeal. In a set of religious meditations that he wrote in 1840, he rails against those who see the body as the devil's domain, exhort its mortification through ascetic practices, and thus believe "that Satan is the author of whatever, [sic] is productive of pleasure, of health, vigour and cheerfulness" (3: 254, 255). Still, a dimension of the body that has not changed for him is its close relationship with the imagination. For the body is the ultimate cause of religious enthusiasm, which he sees as depending on physical and pathological causes that excite the imagination, a "treacherous faculty" that incites men to surrender to religion (3: 115, 38).[40] Whether of the flesh or of the mind, the passions are for him allied to the imagination, and now, at this final stage of his life, he insists not on the intrinsic malignancy of the senses but on the need to govern them through reason (3: 121–22). Here he echoes Marcus Aurelius, who proposes a similar rule of governance: "not to yield to the persuasions of the body, for it is the peculiar office of the rational and intelligent motion . . . never to be overpowered either by the motion of the senses or of the appetites, for both are animal; but the intelligent motion claims superiority. . ." (Meditations, VII.55, 541). The very last incarnation of his body is thus as a palaestra where his reason wages an agonic battle. In the last years of his life his bodily sufferings must have been overwhelming, as attested by the constant references in his journal to his physical tribulations. But even in the midst of the most terrible pain, and especially then, he is not so much obsessed with the pain itself but with the thought that it threatens to overpower his reason. His references to his physical ailments are interspersed with constant allusions to them as a trial "to conform to the will of God," to the need to exert self-government, and to maintain himself under the control of reason in the face of unbearable pain (3: 47, 163, 215). His delirious, sublimating self-imagining as a martyr is a fitting embodiment of his final truth, as is the last entry in his journal, "Got up," a terse but touching testimony to his unremitting will to self-governance, written on February 6, 1841, just a few weeks before his death. Thom takes up the task of giving testimony when Blanco was unable to continue doing so, and he records the progress of Blanco's disease as well as his final thoughts: "In the midst of my sufferings, all the leading thoughts are present with me. . . . I have contributed my mite to the Liberty of mankind. . . . God's providence is carried on by the struggles of Reason against the Passions" (3: 302).

Foucault observes that the religious crisis in the sixteenth century led to a rejection of confessional practices and to a reactivation of Stoic doctrines, whose influence, studied by Peter Gay, reached its zenith in the eighteenth century.[41] Blanco White seems to have made a late discovery of the Stoic formulations of a Seneca or a Marcus Aurelius—he refers to them only in the last years of his life—but he does so in a spirit of complete identification. The congruence between Blanco and the Stoics reaches well beyond a mere coincidence of ideas to include also what Foucault calls the care of the self, a form of relationship with oneself, typical of the Hellenistic age, which is much more complex than the mere knowledge of oneself that later became, and still is, prevalent in the West. In opposition to the obsession with the endless decipherment and purification promoted by Christianity, the Stoics proposed a relation with oneself founded on a self-control, or ascesis, that was at the service of practical conduct. In other words, according to Foucault, the Stoics linked together the knowledge of oneself, the structure of the self (proclaiming the superiority of the logos) and practical reason.[42] One finds this exact arrangement in Blanco's self-formulations once he simultaneously discovers Stoicism, embraces Unitarianism, and proclaims the divinity of reason, reaching a form of self-knowledge in which the self is characterized by a hierarchical structure, with "conscientious reason"—a term he prefers to mere "reason" in order to stress its practical dimension—occupying a position of superiority and domination over the passions.[43] From this perspective one can ascertain that Blanco's radical break consists in passing from a consideration of the mind and the body as places to be endlessly scrutinized following the Catholic or Anglican scripts—and therefore as sites with potentially troubling blind spots—to a conception in which, once his "free" inquiry into his self reaches the point of acknowledging its divinity, his task in life becomes one of management of body and imagination so that they never escape the supervision of the superior faculty, reason. In a way Blanco renounces his desire to know body and imagination, conceding that they are realms of darkness that, even if impossible to know, must nevertheless be rationally managed.

Living and Dying by the Book

Blanco White's incessantly revisionary self-reading and self-writing bring home the paradoxical realization that personal truth is never an absolute and reachable goal but just another form of passion that afflicts autobiographers. This insight in no way casts a pall upon Blanco's endless search. On the contrary, it makes that search into an exemplary autobiographical case. Deleuze argues that because all enunciation is social, there is only indirect speech, and thus speaking in one's own name is not "a matter of everyone finding their moment of truth in memoirs or psychoanalysis; it's not just a matter of speaking in the first person. But of identifying the impersonal physical and mental forces you confront and fight as soon as you try to do something. . . . Being itself is in this sense political."[44] As a matter of fact, Blanco White's autobiographical output combines the best of both worlds, for it is a first-person, autobiographical narrative in which the endless search for truth is conducted not by digging deeper and deeper into a storehouse of forgotten or repressed memories but by a constant reformulation or reconstruction of the play of forces that contend to "name" Blanco White, to give content to that proper name. His search is impelled anew, over and over, by his awareness of a disjunction between his feelings and desires, and the commands imposed by the dominant practices and discourses that create the sense of reality where he uneasily dwells. Feeling is a "resisting emotion," argue Deleuze and Guattari.[45] As has been mentioned, in his first autobiographical work Blanco can only register his resistances without being able to give them a shape, and so *The Examination of Blanco by White* can only be a painstaking chronicle of the guilt occasioned by the disproportion between his erotic desires and the imperatives of celibacy, as well as by what he felt was a senseless—even at the time of writing—fall into atheism; however, in *Letters from Spain, Practical and Internal Evidence* and the narrative part of *The Life of the Rev. Joseph Blanco White* he converts into plot his previous feelings of disjunction or resistance. The same can be said for the story of his Anglican years: only in retrospect, once in possession of his Stoic/Unitarian truth, can he really figure his Anglican past and elucidate, under his official story, the no-longer-hidden narrative of his resistance to it during the sixteen years (1818–1834) when he smothered his "truer" Unitarian ideas. In each case, only when he has reached a point of illumination does he manage to tell his past's "real" story, which always features a conflict between practices and discourses that created the "wrong" kind of feelings and desires, and another set of discourses that he fully identifies with at the time of writing—but that is liable to take a new shape in future autobiographical outlooks. Those contending discourses vie to create different types of subjectivation, and Blanco's subjectivity develops at the point where those forces clash or intersect.[46] Blanco's self and body could thus be characterized as battlegrounds, constantly shifting and reshaping in response to feelings of disjunction or disadjustment. His written lives are an incessant replacement of discourses with more fitting ones, a persistent readaptation in search of a truth that in the end, and regardless of his being convinced of its absoluteness, is felt as such by Blanco only because the discourses he speaks through conform with his feelings and desires, give him the capacity to produce a satisfactory self-understanding, make him believe he is speaking with his own voice. In a word: truth is only contented self-deception.

From the point of view of the workings of autobiography, Blanco's case is also paradigmatic in that he reconstructs his identity by highlighting the retrospective role of reading. From Fénelon to Feijoo, from Seneca to Kant, Blanco recreates his life through the painstaking discovery of books and authors whose ideas he can call his own, ideas he cannot resist: when he reaches that point of identification, he revoices them, and they speak his identity. Nothing illustrates this process better than Blanco's relations with the Bible, which he subjects to a relentless historical hermeneusis—a form of reading that only the Enlightenment made possible—until he exacts an apparently faultless reading that leads him to discard its infallible and revelatory nature and to argue instead that it contains not a divine story but only a kernel of doctrine, a true spirit that Blanco disinters from under both the history of the institutional church and the avatars of his faith. In their appraisal of the role played by the book in the process of subjectification, Deleuze and Guattari point out that, with the Reformation, interpretation rejects all intermediaries and specialists and becomes direct, "since the book is written in itself and in the heart."[47] They call this stage "the passional regime of subjectification," and Blanco's defection from Catholicism to Protestantism obeys that logic. But later he takes one more step forward, by placing the book of his heart above the outside one, by making his life a testimony to the historical and institutional corruptions of the Bible. His unerring reconstruction of the Bible's truth is founded on his identification with Christ's doctrine and sufferings and on his presupposition that he carries the spirit within him. When he rejects the Anglican interpretation of the Bible, Blanco is dismissing its historical manifestations in favor of the perfect coincidence, in his self, of nature and divinity, of reason and religion. This congruence allows Blanco to construct his self's ultimate truth, and he finds the final proof of his self's veracity in the accordance between the story in the Bible (Christ's testimony and his final immolation) and Blanco's story, which culminates with his self-imaging as a martyr, as a witness to truth. His repossession of his self demands its immolation in a passion that is also a paradox.

Thus Blanco's life is a journey from witness-victim of erroneous doctrines to witness-martyr of unassailable truth, and consequently, at each stage of his passion, he offers his sufferings as proof: first, of Catholic oppression; later, of the sincerity of his desire to embrace Anglicanism—"what trial of that sincerity could equal that of the internal sufferings which I have for many years submitted to, in the pursuit of a belief which I could never thoroughly obtain?" (*The Life of the Rev. Joseph Blanco White* 1: 402); and finally in his willed martyrdom as proof positive of his having found both the true spirit of Christianity and his real self.[48] And both truths receive their confirmation in the passion of Blanco's body, a passion that mimics Christ's. Blanco's life then is a relentless search for a sacrifice he can gladly accept. In accordance with that search, his body changes from a wild territory of barely controllable impulses (Catholicism), to a painful proof of his sincerity (Anglicanism), and then to a field of ordeals (Unitarianism). But despite Blanco's repeated complaints at the end of his life about the increasing isolation that his creeds and disease have brought him, as a witness to truth a martyr can never suffer in solitude if such sacrifice is to be a public testimony for another.

Forever Confessing

This brings one to another inescapable feature of Blanco's writings of the self, one as unfailing as his obsession with religion and truth: all his writings are structured as responses to, or dialogues with, another. As already pointed out, *The Examination of Blanco by White* is arranged as a confessional interrogation of his past self (Blanco) at the hands of his present one (White). Although he did not sustain the form throughout (a failure that could be attributed to his inexperience at self-writing), what is truly relevant is his initial attraction to this confessional device; at any rate his self-scrutiny is as relentless and unsettling when he uses the confessional form as when he abandons it. In *Letters from Spain,* the Spanish priest tells the story of his life to the traveler Leucadio Doblado in another personality-splitting stratagem in which an objective observer listens to the priest's story. *Practical and Internal Evidence against Catholicism* consists of six letters addressed to those British and Irish Catholics whose education has not smothered in them "a natural passion of truth" (18)—Blanco's replicas, one could say; and this book's digest, *The Poor Man's Preservative against Popery* is structured as a catechismic question-and-answer, a dialogue between Blanco and a representative of the British masses. In a similar dialogical vein, Blanco structured *The Life of the Rev. Joseph Blanco White* as a letter to his friend Archbishop Whately (who encouraged him to write his life), and he launched the project impelled by "the necessity of leaving my friends in possession of every important fact relating to myself, in order that they may refute the calumnies and misrepresentations of my enemies, when I shall be no more" (*The Life of the Rev. Joseph Blanco White* 1: 1). As the reader will remember, his final sustained autobiographical statement is yet another letter that is addressed to Thom, whom Blanco had chosen as his literary executor.[49] Blanco's *The Life of the Rev. Joseph Blanco White,* like all his other autobiographical writings, is a response structured as an apostrophe, that is, addressed to Whately but really destined for a third party.[50]

In sum, Blanco is always writing to another and for another—another who is not simply Whately, Thom, or any of the direct interlocutors in his autobiographical writings. Blanco is responding: all his autobiographical constructions are responses, presentations to the world, for its examination, of his spiritual accounts. In this way, and it could not be any other way for him, his autobiographies are confessions. As Foucault argues, confession is a fundamental technique of subjectification, one of the privileged forms for creating a discourse of truth about oneself, "a ritual that unfolds within a power relationship," for confession takes place in the presence of another who requires the confession "and intervenes in order to judge, punish, forgive, console, and reconcile." It is also a ritual whose enunciation has certain effects on the person who pronounces it (redemption, liberation, etc.).[51] Catholic confession imposes on the confessed the will to a self-knowledge whose shape is determined by the requirements of confession and whose enunciation vis-à-vis the confessor does not merely express that knowledge but validates it: the performative aspect of confession not only is not at odds with its epistemological dimension but in fact determines and supports it in fundamental ways. In a similar manner, as confessional performance autobiography follows, implicitly or explicitly, a dialogical structure of interrogation (one which Blanco assays in *The Examination of Blanco by White* and other writings); but above all autobiography is a manifestation of an imperative that creates a need to respond to the other. As such this imperative is a form of subjectification that also determines autobiography's thematics and its confessional form(s). It could be argued, moreover, that confession as the will to take responsibility not only founds autobiography's form and themes, but also sustains the possibility of practices such as Catholic confession.[52]

As already indicated, the side of Catholic confession that Blanco considered pernicious was its demand that one put one's conscience and ideas under the authority of a priest whose function is to perpetuate the church's dominance, thus helping an erroneous Christianity to prevail. Blanco, then, rejects a particular type of noxious confession and will be on guard all his life against its surreptitious subsistence in his psychological makeup. Looking at his life retrospectively, he believes that the persistence in him of a Catholic "ascetic spirit of humility" made him feel, when he wrote *Practical and Internal Evidence against Catholicism,* "as if I had been at the Confessor's feet, entirely under that infantine fear of not being a sufficiently severe accuser of myself, which the early practice of confession raises in a sincere boy" (*The Life of the Rev. Joseph Blanco White* 1: 383–84).[53] But his repudiation of Catholic confession in no way amounts to a renunciation of confessing, and that is precisely what Blanco will do over and over again in his writings. However, once he breaks with all forms of religious orthodoxy, Blanco gains the right not to follow the institutional scripts of confession but to follow his own guidelines, and consequently he achieves the freedom to say anything, to say finally and exactly what he has been striving to say all his life— and so, after leaving the Whatelys, he not only redoes *Heresy and Orthodoxy* but also writes "A Sketch of His Mind in England," the "Letter to . . . Thom," and all his other religious/autobiographical manifestos that have been mentioned here.

Derrida suggests that a revolution in law and politics granted literature "the right to say anything, and it is to the great advantage of literature that is an operation at once political, democratic and *philosophical,* to the extent that literature allows one to pose questions that are often repressed in a philosophical context. . . . In this responsibility to say anything in literature, there is a political experience as to knowing who is responsible for what and before whom."[54] This linkage between responsibility and the freedom to say anything pertains with even more propriety to autobiography, as Blanco White's writings exemplify. Derrida's belief that literature has a more questioning ability than philosophy leads back to Loesberg's thesis about Victorian autobiography being a (superior) substitute for philosophy: "One turns to the fictions of autobiography as a result of the flaws in the philosophy. One turns to autobiography to substantiate through narrative description what cannot be substantiated through philosophical discourse" (14). Loesberg's proposal must be refined for it to be valid in Blanco's case. It would not be accurate to say that Blanco substitutes autobiography for philosophy: he does not simply exchange one for the other. On incorporating philosophical ideas into the fabric of his autobiographies (to the point that in the end the philosophical seems to take the place of the biographical), he brands philosophy as an autobiographical enterprise and instills into it the marks of the personal that philosophy as a genre avoids or rejects. And it is not merely a matter of subjectivizing philosophical discourse or of bringing to the fore a signature that would normally remain anonymous (as if philosophy were a discourse that generated and sustained itself in a political and personal vacuum). Nor is it a matter of Blanco borrowing philosophical ideas in order to confirm and recuperate what he considers was always in him, that natural state that he believes his Catholic education smothered under layers of perverted feeling and spurious dogma. By making Kant's or Seneca's ideas into his mind and flesh, Blanco responds for, and to, those philosophies, infusing them with a personal/religious history that has nothing to do with so-called history of philosophy. In conclusion, rectifying Loesberg's assertion, Blanco makes autobiography philosophical and philosophy autobiographical. Blanco does not make philosophy personal: he makes it responsible. He does not merely borrow philosophy's themes: he suffuses them with responsibility; he makes them respond for his self by incarnating them in his written life.

"I am I in the sole measure that I am responsible, a non interchangeable I. . . . Such is my inalienable identity of subject," writes

Levinas.[55] This responsibility, which constitutes the fiber and foundation of the self, manifests itself supremely in autobiography and makes
the latter inseparable from confession, thus imposing the need to
reassess the meanings of *confession* and of that other, closely related
term, *apology,* which in many nineteenth-century titles stood for autobiography. By reducing it to a category imbued with suspect connotations or to an autobiographical subgenre whose heyday is well past,
apology is taken for granted. But some luster needs to be restored to
the word because no other word embodies better (together with *confession*) what autobiography is about. An apology is the preeminent
autobiographical act because it represents taking responsibility for
one's truth, even when the apologist is consciously lying or is wrong,
misguided, or deluded, because it is primarily a saying and not a content; an exposure to another of the autobiographer's truths; and a
response to the primordial ethical demand for responsibility.[56] This
responsibility that makes the self unique, not substitutable, also constitutes the foundation of the subject as subjection to another, as subjugation to the commands that, coming from the outside, the self
makes its own, thus hearing them as coming from the inside. This blurring of the borders between inside and outside is an absolute necessity
when we posit a subject, and it makes of interiority "not a secret place
somewhere in me" but an internalization of the exterior that commands me "by my own voice" and testifies to the internal fission of the
subject and points to the other.[57]

    Without this blurring internalization there would not be a foundation
for any political (re)constitution of the subject nor would there be any
reason for the subject to engage in what Deleuze calls indirect speech or
for it to heed what Althusser denominates "ideological interpellation,"
the ideological call from the other outside that constitutes the subject,
according to Althusser, as primarily political.[58] Deleuze and Guattari
argue that in modern forms of subjectification power no longer emanates
from a transcendent center but is instead immanent, operating through
normalization, which leads to the paradox that "the more you obey the
statements of the dominant reality, the more in command you are as subject of enunciation in mental reality, for in the end you are only obeying
yourself."[59] But why should the subject obey such statements or heed the
call of "ideological interpellation," unless one posits a primordial ethical
instance of responsibility that antecedes, grounds, and makes possible the
political?[60] Without an ethical foundation politics would be unable to

impose any order. However, while the political needs the foundation of the ethical, it would be a delusion to pretend to live in the latter and ignore the former. This pretension is Blanco's last illusion. Blanco constructs his life as a progressive rejection of the outside commands of religious establishments and a concomitant reconquest of the right to maturity, of the freedom to obey solely the commands of the natural/divine—an exterior that he interiorizes and makes into his own self. However, Blanco accomplishes this right to self-mastery only at the price of an increasing self- enclosure and isolation that amounts to an idealized confinement in the ethical and an oblivion of the political. Obviously his disease restricted him to the confines of his house (and even to his bed), but there is another kind of self-enclosure. The changes in his ideas impose on him a number of displacements toward a geographical and social periphery; however, this increasing marginality, while granting him a privileged view into the workings of the religious establishments, pushes him further and further into the realm of his own ideas, which end up acquiring the stiffness of dogma. The fact that Channing, who shows in his letters a fervent admiration for Blanco, ended up rebuking him for his narrow and obdurate concept of imagination illustrates Blanco's progressive and pigheaded isolation.[61] The attempt to find the perfect confessor, the faultless reader that would make all other superfluous, that would make confession a one-to-one affair, seems a natural temptation for autobiographers. Augustine confesses directly to God, and Rousseau, moved to despair in the face of his contemporaries' misunderstanding of his life, ends up by invoking God as infallible granter of justice. Going further than those two predecessors, in "The Rationalist A-Kempis, or The Religious Sceptic in God's Presence" (1840)—arguably his last doctrinal statement—Blanco not only confesses to God ("to Thee I may venture to speak humbly but freely, in the sanctuary of my soul," 3: 231) but also affirms a coincidence of identities ("Thou hast identified me with Thee," 3: 231) that allows him to perform a stunning reversal of roles by which the life that becomes contentious is not Blanco's but God's: "I speak the truth before Thee, oh my misrepresented God" (3: 266). By this identification and reversal, God becomes the guarantor of Blanco's truth, and conversely Blanco assures the right representation of God to the point of martyrdom. But the very dialogical pattern of Blanco's writings, duplicated by his intentions of having all his papers published posthumously, supersedes this unsustainable ethical bliss and puts his life and truth in the hands of others.

Blanco's awareness that he does not control his self's fate impels him
to write *The Life of the Rev. Joseph Blanco White,* as he himself states at
its beginning. It could also be said that all his life Blanco was looking
for the perfect reader, one that at a certain point he thought he had
found in Whately, to whom Blanco not only addresses *The Life of the Rev.
Joseph Blanco White* but of whom he also writes in that same work: "The
rest had to study me; you read me without preparation" (1: 2). Blanco
surely found his readers, although it seems that the majority failed to
prepare adequately to read the *The Life of the Rev. Joseph Blanco White.*
None was worse prepared than the Spanish philologist Menéndez
Pelayo, a stentorian and influential nineteenth-century mouthpiece for
a conservative, Catholic vision of Spain, who denounced Blanco's life as
a perpetual error: ""Toda creencia, todo capricho de la mente o del
deseo se convirtió en él en pasión; y como su fantasía era tan móvil
como arrebatado y violento su carácter, fue espejo lastimosísimo de la
desorganización moral a que arrastra el predominio de las facultades
imaginativas sueltas a todo galope en medio de una época turbulen-
ta"(Every belief, every fancy conceived by his mind or his desire became
for him a passion; and since his fantasy was as voluble as his character,
he was a painful example of the kind of moral disorganization produced
by the predominance of the imaginative faculties, set free on the gallop,
in a tumultuous age).[62] Menéndez Pelayo's accusation is nothing short
of paradoxical, given Blanco's unremitting exaltation of reason and his
equally persistent condemnation of the passions and the imagination.
On the other hand, however, it could be said that Menéndez Pelayo
faithfully followed the directives for the reading of autobiography that
Blanco advocated when, commenting on the memoirs of the Quaker
John Woolman, he wrote: "Autobiographies are instructive, almost
without exception, provided that the reader knows how to study
mankind. . . . [A]s the prejudices and passions of the reader can scarcely ever be identical with those of the writer, there is the greatest probability that the delusions of the latter will generally be apparent to the
former, merely from the circumstance that he is placed in a different
position" (*The Life of the Rev. Joseph Blanco White* 3: 366–67).

After more than half a century of silence on his work—finally broken mainly by Vicente Llorens's distinguished and sustained contributions—Blanco would seem to have found a very receptive reader in
Juan Goytisolo, who, writing in 1972, tries to rescue him from the
"dungeon" to which he was confined by Menéndez Pelayo: "Separados

de la obra de Blanco por el denso telón de silencio y oprobio de nuestros *zombis*, sus eventuales lectores no han podido arrancarle de la casilla en que lo encerrara el conocido celo apostólico del polígrafo montañes. Mazmorra o sepultura más bien, ¡y vaya una!—la de apóstata, renegado, abominable y antipatriota, que justificaría por sí sola la mortaja piadosa que lo cubre" (Separated from Blanco's work by the thick curtain of silence and ignominy of our zombies, his chance readers have been unable to move him from the box where he was imprisoned by Menéndez Pelayo's apostolic fervor. A dungeon or a grave, more likely, and what a grave!—that of the apostate, the renegade, the abominable antipatriot, the latter alone being enough to justify the pious shroud that covers him).[63] Goytisolo's reading, however, is as biased as that by Menéndez. By privileging Blanco's early rejection of Spain and his final condemnation of all orthodoxies, Goytisolo ignores the religious search that consumed most of Blanco's life. It seems as if this apostate will never find a way to return home if only because, following the logic of the passions that he proposes, his reading of himself will only be the first in an endless chain of readings that will correct and engender one another. Thus, writing his autobiography in order to correct false future readings of his life appears to be a pointless gesture that will be able to stop neither that interminable reading nor the misunderstandings that it inherently provokes. By laying out his faiths and faults in writing, Blanco simultaneously unleashes and tries to contain the terror of that infinite reading; but he cannot escape the testamentary nature of autobiographical writing, and, as the fate of his work illustrates, politics never fails to reclaim the self.

MARÍA TERESA LEÓN
The Ruins of Memory

An extraordinary group of women, born at the turn of the century, reached a distinction in Spanish politics and the arts that was unprecedented in its scale. Most of them sympathized with liberal positions, and the defeat of their side in the Civil War forced them into exile, where many of them wrote autobiographical texts focusing on their experiences during the war and exile or chronicling their whole lives or at least a significant part of them. Most of the numerous works that deal with the war and/or exile are straightforward chronological narratives that hold significant interest for what they tell about the private and public vicissitudes of their authors at a distressing time.[1] Some of those women who, not coincidentally, were also "professional" writers, authored autobiographical texts whose significant informational interest is enriched by their narrative complexity. Among them stand out Rosa Chacel (1898–1994), María Zambrano (1904– 1992), and María Teresa León (1904–1988), whose autobiographical works are among the most fascinating ever written in Spain.[2] Those works are vastly different from each other, both in terms of the periods covered and in their narrative strategies. Chacel deals only with the first ten years of her life; and while Zambrano reaches until her twentieth year, León covers some sixty years, from her childhood until about 1967. As far as their narrative organization, Chacel's text adheres to a straight chronology more than the other two do, although it is by no means devoid of complex layerings; owing much to the vanguardist style that proceeds through indirection, Zambrano's text is the most elliptical of the three and lacks almost any temporal bearings, while reflection prevails over strict narrative. Although many parts of León's work follow temporal linearity, many others are presented through a complex chronological interweaving; and although the first person dominates, the narrator switches occasionally to the second and third persons.

Rosa Chacel has had a somewhat prominent, if constantly belea-guered, intellectual reputation in Spain since the early thirties, and her work has generated an abundant critical bibliography. Zambrano, who like Chacel grew intellectually under the long shadow of Ortega y Gasset, fell into relative oblivion in Spain during her exile years, despite her numerous publications in Spanish American countries, and she did not start to receive critical attention again until the early seventies.[3] Her rediscovery reached a high point in the eighties, when many of her books were reprinted or saw the light of day for the first time and when she received numerous accolades, among them the 1981 Premio Príncipe de Asturias, the highest literary prize granted in Spain. Although María Teresa León began writing and publishing very early in her life, her political activities have always taken the spotlight from her artistic activities, which have also been overshadowed by the extraordinary literary prominence of her second husband, the well-known poet Rafael Alberti. León began publishing in newspapers in 1924, and between 1928 (when her first book of stories appeared) and 1978, she published a considerable number of works. She wrote several collections of short stories, two novels, four novelized biographies (of the Cid; his wife, Jimena; Bécquer; and Cervantes), and a travel book, *Sonríe China* (1958), coauthored with Alberti, although his contribution seems limited to the book's illustrations and to some poems included in it. Although her literary production is uneven, some of her works certainly deserve close attention, among them some of her short stories, her extraordinary *Memoria de la melancolía* (1970; Memory of Melancholy), and the multi-voiced autobiographical novel, *Juego limpio* (1959; Fair Play), based on her experiences during the war (some of which are also narrated in *Memoria de la melancolía*).[4]

María Teresa León was born in the city of Logroño in 1903, in an upper-middle-class family. The itinerant life of her military father kept the family constantly on the move (Madrid, Burgos, Barcelona) in León's first fifteen years, a nomadism that seems to have had a profound impact on her life. She married and had her first child at age seventeen, with a second one coming in 1925. While still in her early twenties she separated from her husband and lost custody of her two children. In 1929 she began a relationship with Rafael Alberti, and they married in 1933. She shared with Alberti a committed Leftist militancy that found expression in the revolutionary journal *Octubre,* which they coedited in the early thirties. Together they traveled extensively throughout their lives, starting in 1932, when they went to Russia (where they would return) and northern Europe with a fellowship to study contemporary European theater. In 1935 they traveled to the United States to disseminate the truth about the brutal military repression of miners in Asturias in 1934, also visiting several Spanish American countries. They lived for most of the Civil War in the headquarters of the Alianza de Intelectuales Antifascistas (Alliance of Antifascists Intellectuals) in Madrid, where they performed a series of tasks, the most important of which was being in charge of moving the Museo del Prado collection, first to Valencia and later to France, in order to avoid its possible destruction. Under attack by international experts who questioned their qualifications to take care of such an important task, León defended that operation in a booklet published in 1944.[5] Alberti and León left Spain at the end of the war in 1939; they lived for one year in Paris, working for Radio France, moving in 1940 to Buenos Aires, where they lived for more than twenty years and published many of their books, while they kept traveling, among other places to China (1957). The political and artistic censorship imposed by Perón forced them to move again in 1963, this time to Rome, until the legalization of the Spanish Communist Party in 1977 allowed their safe return to Spain, where they arrived that April.[6]

The Pitfalls of Melancholia

Memoria de la melancolía is a most apt title for María Teresa León's autobiographical text. In its double meaning that title gathers all the rich and wrenching contents of the text, while opening a number of venues to explore not only León's personal narrative but also the workings of autobiographical memory in general. As the title suggests, at first sight the book can be considered as a memoir in which León is the subject who remembers her past with melancholy. This is in line with the expected, straightforward meaning of the typical autobiography: a subject who remembers. But the title admits a second possible reading, which adds a peculiar dimension to the book: in that interpretation of the title, "melancholy" remembers, it is the subject of a memory that is then no longer ascribable to María Teresa León. Exploring the book from this perspective of the memory of an impersonal subject complicates the interpretations afforded by the first, more conventional view of the title. At stake are questions about the properties of memory, about the proper relationship between the subject and its memories, and in particular about the problematic nature of that possessive, *its*, that links the subject and memory. Any interpretation of León's text must pay attention to the clashes and connections of those two memories, León's and melancholy's, and thus to what León's memory and memories tell one about how melancholy can haunt and shape remembrance.

First of all, however, one must make sure that "melancholy" belongs in the title, since it could well be that such a state does not accurately represent the experiences recounted in the narrative. Such healthy distrust is allayed by even the most cursory reading of León's book, suffused as it is by loss and longing, by the pains and pleasures of melancholy. The question, then, concerns the consequences and desires involved in the act of melancholy recalling, of recalling melancholy. In particular one must explore whether the melancholy subject really desires to eradicate melancholy. León invokes melancholy as if she were its prisoner, but her melancholic narration of melancholy, her open indulgence in the puzzling pleasures of extreme sorrow, seems to indicate that after all melancholy might have some saving grace.

A second area replete with potential pitfalls concerns the role of politics in León's melancholy. The temptation to look for the origin of León's melancholy in particular political circumstances is very strong, given the fact that the book was written in exile and focuses in good measure, although by no means exclusively, on the Spanish Civil War and the travails of exile. A simplistic political reading would see the origin of melancholy in the lost war, the defeated ideals, and the ensuing exile, with its painful separation from a lost homeland that León constantly evokes and longs to return to. In this view war and the forced exit from Spain would be a traumatic experience, a loss of hope and homeland that León refuses to accept, thus falling into melancholy. This possible reading, however, would leave out of consideration the parts of *Memoria de la melancolía* devoted to León's life before, and outside, the war and would thus leave in darkness her lifelong obsession with severance, displacement, abandonment, and loss.

Freud's understanding of melancholy provides a good start for delving into the complexities of León's affliction. As it is well known, in *Mourning and Melancholy* Freud ascribes melancholy to the inability of the self to let go of a lost object (generally a dead person), to its reluctance to loosen the links with the vanished object. Instead of engaging in the work of mourning, which slowly breaks the affective charges binding the subject to the vanished object, the melancholic, refusing to accept the loss, introjects the lost object while simultaneously experiencing aggressive feelings toward it (Freud adds that the subject ends up turning against itself the aggression directed at the now-introjected object, resulting in the subject's self-devaluation and guilt). The stubbornness of the subject prevents mourning from performing its normal function of gradually assuaging, and accepting, the loss, a failure that transforms the labor of mourning into the permanent process of grieving known as melancholy.[7] Haunted by wrenching separations, León's written life fits this description; however, still left is the task of identifying the loss(es) she never accepted, the moment of trauma after which nothing was ever the same. Such wholesale modification will start by altering the experience of time itself, melancholy being mainly about time and timing.

Far from being the only episode of loss endured by León, the war is one more, albeit very important, experience of privation in a life story periodically punctured by ruptures and separations. León's remembrances could be grouped in three distinctive sets that correspond to three different periods of her life: her memories before the thirties; those of the years leading to the Civil War and of the war itself; and finally the recollections of her exile from 1939 to approximately 1967.[8] León's experiences in the first and third periods are strikingly different from each other, but they have in common her insistence on separation, severance, and uprootedness. As such those experiences are pervaded by melancholy, by her feeling of having suffered irreparable losses, although with the passing of narrated time it becomes increasingly difficult to specify what those losses are, to the point that *Memoria de la melancolía* ends up resembling the representation of a pure and permanently ongoing experience of loss. Correspondingly *Memoria de la melancolía* gradually shifts its focus from the grief generated by a loss of object that she misses to the sorrow engendered by the thought of getting lost, literally, without being missed.

Although *Memoria de la melancolía* does not follow a strict chronological sequence, it starts out with the narrative of León's childhood experiences and thoughts. From its beginning the stress falls on the constant separations and readaptations that marked her early life: "Niña de militar inadaptada siempre, . . . con amigas de paso. . . . La vida parecía hecha para acomodar los ojos a cosas nuevas" (Forever a maladjusted army brat, . . . with transient friends. . . . Life seemed made to accommodate one's eyes to ever-changing things.)[9] Some of her most significant experiences and impressions corroborate or reinforce that assessment: her gripping fear that one day her family might forget to pick her up at school; her anxiety when confronting family squabbles caused mainly by her father's infidelities; her early, traumatic sexual experiences with boys, incomprehensible to her (both the boys and the experiences); her separation from her husband, which forced her also to part company with her two children (she lingers with harrowing detail on her son's close encounter with death after the separation). Perhaps all those diverse experiences are best summarized by León in the passage that opens her autobiographical account, in which she tells of one more family move: "Llegaba decidida a todo. . . . Había decidido dentro de sí la urgencia de agarrarse con las dos manos a todo lo que había huído desde tiempo remoto, pues todo para ella había consistido en llegar, cambiar, echar a andar, encariñarse e irse" (11; She arrived determined to everything. . . . She had decided inwardly to clutch with both hands to everything that had escaped her from early on, since so far her life had been to arrive, to change, to get on the move again, to get attached to things, to leave again). After this observation León reproduces the quote from Lucian of Samosata that she uses as epigraph for *Memoria de la melancolía:* "Las cosas de los mortales / todas pasan, / si ellas no pasan somos nosotros / los que pasamos"(All that belongs to mortals is mortal. . . .)[10] It would seem that León finds in Lucian's affirmation of universal transience a good expression of her depriving experiences, but the significant differences between León's and Lucian's views of transitoriness will become clear.

In contrast with the emphasis on displacement in her account of the first twenty-five years of her life, León's reminiscences of the period that encompasses from 1929, when she began her relationship with Alberti, until 1939, when the war ended, are characterized by an almost feverish sense of purpose, of elated belonging, of glorious plenitude. Especially the years of the war, seemingly the happiest in León's life, are dominated by manic elation—the antithesis of sorrow and the other side of melancholy according to Freud: "Los días más luminosos de la vida fueron aquellos tres años de ojos brillantes, cuando la palabra camarada sustituyó al señor y la vida generosamente dada sustituyó a la mezquina" (28; The most luminous years of our lives were those three years of shining eyes, when the word 'comrade' replaced 'lord,' and life generously sacrificed replaced selfishness).[11] It could be surprising, at first sight, that such a tragic and deadly episode as the Spanish Civil War would be considered as a time of plenitude, but this is the way León, anticipating such objection, unhesitantly characterizes it: "Días felices. ¿Felices los días de guerra? ¿Está usted loca? Y yo añado . . . : los mejores de nuestra vida" (222; Happy days. Happy the days of war? Are you deranged? And I add . . . : the best of our life). León's singular and momentous view of the Civil War calls for a peculiar reading, one which should also become a keystone in any interpretation of her autobiographical text.

In opposition to the elation of the war, the years of exile impose on her a return to the predominant mood of her childhood and early adulthood. One of the preeminent experiences of severance, exile frequently leads to a feeling of displacement and uprootedness that inflects the exile's psychological makeup to a greater or lesser extent, but whose effects are nonetheless mitigated by the passage of time. Framing exile along the lines of the Freudian contrast between mourning and melancholy (a comparison that exile, as experience of loss, fully warrants), it could be said that in most cases the exiled person, while not forgetting the lost homeland, becomes gradually accommodated to the new settings, eventually accepting, as the person in mourning does, the reality of the loss. This was the case with most of the exiles of the Spanish Civil War, although they, like most expatriates, at first thought of their banishment as only a temporary condition and were constantly making plans for their return to the homeland.[12] Not so León. In the thirty years of exile spanned in *Memoria de la melancolía,* her sense of loss and uprootedness only increases with time, ending up by encompassing new, similar experiences, one of the most salient being the new exile imposed because of Perón's censorship. Her description of Rome upon first arriving there from Argentina uncannily resembles her account, quoted above, of arriving in a new town during her peripatetic childhood:

> Había llegado a la ciudad [Roma] decidida a besar las fachadas. . . . Años y años sintiéndose expulsada, rechazada, herida por los aleros y los balcones y los filos de las puertas y las calles asfaltadas nunca suyas y todo siempre huyéndola. . . . Se le había caído el alma, la había perdido, la encontró diseminada y rota . . . ¿Por qué no se acababa todo, se olvidaba . . . ? El último grano de la tierra española se le había caído de los zapatos. . . . Memoria para el olvido, por favor. No me dejen ante una ventana extranjera, mirando. . . . Sintió terror de que le hubieran cerrado los postigos de la ventana,

y de las ventanas [sic] de la vida. . . . . Durante años, únicamente sus amigos judíos comprendieron su soledad y hubo
un momento en que creyó podría fabricarse un mundo de
esperanzas, teja a teja. Luego. . . ." "Luego sintió que la
expulsaban de la sociedad como un objeto maligno . . . ¿Otra
vez andar? ¿Hacia dónde? . . . Por eso, cuando apareció la ciu-
dad, sintió deseos de besar las fachadas y las esquinas. . . . Una
patria, Señor, una patria pequeña como un patio. . . . Una
patria para reemplazar a la que me arrancaron del alma de un
solo tirón.(16–17)[13]

In addition to this renewed feeling of uprootedness and exclusion,
her chronicle of those same years (the early sixties) becomes increasingly steeped in death. Toward the end of the book, on page after
page (287–319) she reminisces about dead friends and acquaintances, offering a brief personal obituary of recently deceased people,
such as (in the order she mentions them) Paul Eluard (1895–1952),
Hemingway (1899–1961), Cernuda (1902–1963), Oliverio Girondo
(1891–1967), Zenobia Camprubí (1887–1956), Ilya Ehremburg
(1891–1967), Gómez de la Serna (1888–1963), and a number of less-
er-known friends, some of whom shared time and efforts with León
and Alberti in the Alliance of Antifascist Intellectuals.[14] All that separates these thirty pages of funereal remembrances from León's final
reflections in *Memoria de la melancolía* are some ten pages devoted to
Picasso (which seem oddly out of place, since Picasso would still live
for a number of years). If severance and loss dominate a good part of
Memoria de la melancolía, death presides over its end. But perhaps
death has been lurking between the lines from the narrative's beginning.

Even after such a brief overview of the book, it should be clear that
rupture, displacement, and a struggle to connect and belong play a fundamental role in León's view of her life, not only during her time in exile
but also, and more importantly, in the first twenty-five years of her life.
And yet it could be argued that the trauma of exile imposed retrospectively on the whole of León's life a melancholy view that did not exist
before the experience of exile. However, an examination of the ideological statements that León makes in *Memoria de la melancolía* and other
writings, together with an analysis of her autobiographical representation of the Civil War, elicits a number of inescapable conclusions,

one of them being the realization that for all its severity the exile caused by the Civil War is not the primordial experience of loss in *Memoria de la melancolía.* Conversely her entire life consists of nothing but a sustained exile.

Ideology: Between the Lines

Overall León's ideological pronouncements follow roughly the line of the Spanish Communist Party at the time.[15] Although her political ideas do not show great sophistication in any of her writings, it is still striking how naive they appear to be in *Memoria de la melancolía.* León suppresses any possible discordant note, any semblance of ideological complexity, in order to ground her political vision in solidarity, fraternity, community, and communion of affect: "Ser un revolucionario es cumplir un servicio, se necesita un aprendizaje, tenemos que volver a la obediencia, al abecedario del amor al prójimo" (213; To be a revolutionary is to fulfill a service, we need training, we must return to obedience, to the abc of the love for others). In this way her 1957 visit to China with Alberti is summarized as a vision of "deslumbrante fraternidad" (283; dazzling fraternity).[16] Even more telling is her account of their interview with Stalin in Moscow in 1937. Describing him as a worried but reassuring leader, León ends that episode hinting at, but ultimately avoiding, the pressing issues she knows the figure of Stalin will surely generate in her readers: "Todo lo que pasó después, la Historia grande de ese momento de la Unión Soviética y de Stalin queda para los historiadores" (86; Everything that happened later on, the History with capital H of the Soviet Union of that time, and of Stalin, is a task for historians). Her ideological hedging appears most distinctly in her narrative about a couple she met during the Civil War, a Russian man and a German woman who came to Spain with the International Brigades. León uses the story of their adoption of an orphan child they found abandoned in Madrid to show that war can bring out the best in people—a constant theme in her war anecdotes. They were later purged by Stalin, and this is León's reaction when she finds out about their fate, in her trip to Russia in 1956:

> Perdidos en la última noche staliniana. . . . Cuando pregunté por ellos, vi que los párpados de los preguntados se bajaban con cierta resignación de víctimas salvadas sin razón. . . .

El Partido Comunista se reunía para ensayar una respiración nueva [XX Congreso]. . . . Iban a regresar los olvidados, a aparecer los desaparecidos y los muertos. El gobierno soviéti-co acababa de ponerse de pie para decir la verdad, cosa que otros gobiernos no se hubieran jamás atrevido a hacer. Pero la gran Rusia había sabido arrodillarse, devolviendo la palabra a los muertos y a los olvidados. . . . (191-92)

By weaving her autobiographical account of the war around people such as the Russian-German couple just mentioned, León truly deliv-ers on her stated promise to center her war narrative on the anony-mous people and the small occurrences neglected by historiography. And yet one wonders whether León's motivation for writing that type of history is simply to pay its due to a neglected but crucial area, or whether the reasons that impel her to follow such a program are the same that undergird her "political" analysis (actually not political at all, but ethical instead). In other words, she sets out to prove the somewhat paradoxical idea that an uncontrolled event like war, which most peo-ple would describe as dominated by horror and irrationality, is for her a fundamental event that is not adequately represented by battles, political alliances, or the actions and decisions of influential leaders, but by the generosity, fraternity, and sense of purpose that "her" people show more prominently in war than in peace.[18]

Her ideological omissions and simplifications, avoidances and dis-tortions, cannot be ascribed simply to political naïveté. León's "glorifi-cation" of war has to be explained jointly with her self-interested aversion to delving into the conundrums of her professed ideology, because both emanate from the same source. Her political fuzziness requires an ideological explanation, but one that starts by explaining ideology, by exploring how its strength and also its weakness reside not in its ostensible assertions but in what underlies them.[19]

In Self-Defense: War and Melancholy as Symptoms

Laclau and Mouffe propose that every social practice operates within what they call a "field of discursivity," a notion that implies "the nec-essarily discursive character of any object and, simultaneously, the impossibility of any given discourse to implement a final suture."[20] Social practices can establish themselves only by exerting a limitation on the "surplus of meaning" that characterizes the field of discursivity;

however, given that such surplus cannot be exhausted or sutured by any practice, it will always subvert the practices that try to delimit it, making them unstable and provisional. This leads Laclau and Mouffe to postulate the existence of an inherent negativity in the social, a limit they call "antagonism." If on one hand antagonism makes the social unstable, on the other it guarantees the subject's ability to operate, an agency that would be radically denied by a hypothetical practice that presumably could suture the field of discursivity.[21] Žižek establishes a parallelism between Laclau and Mouffe's ideas and Lacan's: the discursivity of all social practices would be akin to Lacan's symbolic; and antagonism, the limit that haunts the social, would be equivalent to Lacan's Real. Following on these premises, Žižek proposes a thorough reconsideration of the classic Marxist understanding of ideology as false consciousness: "Ideology is not a dreamlike illusion that we build to escape insupportable reality; in its basic dimension it is a fantasy-construction which serves as a support for our 'reality' itself: an 'illusion' which structures our effective, real social relations and thereby masks some insupportable, real, impossible kernel."[22]

In order to impose itself, any discursive/symbolic/ideological formation has to privilege certain signifiers, certain centers that structure that discourse, while simultaneously rejecting (foreclosing or repudiating, in psychoanalytical language) from the symbolic surpluses of meaning that would compromise the integrity of that discourse. The Real is precisely that which the symbolic cannot accommodate because, if it tried to do so, the symbolic would risk being subverted: thus Žižek defines the Real as "that which resists symbolization: the traumatic point which is always missed but none the less always returns, although we try . . . to neutralize it, to integrate it into the symbolic order" (69). But, as Lacan argues, what is repudiated from the symbolic reappears as symptom. The symptom therefore functions as a representative of the Real in the symbolic, as the only form in which the Real can make its presence felt in the symbolic. In late Lacan, argues Žižek, "it is precisely the symptom . . . which persists as a surplus and returns through all attempts to domesticate it . . . to dissolve it by means of explication" (69).

That which a discursive/symbolic/ideological order cannot suture, integrate, or explain is therefore repudiated, but it returns as symptom. Far from considering it simply as a pathology, Žižek stresses that a symptom is a signifying formation that gives meaning to what no discourse/ideology can formalize: thus some societies make of the Jew a social symptom, and it becomes "the point at which the immanent social antagonism assumes a positive form, erupts on to the social surface, the point at which it becomes obvious that society 'doesn't work'" (127). By charging the "Jew" passionately with significance, society finds a way to give (perverse) meaning to a constitutive lack, thus making possible its own functioning; but simultaneously the "Jew" as symptom evinces society's inherent limitations, the impossibility of any social formation to ever reach stability. Consequently Žižek argues that a basic procedure of a criticism of ideology should be "to detect, in a given ideological edifice, the element which represents within it its own impossibility" (127).

One gains nothing, other that a dubious complacency, by merely judging as utopic, naive or, simplistic, León's ideology/fantasy of universal fraternity and empathetic communication beyond differences. One should explore instead what is dissimulated by those ideological distortions, what are the threatening forces those blind ideological spots attempt to suppress. Ostensibly León's "distorted" ideology aims at containing the opposite of what it preaches, the threatening "real" of permanent disunity and struggle, the obscure, ineluctable forces that presided over her life before the Civil War and that will again govern her existence in exile. Upon meeting Alberti, León finds a political cause that will temporarily keep at bay her personal predicaments.

León's ideological illusion protects her from the threat of disunity and disjunction, but, repudiated from León's ideological fantasy, that "traumatic kernel" of discord returns as the surplus of the symptom. As the guarantee of meaning, the symptom is "the embodiment of a lack, of a chasm of non-sense gaping in the midst of ideological meaning," writes Žižek (100). Actualizing the lack, standing for it and over it, covering it up, the symptom is the last defense against the irruption of nonsense, the last self-defense. One can then easily comprehend that the subject will embrace the symptom passionately. However, while the symptom points to the radical impossibilities of any given ideology or social construct, it simultaneously exerts an absolutely indispensable, meaning-granting task, and as such it possesses a "radical ontological status:" thus conceived, argues Žižek interspersing his words with quotes from Lacan, the symptom "is literally our only substance, the only positive support of our being, the only point that gives consistency to the subject. In other words, symptom is the way we—the subjects—

'avoid madness,' the way we 'choose something (the symptom-forma-
tion) instead of nothing (radical psychotic autism, the destruction of
the symbolic universe)' through the binding of our enjoyment to a certain signifying, symbolic formation which assures a minimum of consistency to our being-in-the-world" (75).

"War" and "melancholy" fulfill those symptomatic functions in
León's ideological fantasy, although in opposite, contrasting ways.
While León's war is a time of supreme, manic elation ("the most luminous years of our lives," "the best"), melancholy is a time of morbid
dejection. Although they stand on opposite poles in the scale of affects,
war and melancholy have in common León's passionate investment on
them, her deep "enjoyment" of both (peculiar as the enjoyment
involved in melancholy is, as noted later). For León the suppression of
discordance reaches its supreme point, paradoxically, during the Civil
War. How can war be the highest moment of fraternity, when it is precisely a civil war? What seems to count the most in her representation
of the war, what she heavily emphasizes, is the spirit of dogged resistance, the unity of purpose she sees on the Republican side. Construed
by León as an event that brings sense of purpose and fraternity, the
Civil War is an emblem of provisional unity; what León refuses to mention or acknowledge is that the Civil War, by definition, will some day
end with the victory of one of the sides. All of this can perhaps explain
why in *Memoria de la melancolía* the enemy, scarcely mentioned, does
not appear as what it is, a compatriot, but is portrayed instead, above
all, as a rather distant and diffuse representative of the true enemy, cap-
italist exploitation and inequality.[23] Impelled by the same necessity to
stress present and future unity, León never alludes to the chronic,
ingrained divisions among the parties that supported the Spanish
Republic. Avoiding the disturbing details of the political, León prefers
to concentrate on the abstract terms of an ideal of fraternity that in her
opinion will bring an end to history's sorrows. In this way, more than a
defense of ideals, war is for León an act of self-defense and hence the
affirmative passion that it elicits in her.[24]

Žižek argues that "[t]he process of interpellation-subjectivation,"
which consists "in assuming a symbolic mandate, in recognizing himself in the interpellation," is a way to eschew the traumatic kernel of
the Real (181). Identification with a given ideological interpellation
constitutes the subject as the blockage of the Real. As proposed in the
first chapter, the processes of symbolization/interpellation can take

place only because they are preceded by an ethical stage that, originally constituting the self as a response to the call of the other, sets the
grounds for the processes of symbolization/interpellation that wrestle
the subject from its adoration of the other, integrating it in the field of
the social/political. Starting as an obligatory response to the call of the
other, afflicted first by responsibility towards the other (this is the gist
of the ethical), the subject can later be "affected" by, and identify passionately with, the political interpellation that completes the process of
subjectivation.[25] The political, then, builds on the ethical and simultaneously displaces it but without completely erasing it. The ethical continues to operate in the midst of the political, interfering with its cold
reasons and calculations, haunting it, establishing with it a complex
and often conflictive relationship. For all its rightness, however, the
ethical cannot aspire to guide or supplant the political.

León's ideological mystifications originate precisely in her confusion
of the ethical and the political. Her self-interested ideological beliefs
derive from, and display, an overwhelming affect of the other: her
affliction is her affection, stemming as it does from the inordinate
ascendancy the ethical has over her, which leads her to conflate it with
the political. Therefore her glorification of war is not generated by
political self-righteousness, but comes from her need to right her self,
to say how much is right about the self. *Ethical* is then the word that
best explains León's condition: she is obsessed by her debt toward the
other, she is consumed with guilt and obligation, and thus her ideological distortions originate in the unwarranted infringement of the
ethical on the political, in the error of understanding the latter in the
former's terms. But if this is León's mistake, it is also her salvation,
because granting the ethical command over the political is her peculiar
strategy to ward off the Real. By holding on to the illusion that unity
and fraternity might one day rule the world, León manages to elude
temporarily the unbearable burden of loss and severance that haunted
her life before she heeded the call of political activism. Exile, one of the
crudest forms of severance, will upset León's ideological stratagems,
and the repudiated Real will return with a vengeance.

While war, exemplifying for León the moment of supreme fraternity and unity, brings a maximum of meaning to her life, melancholy
constitutes the exact opposite, a time of radical separation and deprivation, of absolute lack of meaning. As symptoms, however, both war
and melancholy support León's self. Read as symptom, war as time of

raving rapture simultaneously forecloses and betrays the unnamable fear of separation, the unthinkable disunity that, haunting León all through her life, becomes a harsh, unavoidable reality in exile. As unqualified realization of loss and separation, melancholy is for León the obverse of war, the nightmare that León kept at bay through her enjoyment of war as symptom. Despite being the consequence of the dismantling of the war as symptom, melancholy also works nonetheless as symptom, but as the symptom stripped to its bare essentials. Once the feared abyss of absolute separation that war repudiated has become real with exile, León still has a final form of self-defense in the sadness proper to melancholy that in Kristeva's view is a way to ward off self-destruction: "sadness reconstitutes an affective cohesion of the self, which restores its unity within the framework of the affect. . . . Because of that, the depressive affect makes up for symbolic invalidation and interruption . . . and at the same time protects it against proceeding to the suicidal act."[26] Melancholy's strong emotional investment on the self, the deep sadness that burdens the subject, is actually the last defense against madness, against a total breakup of the links between self and world: in the paradoxical "joy" of melancholy, in its self-centered sorrow, León finds the last stopgap against non-sense, against the real of separation, of separation as manifestation of the Real.[27]

Sadness works as a counterbalance to the other side of melancholy, the ostensible ravages of loss. Accordingly, the "memory of melancholy" also has two distinct and contrary sides, simultaneously producing dejection and delight. When melancholy is the subject that reminisces, when melancholy remembers, it shows its chilling cognitive side, the depths of the abyss of separation, causing León to be at the mercy of unpleasant memories she would rather suppress or forget:

> La memoria puede tener los ojos indulgentes. Ya no llegan a nosotros los ruidos vivos sino los muertos. Memoria del olvido, escribió Emilio Prados, memoria melancólica, a medio apagar, memoria de la melancolía. No sé quien solía decir en mi casa: hay que tener recuerdos. Vivir no es tan importante como recordar. Lo espantoso era no tener nada que recordar. . . . Pero qué horrible es que los recuerdos se precipiten sobre ti y te obliguen a mirarlos y te muerdan y se revuelquen sobre tus entrañas, que es el lugar de la memoria. (51)[28]

"Memory is a passion no less powerful or pervasive than love," writes Elie Wiesel.[29] The passion of memory, however, can have two different manifestations: the passion not to forget, the passion for remembrance, but also memory as suffering, as the inability to forget attested by León in the quote just reproduced. In this way when melancholy remembers, desolation reigns; when León remembers, sorrowful hope dominates, given that, as memory of lost unity, melancholy holds the promise of reunion, of restoration of plenitude. In the meantime the self is sustained by sadness. And without this melancholy sadness the self would sink into the black hole of the unabated, unmediated Real. León's passionate commitment to the symptom of war as paradise is now matched by her melancholy sadness, by the sadness of repeatedly reminiscing about the times of fraternity. And the writing of *Memoria de la melancolía* is yet another form of repetition, of recollection, but one in which memory is radically overcome by a surplus that takes the form of communal testimony, of cathartic communication with the many addressees it invokes. In the act of writing, memory as cognition is exceeded, and to a certain degree also redeemed, by the ethical dimensions of autobiography.

León's mystified ideological vision and her awry view of war are the result of a massive sublimation, of an enormous forgiveness that provisionally sutures the wound of time. As Kristeva argues, melancholy blocks the flow of time: "Riveted to the past, regressing to the paradise or inferno of an unsurpassable experience, melancholy persons manifest a strange memory: . . . there is no future"; and she concludes: "A dweller in truncated time, the depressed person is necessarily a dweller in the imaginary realm."[30] León finds solace in the world of generosity and fraternity that does not make it to the history books, but as Philip Roth states, "[m]emories of the past are not memories of facts but memories of your imaginings of the facts."[31] León's imagination of her past is constructed by a specific political discourse about Spain, its Civil War, and exile in which the facts of the war are not imagined as episodes of a fratricide fight to the death, but as the establishment of a utopian space of fraternity. But that contented, timeless utopia is brought into movement by the lost war. Exile makes it impossible for León to dissimulate loss: as in the primordial expulsion from paradise, exile imposes temporality on León, and hence loss becomes cognoscitively inescapable. Ultimately exile from paradise entails also the triumph of transience, of death. However, as introjection of loss, as denial of severance, in what it has of immersion in sorrow, melancholy stops the passage of time. Counterbalancing the cognoscitive imposition of loss and temporality, timeless sorrow offers the melancholic a final form of self-support.

Constituting Exile

As the apex of a plenitude that, later in exile, is obsessively remembered, war is a symptom that lets one see that, before war, infinitely before war, there was something amiss, something León attempts to cover up with her naive ideology: what is amiss, what León refuses to accept is a radical, originary cleft that nonetheless ultimately returns to haunt her. As already indicated, León obstinately persists in living in the terrain of the ethical, in the realm of unbounded responsibility for the other. As a result her access to the political is partial and peculiar, and her insistence on guiding her political practices and declarations with ethical goals and beliefs is what makes her case appear simultaneously poignant and naive. But if one remembers that the ethical emanates in a preontological and prepolitical domain, the fact the León moves predominantly in that terrain indicates that her melancholy has to be located before and beyond history. Her melancholy has a history, but one whose origins and beginnings cannot be located and do not need to be located: it is enough to reveal the traces it has left in León's memory and memoirs.

León is afflicted by one of the types of melancholy postulated by Kristeva, that which emanates from the trauma of a primordial separation that is never overcome by the subject. Using a biological metaphor, the primordial separation could be figured as the weaning from the mother the infant needs to go through in order to individuate. However, there is no need, and probably no possibility, of tracing the separation's precise origins: it is enough to perceive its manifestations, to see that León's life is haunted from its beginnings by an irredeemable loss, that her autobiographical text foregrounds severance from beginning to end, that *Memoria de la melancolía* can be understood only it one assumes an originary separation in León. As Kristeva writes, the "initial deprivation" is not "the deprivation of a 'property' or 'object' constituting a material, transferable heritage, but the loss of an unnameable domain, which one might, strangely enough, evoke or invoke, from a foreign land, from a constitutional exile."[32] León's affliction is a constitutional melancholy, the immemorial memory of a primordial loss which undergirds a life that is thus lived gripped by the perennial terror of loss and disunity.[33]

"The exile . . . exists in a median state, neither completely at one with the new setting nor fully disencumbered of the old, beset with half-involvements and half-detachments, nostalgic and sentimental on one level, an adept mimic or a secret outcast on another," writes Edward W. Said.[34] Not all exiles of the Spanish Civil War fit Said's description, whose exile as "median state" corresponds to the type that Naharro-Calderón calls "exilio latente" (latent exile), in which the exiled person "pretende equilibrar memoria y olvido" (tries to balance memory and forgetfulness). While a good number of the Spanish Civil War expatriates lived in this state of latent exile, León's resembles the condition of "infra-exilio" (infra-exile), which Naharro-Calderón characterizes as a "constant ritual for the imagination"; riveted to the often unrealizable dream of returning home, the exile lives enthralled by the past.[35] A telling contrast with León's case is that of Rafael Alberti. Although Alberti seems to have missed some aspects of life in Spain (one of the things Alberti constantly reminisced about in exile were certain landscapes of southern Spain), neither in his memoirs *La arboleda perdida* (The Lost Grove), nor in a series of interviews held in Italy in 1969, when León had just finished *Memoria de la melancolía*, is there a hint in Alberti of the desolation that pervades León's account of her life. He comes across instead as a reasonably well-adjusted exile, one who has made the most of the professional opportunities his numerous and influential connections have afforded him. The contrast between León's and Alberti's autobiographical works has been described by Randolph Pope with perceptive succinctness: "Mientras que Alberti describe una carrera, León da una fiesta, una fiesta en que la mayor parte de los invitados han sido segados por la muerte" (While Alberti describes a career, León holds a party, one in which most of the guests have been cut down by death).[36]

And yet not even infra-exile describes León's situation, because that would be tantamount to making the specific exile of the Civil War responsible for León's melancholy. As already argued, León's affliction is older than the war, and thus, antedating 1939, her exile is the type that Joseph Brodsky characterizes as "a metaphysical condition."[37] Differentiating between the exile, the refugee, and the banished, another expatriate of the Spanish Civil War, María Zambrano, proposes as does Brodsky an ontological exile, which she links to a feeling of "abandono" (abandonment) and "desamparo" (shelterlessness) that neither the refugee nor the banished endure.[38] In sharp contrast with León and more in tune with reality, Zambrano does not see any unity among the Spanish exiles (a view also endorsed by Andújar), but far from seeing it as a drawback, Zambrano believes it to be the necessary springboard "[para] tener cada uno de nosotros el valor de vivir entregándonos a nuestra propia desolación y buscando en ella; sólo así podremos estar cerca, sólo [así] podremos encontrarnos" (so that each one of us has the courage to live giving in to our desolation and searching for ourselves in it; only in that way can we be close to each other, only in that way will we be able to re-encounter ourselves/each other).[39] Holding to the belief in a communal, fraternal paradise is León's strategy for denying the sense of loss and desolation that ravaged her life from its beginning: León is an ontological exile in denial. Kristeva argues that melancholics "are potential exiles" (64), a statement in which "exile" is not to be understood in a literal, physical sense, but as a state, akin to Zambrano's radical exile, in which someone afflicted by melancholy is prone to fall. Underneath León's averting strategies, everything points to a radical, originary sense of exile, to a constitutional melancholy. One can conclude, then, that besides being a concrete experience in her life, exile provides the basic figure to characterize most of her life, even before her expatriation in 1939.

The Pillars of the Past: Exile and Homeland

Zambrano also describes the time of the Civil War as the happiest of her life, but, in a drastic contrast with León's reasons, she ascribes her happiness to "la proximidad de la muerte constante, la soledad y el haberme por completo evadido de burocracia, de *necesidad*" (the permanent proximity of death, solitude and to having gotten rid of bureaucracy, of *necessity*; *Cartas a Rosa Chacel*, 40; letter of September 5, 1941). Zambrano lives exile in the way she preaches it, as the search for a lost "home(land)" that is nowhere but whose faint gleam she perceives everywhere. Zambrano links exile to what she calls true homeland: "El exilio es el lugar privilegiado para que la Patria se descubra. . . . Cuando ya se sabe sin ella, sin padecer alguno, cuando ya no se recibe nada, nada de la patria, entonces se le aparece" (Exile is the privileged place for discovering the homeland. . . . When the exile has already renounced it, when one doesn't suffer any longer, when one doesn't receive anything, anything at all from the homeland, at that moment the homeland discloses itself to the exile). Zambrano adds that "[t]iene la patria verdadera por virtud crear el exilio" (the homeland has as its hallmark the creation of exile),[40] thus indicating that exile is the limit of the nation, which makes exile the destiny, but also the biggest fear, of the patriot. The threat of exile, immanent within the idea of homeland, evinces the precariousness of both homeland and the patriot.

Michael Rowlands argues that in moments of danger for a nation, "what are chosen as diagnostic iconic images . . . are precisely those acts of sacrifice, the creation of heroes and martyrs around which conviction of the just cause and longevity of a national identity is forged."[41] Exile always bespeaks some form of national convulsion and thus necessarily imposes the reconstruction of the nation by means of figures that would presumably embody its essence. As Michael Ugarte points out, many Spanish writers (Ayala, Bergamín, Durán, Zambrano, etc.) searched in exile "for the emblems of a national consciousness."[42] León has close at hand the elements to link exile, homeland, and patriotism in the preeminent epic hero of Spain, the Cid, and his wife, Doña Jimena, who are the subject of two novelized biographies León wrote while in exile. León's mother was from Burgos, the Cid's native province, and León herself lived there for several years. Even more importantly, Menéndez Pidal, the preeminent twentieth-century expert on the Cid, was married to an aunt of León, María Goyri, and León spent part of her childhood with their daughter Jimena.[43]

In the traditional version of the story, from which León does not veer, Rodrigo Díaz de Vivar, the Cid, is the loyal patriot who forces King Alphonse VI to swear solemnly that he had had no part in his brother Sancho's death (after which Alphonse annexed Sancho's kingdom of Castille to his own crown of León). Exiled by a resentful Alphonse, Rodrigo embarks on an itinerant warfare, and he proves his unassailable loyalty by sending to the king, as a tribute, part of the booty he collects after each of his victories. The Cid has been traditionally held by Spanish conservatives to be a paradigmatic Christian crusader against the Moor invaders, who are often portrayed with xenophobic notes of which León's biography is not exempt. Although it would be indispensable for any reflection on the construction of the nation in twentieth-century Spain to explore the consequences derived from the fact that both the Francoists and the exiles extolled some of the same highly problematic figures of Spain's past, it is more to the point here to see the particular slant that León gives to her biographies of the Cid and Jimena.

León's novelized biography of the Cid draws on a number of well-known sources, which she acknowledges (Guillén de Castro, Corneille, the *romancero, Poema de Mío Cid,* Menéndez Pidal;see *Rodrigo* 203). She ascribes to him a dubious moral exemplarity—"El personaje es tan grande que puede siempre servir de lección y estímulo a la juventud de cualquier época y de cualquier país" (*Rodrigo* 203; Such is his greatness that he can

serve as a lesson and a stimulus to the youth of all periods and countries)—which is understandable in part because the book is aimed at children. The Cid is depicted by León as a defender of his family honor, loyal
to the king despite his banishment, thirsty for glory, brave, just, and patriotic.[44] Above all these features, León sees the figure of the Cid primarily as
an exemplary exile, drawing from his figure comfort and assurance about
the moral rightness of the Spanish Civil War expatriates. León stresses that,
as all exiles, the Cid suffers great pain upon being banished from the homeland;[45] but, more important, and in tune with her representation of her fellow expatriates, the Cid embodies for León a sense of justice that, lacking
in Alphonse's court, caused his exile, thus establishing a parallel with the
condition of social injustice prevalent in Spain at the time of the Civil War.
León will affirm in *Memoria de la melancolía* that the exiles of the Civil War
took with them the "laws of living together" (implicitly comparing their
situation to that of the Cid), and only their return will raise Spain from its
ruins. León's interpretation of the Cid's exile is remarkably close to that of
Robert Edwards, who argues that one type of narrative generated by exile
in the Middle Ages depicts the "creation of a parallel society from exile,"
which is brought about by "an impulse toward restoration instead of
predicament. Whether a second world or underground kingdom, the society created from exile attempts to rediscover and enact the values that are
presumed to have governed the original order from which it has been
expelled." And he considers that this type of narrative is best exemplified
by the "chanson de geste" and particularly by the twelfth-century epic
Poema de Mío Cid.[46] Unjustly banned from the homeland but nonetheless
still loyal to it, like the exiles of the Civil War, the Cid would be the exemplary exile/patriot: León's Cid is "[Un] Rodrigo rebelde, un Rodrigo que
nos representará a todos siempre cuando haya que hacer respetar—como
él hizo al rey—los derechos del pueblo de España" (a rebellious Rodrigo,
a Rodrigo that will represent us all whenever we must ask—as he asked the
king—that the rights of the Spanish people be respected), she writes in
Memoria de la melancolía. And she adds, establishing a parallelism between
the exiles who call for their wives and the Cid, who asked Jimena to join
him in the recently conquered city of Valencia: "Hasta que un día llegaba
una carta. Venía de México, de la Argentina, de Chile. . . . Ven. Ven mujer,
con los niños. Venid a recomenzar la existencia. . . . Los desterrados
españoles, también a su manera, habían conquistado un reino" (Until a day
a letter arrived. It came from Mexico, from Argentina, from Chile. . . .
Come. Come and bring the kids, my dear. Come to start life anew. . . . In
their way, the Spanish exiles had also conquered a kingdom.)[47]

Unlike her biography of the Cid, *Doña Jimena* is addressed to a mature audience. As the sources on Jimena are sketchy, León has much more freedom to veer from tradition, portraying Jimena as a somewhat tortured figure, one undoubtedly much closer to her heart than the Cid. When she reflects on the solitude of the wives the exiles had to leave in Spain, León writes, "Pensé en Doña Jimena, ese arquetipo de mi infancia" (I thought of doña Jimena, that archetype of my childhood), who was left behind in Castile, alone, sad, and desolate, like the exiles' wives: "En esta dispersión española le ha tocado a la mujer un papel histórico y lo ha recitado bien y ha cumplido como cumplió doña Jimena, modesta y triste. Algún día se contarán o cantarán las pequeñas historias, las anécdotas menudas, esas que quedan en las cartas escritas" (In this Spanish diaspora women have been assigned a historical role and they have performed it well, and they have lived up to it as did Doña Jimena, modest and sad. Some day, someone will tell the small stories, the minor anecdotes, those inscribed in letters).[48]

Jimena's portrait differs markedly from *Rodrigo* to *Doña Jimena*. In both she fulfills the role supposedly assigned to women like her, that of solitude and duty: "la vida de una mujer en el siglo XI es aguardar" (life for an eleventh-century woman consists of waiting).[49] Besides being the loyal wife who waits for her exiled husband in the Cardeña monastery, taking care in the meantime of their son and daughters, in León's biography Jimena cuts a somewhat romantic, desolate figure, one that resembles León in her Roman self-portrayal in *Memoria de la melancolía* (remember that *Doña Jimena* appeared in 1960, shortly before León moved to Rome). After resignedly waiting for years to reunite with the Cid, when he calls her to Valencia, Jimena spends her days missing her simple life in Cardeña, while being apprehensive about her husband's constant warring designs. Her unhappiness is compounded first by the loss of her son in battle, later by her husband's death, and finally by the gradual demise of everyone and everything associated with the Cid. In her final days Jimena wistfully reflects about life being brief, full of duties, solitude, and silences (195) and romantically regrets still being alive (210). As will become evident later, this obsession with separation, uprootedness, transience, loss, and grief parallels and forebodes similar obsessions present in León's depiction of her own life in *Memoria de la melancolía*. Although both in her autobiography and in her book on Jimena, León's melancholy meditations are counterbalanced by an opposite insistence on the hope of reunion and restoration, in both works transience ultimately prevails.

Being beyond politics, transience (and death in particular) is a nonpolitical threat to the homeland, an absolute threat in that it does not admit a response. Viewed as temporary, exile is a more manageable enemy. It is instructive to compare the highly disparate reactions to exile offered by Rodrigo and Jimena in León's accounts. Rodrigo responds to exile in a common way: "¡Ay, pena amarga de los desterrados que no pueden regresar por ninguna cosa que se les olvidó! ¡Nuestro Cid llorando por ese bien de todos los días y esa costumbre que se llama patria!" (Ah, bitter grief of the exiles, who cannot return to gather anything they left behind! Our Rodrigo crying for that daily good and that custom called Spain!).[50] In contrast, Jimena's answer to the mere idea of exile is a highly personal one, an illustrative representation of a particular brand of patriotism:

> En una ocasión, cuando el fraile le leía en el libro de Idiáquez "¿Qué importa que no estés en tu patria? Tu patria es la tierra en que has encontrado bienestar y la causa del bienestar no radica en el lugar, sino en el corazón del hombre," Doña Jimena gritó altivamente: "¡Mentís, o léeis falsía!" Y aunque el buen Abad trató de calmarla mientras el perplejo monje cerraba el libro de buena piel de becerro: "Mentís, ¿quién será capaz de traicionar el regazo de su madre?," gritó. . . .(36)[51]

Although appearing commonplace, the figuration of Spain as a mother reveals more about León's melancholy than about Jimena's plea. At several points in *Memoria de la melancolía* Spain is personified either through prosopopeia or apostrophe. From Quintilian until at least the nineteenth century, those figures were classified under the figures of passion, the reasoning being that the speaker resorts to them during high excitement or ardor. One such case of passion is found in León's depiction of the staging of Cervantes's play *Numancia* by the "Guerrillas del Teatro del Ejército del Centro" (Guerrillas of the Central Army Theater), a company in which León was involved during the war: "Había un heroísmo en la sala tan atenta que correspondía a los personajes. . . . Nunca hubo mayor correspondencia entre una sala y un escenario. Allí los numantinos, aquí los madrileños. . . . Nos sentimos todos ligados, ligados y felices. Ya podían los aviones franquistas hacer temblar los tejados viejos del teatro de la Zarzuela" (There was a heroism in the transfixed audience that corresponded to that of the characters. . . . There has never been a highest correspondence between an audience and a stage. There the Numantines, here the people of Madrid. . . . We all felt united, united and happy. Let the Froncoist planes make the old roof of La Zarzuela theater rattle).[52] Commenting on those performances, León addresses Spain in *Memoria de la melancolía:* "Sí, todos te deben llorar, eso sí, llorar es diferente. Llorar de emoción por ver a España, magnífica y alta. . . . Muchas noches, mientras representábamos Numancia, María Teresa León lloraba entre bastidores viendo subir a su pueblo hacia la hoguera de la muerte común" (Yes, everyone should cry for you, yes, to cry is different [from pitying Spain]. To cry out of the emotion of seeing Spain, grand and majestic. . . . Many nights, while we performed Numancia, María Teresa León would cry offstage seeing her people mount the pyre of collective death).[53] Even more to the point is her playing the role of Spain in Alberti's "Cantata de los Héroes y la Fraternidad de los Pueblos" (Cantata about Heroes and Fraternity between Nations), offered as homage to the International Brigades when international pressure interrupted their participation in the Spanish Civil War in support of the Republican side. Tears streaming from her eyes, she recites lines in which Spain tells about its "penas" (42; grief).[54]

Carolyn Boyd indicates that a favorite image of the national Catholic literature on history "was that of 'Mother Spain,' which conveyed involuntary and primordial obligations of respect, loyalty, and uncritical love."[55] Belying the worn image, León gives special meanings to her personification of Spain as a mother or simply as a female figure. León, obsessed with separation, sees Mother Spain as a figure of unity and not necessarily just national unity. It could be that "Mother Spain" plays for León the same role that war as symptom does. Both are invested with passion and pleasure, because they are the last line of resistance, the last figuration against the threat of cleavage that permeates León's life. Therefore the image of the nation as mother of fraternal beings is just another passionate illusion, another useless stopgap to avoid confronting severance and transience, the stark realities dissimulated by the prosopopeiac mask of the nation as female figure. And given the radical nature of the enemy (of the limit of León's construction of the social), the nation has to be figured as something sacred, something that generates feelings of allegiance strong enough to be at the level of the terror the nation is constructed to ward off. The Cid, Jimena, Numancia, and the personification of Spain are prominent figures that León resorts to give meaning to her dilemmas. Looking towards the past for orientation, "towards an idealised sacrificial role" best exemplified by the past, is a common maneuver when the nation faces some cataclysmic change, argues Michael Rowlands, who adds: "the wider issues raised concern how people make sense of terrifying memories and events involving a sense of loss, grief and contradiction that remain forever."[56] Does this mean that behind León's ostensible political commitment to Spain we should see only a shield for her personal predicaments? Not at all. However, transience will be for León the great equalizer, the one for which there is ultimately no personal or political answer. Beyond the reach of personal and political comprehension, transience marks the limits of both fields while also calling into question their complicities.

Ruinous Melancholy

The look to Spain's past to search for meaning is complemented by a look at the present. León makes frequent references to Spain, but she finds it unrecognizable: "Las imágenes actuales de España nos llegan como paralíticas. ¿Eran así en tu tiempo? No, eran aceras partidas, casas rotas, huecas, camas desventradas con el sudor del miedo aún, cañerías vomitanto. Y todo en una escenografía de catástrofe. Así me quedó todo dentro. . . . Se deslizaban casi tres años de una apasionada aventura humana, la más entrañable aventura española que corrió nuestro pueblo. Y yo quería llevar todo bien atado, para no perder nada por ahí" (The current images of Spain come across as paralytic. Were they like that in your time? No, they were broken sidewalks, gutted houses, disemboweled beds still with the sweat of fear, pipes spewing. And everything in a scene of catastrophe. That is the way everything was left impressed within me. . . After three years, a passionate human adventure, the most deeply felt adventure our Spanish people has ever lived, was coming to an end. And I wanted to take everything well tied up, so as not to lose anything).[57] *Paralytic* is here synonymous with *unrecognizable* and *meaningless,* and with this lack of sense León contrasts the glorious suffering of the exiles:

> Nosotros somos los desterrados de España, los que buscamos la sombra, la silueta, el ruido de los pasos del silencio, las voces perdidas. Nuestro paraíso no es de árboles ni de flores permanentemente coloreadas. Dejadnos las ruinas. Debemos comenzar desde las ruinas. Llegaremos. Regresaremos con la ley, os enseñaremos las palabras enterradas bajo los edificios demasiado grandes de las ciudades que ya no son las nuestras. Nuestro paraíso, el que defendimos, está debajo de las apariencias actuales. También es el vuestro. ¿No sentís, jóvenes sin éxodo y sin llanto, que tenemos que partir de las ruinas, de las casas volcadas y los campos ardiendo para levantar nuestra ciudad fraternal de la nueva ley? (*Memoria de la melancolía,* 30)[58]

In León's recollection, the ruins are not the remembrance of the real ruins of wartime Madrid; instead they are beyond memory because they block memory and paralyze time. They are the phantasmic trace of León's supposed paradise, and she depicts them as a shared property that the community of exiles has safely tucked away outside of Spain. But the price of salvaging the ruins as remembrance of paradise is their burial in the memory ofLeón, who remains a prisoner of the melancholic introjection of the object whose loss she cannot accept. "Our" paradise of ruins, insists León, is kept intact under the unrecognizably glittering new buildings, and the community of exiles, "Nosotros, los del paraíso perdido" (29; We, of the lost paradise), will one day return and, starting again from the ruins, will wake Spain from the bad dream it has been living (70).

León's ruins obsessively remain deadly alive, unchanged and imposing, demanding that one return to them, thus obliterating all, good or bad, that was built upon them. León's talk of the freedom to be restored to Spain (29) could lead one to think that she identifies the restoration of the ruins with the return of democracy to Spain, but several observations debunk that hypothesis. First, León's "we" imposes over the community of exiles a privilege that is her burden only—and those whom she portrays as unified actually took into exile, as is well known, many of the sharp divisions that plagued the Republicans during the war. It could also be said that, almost thirty years after the war, very few exiles, if any, could still share, if they did at any time, León's obsession with returning to a ruinous time that for her embodies paradise. Besides, by then the exiles were mostly a dying community, as León chronicles repeatedly toward the end of *Memoria de la melancolía* (287–319). A paradise is always a lost paradise, and León admits that she longs for a freedom that perhaps did not exist but that she nonetheless remembers as a lost good (239). By making her plea a collective one, León does not have to accept that the promise of redemption she entrusts to a whole community is a way of making collective the burden of securing for herself a place oblivious to the catastrophe of history and the decay of nature, safe from loss and severance, from time and death.

León's quandary concerns the establishment of links between the past in ruins and the passage of time, between the past and the future of Spain. However, her troubling disquiet regarding current Spain is not political, and she ultimately tropes it as her inability to read Spain: "Cuando ahora abro los periódicos que me llegan de aquel país pienso que todo se ha petrificado. . . . ¿Por qué nada contesta?" (26; When I now open the newspapers that arrive from that country I have the impression that everything has petrified. . . Why doesn't anything answer to me?). Similarly she cannot relate to the progressive youth that, according to her, will bring about "la Resurrección de España" (37; the resurrection of Spain): "¿Por qué me faltan las palabras claves para dialogar con ellos?" (34; Why do I lack the key words to dialogue with them?). Her inability to hold a dialogue with her young visitors despite their common political ideals and her incapacity to read Spain indicate that something would be amiss if one insisted, following León's hints, on a political reading of the ruins. Restoration of democracy should politically be enough for León, but her imperative insistence on a return to "her" ruins as the only possible solution shows that hers is not a political plea but one older than the war itself. Therefore her ruins do not stand for the promise of a democratic reconstruction of Spain, but dissimulate some unspeakable, unrepresentable fear, the terror of a primary loss that León seems reluctant to confront because its threat is more powerful than any political oppression.

At first sight León's eulogy to the "paraíso perdido" (lost paradise) of the ruins (29), with its emphasis on the destructive passage of time, connects with the quote by Lucian of Samosata that she uses as epigraph for *Memoria de la melancolía* ("All that belongs to mortals is mortal, and all things will vanish; or if not, we'll be the ones to perish").[59] In their similarities and contrasts, León's celebration of the ruins and Lucian's affirmation of transitoriness neatly summarize the conundrums of time and memory that haunt *Memoria de la melancolía*. But while Lucian's words proclaim an irremediable absolute decline, the ruinous image of Spain that León carries within her, as image/remainder of a lost paradise, holds forth the promise of restitution. A closer look, then, reveals that Lucian's irrevocable decay contrasts sharply with León's ruinous affirmation: against the destructive passage of time León, in her fierce attachment to the ruins, proclaims an emendation to the ravages of time that is ultimately equivalent to the abolition of time itself. Caught in a temporal predicament, *Memoria de la melancolía* oscillates between transience and timelessness, between vanity and glory, the two temporal extremes whose confrontation Benjamin sees behind the practice of allegory: "Allegory established itself most permanently where transitoriness and eternity confronted each other most closely."[60]

Benjamin argues that allegory reached one of the highest points of appreciation in the baroque, precisely because in that epoch people saw nature, and history, as "eternal transience," as inevitable decay. Beholding everything as destined for ruination, those exemplary melancholics could not see any meaning linking the self with nature or history (a link the romantics, on the contrary, believed to have found in their theory of the symbol), and their melancholy impulse to allegorize springs forth from such a calamitous realization, in an effort to rescue self, nature, and history from the abyss of meaninglessness:

"For an appreciation of the transience of things, and the concern to rescue them for eternity, is one of the strongest impulses in allegory"; hence the baroque's appreciation for ruins, the only setting where its "saturnine vision" recognized history (Benjamin 223, 179). Allegory, then, always starts from melancholy. As experience of loss, as proclamation of universal transitoriness, melancholy results in a *"modification of signifying bonds,"* in a symbolic collapse that drains meaning from the world.[61] The first step toward allegory therefore is the melancholy contemplation of things, "the moment where the subject beholds a world that has been drained of all its 'inherent' meaning."[62]

Pensky indicates that "the emotive dimensions of the melancholy experience, the desolation, sadness, and mourning . . . have always received preponderant attention to the detriment of melancholia's properly cognitive dimension" (116), a facet of melancholy that manifests itself as the practice of allegory: "Allegory is thus a creative cognitive mode inseparably connected to the melancholic disposition."[63] What melancholy ruins and empties of meaning, allegory attempts to redeem and make signify. Melancholy is a lucid vision of the world as regards what the latter has of immediate senselessness, and allegory establishes itself over the abyss that separates appearances and meaning, world and sense. Those who perceive this breach in its stark, unmediated reality, are doomed to live it as melancholy, as lack of meaning before the inescapable spectacle of the irrevocable decay of nature and, primordially, before the individual's realization of his/her subjection to death. The melancholic is afflicted by a keen perception of nature as decay and history as catastrophe. As a meaning-giving operation that attempts to salvage both nature and history, allegory aims ultimately at redeeming the self.[64]

Although allegory is often presented as a sustained narrative, in the long tradition of that figure either an episode, a cluster of images, or even a single figure has also been used allegorically. Ruins are a paradigmatic allegorical emblem: any melancholic, and not simply León, always departs from some form of ruins. León's clamoring for a return to the ruins does not stem from the need to offer historical continuity, to start exactly at the point when politics took a wrong turn in Spain. The war was only a temporary reprieve for a sense of loss that harks back to an indefinite time before the war: León's imperative need to return to the ruins has to do with time and meaning, with giving meaning to time, with rescuing things from the destructive passage of time.

Melancholics such as León have an ambivalent view of ruination: privileged witness to the ravages of transience, their lucidity imposes on
them the realization of its inexorability; but simultaneously they love
ruins because that is their last line of defense, the only way their lost,
ruined object is preserved.[65] No longer alive, the only chance their
object has of being preserved and restored is by keeping its ruins, by
cherishing its deathly remains: "If the object becomes allegorical
under the gaze of melancholy, if melancholy causes life to flow out of
it and it remains behind dead, but eternally secure, then it is exposed
to the allegorist, it is unconditionally in his power."[66] By making the
lost object definitely theirs, by introjecting it, melancholics assume
the power to grant it meaning, to rescue it from decay. But although
unconditional, this capacity of the allegorist to give meaning to loss is
simultaneously fraught with precariousness, and it needs ultimately to
claim an uncontested foundation in order to be a truly redemptive
power.[67] Thus León grants ideology—her peculiar view of commu-
nism as fraternity—the role that baroque theater reserves for divine
intervention or will. Emanating as they do from a dream of fraternity
and reconciliation, León's memory and melancholy share in the theological, albeit she avoids that connotation, preferring to dress it up as
ideology. Implicitly, however, her text is pervaded by the theological,
as readily evinced by her obsession with such ideas as transience, lost
paradise, intemporality, redemption, and resurrection. And one can
now understand better what stands behind her passionate figuration
of the nation as mother. Benedict Anderson links the rise of nationalism with the waning "of religious modes of thought": "With the
ebbing of religious belief, the suffering which belief in part composed
did not disappear. Disintegration of paradise: nothing makes fatality
more arbitrary. Absurdity of salvation: nothing makes another style of
continuity more necessary. What then was required was a secular
transformation of fatality into continuity, contingency into meaning."
And, he adds, "few things were (are) better suited to this end than an
idea of nation."[68] León's paradise, and its ruins, originates in an ethical imperative and not in a political necessity; and her reading of the
ruins shows itself not to be grounded in the political but ultimately in
the need to offset transience. Hence her motherly nation is not from
this world.

   And yet León's self-interested obfuscation does not block totally a
voice whose searing lucidity disrupts León's allegory of the ruins,

bringing into the open their arbitrary meaning. As already noted, the first stage of melancholy allegory appears when meaning is drained out of things, with the devaluation of the world of appearances. This initial moment "is related to another consistent feature in the discourse of melancholia: the social and personal isolation of the melancholic, the real or imagined exclusion or marginalization of melancholics from their social milieu."[69] Writes León:

> "Es como si yo no perteneciese a ese país [España] del que leo los periódicos. . . . Siento todo fuera de mí, arrancado. . . . Estoy como separada, mirándome. No encuentro la fórmula para dialogar ni para unirme. . . . He sentido muchas veces angustia al mirar, sentados junto a mí, a seres que dicen son mi gente [españoles] y no los reconozco . . . , tan distinto es todo de lo que a mí me dejaron las horas de la vida." (18)[70]

To this sense of separateness, which stems from and reinforces the separation proper to melancholy, corresponds a memory different from the one that glorifies the ruins as the token of a political promise. This second memory is truly a memory of melancholy, and—in contrast with León's willful and militant political memory, which insists on remembering—this other unbearable memory painfully wishes for its own dissolution: "Yo quisiera verlo todo diferente para que se levantasen en mí amores nuevos, cosas que me sacaran el pasado de la memoria" (26; I would like to see everything differently, so that new loves would rise in me, things that could remove the past from my memory).

In opposition to the willful voice of León's political memory, which dominates the central part of her autobiography (as mentioned, some of those middle pages were written many years before the publication of *Memoria de la melancolía*), the initial and final pages of the book (which seem to have been written in Rome, in the early sixties) are tinged by a morbidly desolate voice. Fueled by a restorative illusion, the political middle parts of the book do not seem to perceive the signs of universal transience. However, the incessant spectacle of death ends up by imposing itself ineluctably: in this way, towards its end *Memoria de la melancolía* becomes a funereal text haunted by a spectral community of ghosts, an unending string of obituaries that provides León with the last chance to remember her dream of fraternity, which now, unambiguously, shows its incongruity. But perhaps the most radical reminders of dissolution are found in the initial pages of *Memoria de la*

melancolía, where León announces that her autobiographical writing is
closely linked to her increasing sense of self-estrangement:

> Me asusta mirarme a los espejos porque ya no veo nada en
> mis pupilas y, si oigo, no sé lo que me cuentan y no sé por
> qué ponen tanta insistencia en reavivarme la memoria. Pero
> sufro por olvidar y . . . siento que me empujan hacia ade-
> lante, hacia la pena, hacia la muerte. Entonces prefiero ir
> hacia lo que fue y hablo, hablo con el poco sentido del
> recuerdo, con las fallas, las caídas, los tropiezos inevitables
> del espejo de la memoria. (18–19)[71]

While the parts dominated by political melancholy (the middle section) are more straightforward, the overwhelming melancholy of
transience that pervades the beginning and the end of the book causes
the narrative to become fragmented, to overlap times and themes. This
is not a flaw, as León seems to believe, but a sign of uncontrolled lucidity. The predominance of the fragment and chronological disjointed-
ness evinces a lack of resolution, an impossibility of threading a
conventional chronological narrative that emanates from a loss that
leaves everything unlinked. However, although León's story is the
record of the endless repetition of loss and separation, it is also the last
effort León makes to vouch for her very identity. Jagged and jarred,
León's narrative of fragments belies also her lamentations about her
painfully limited memory: as a matter of fact, haunted by an irredeemable melancholy, León remembers too well and too painfully. Thus
her desire to get rid of certain memories, to summon a political memory in order to fight against the memory of loss and the reminders of dissolution, a form of memory that she fittingly inscribes in the heart:
"Todo, todo lo vivido quedó allí clasificado. Tampoco puedo yo leer lo
que a través de la vida quedó en esas tramas sutilísimas que nadie puede
descifrar nunca. . . . Es inútil. Unicamente sé que a veces llora. Cuidado,
es que ha tocado usted mi infancia" (Everything, everything I lived
remains shelved there. Not even I can read what life engraved in that
most delicate of grids, which nobody is able to decipher. . . . It's useless.
I only know that sometimes it cries. Careful, you have touched my
childhood).[72] Against the double threat inscribed in the flesh (the pain
of memory and the reminders of the self's eventual dissolution), writing, in what it has of cathartic reaching out, in a word, as *saying,* is
León's final shelter against oblivion and dissolution.

The Ethics of Memory

Kristeva describes the struggle of the melancholic as a "battle with symbolic collapse," which can result in aesthetic creations or religious discourses that possess "a real and imaginary effectiveness that comes closer to catharsis than to elaboration" (*Black Sun,* 24). Neither properly literary nor religious, *Memoria de la melancolía* participates, however, in both dimensions. León's wartime paradise of fraternity is undoubtedly a creation, not a negligent, gratuitous invention but a fable that invokes a religious transcendence as a defense against unjust loss and transience. Perhaps *literary* and *religious* could be fused in a term that, in León's case, would gather their meanings. That word would be *ethical,* because León's paradise, although manifestly political, in what it has of the utopic and the implausible stands as an impossible ethical dream of fraternity that supplants, and suppresses, thorny political conflicts and contradictions that León, driven by an ethical dream, is bound to oversee. In addition to what the story has of ethical in its content, the ethical manifests itself in *Memoria de la melancolía* as *saying,* a dimension that is most easily discernible in the frequent apostrophes to the most diverse people (and even Spain) that openly reveal the other-directed nature of León's narrative, its dialogical dimension. Although all autobiographies participate in the *saying,* León consciously and constantly foregrounds that dimension, and by so doing she shows unequivocally that the telling of her story adds to the said a supplement that not only thoroughly inflects what is told but is in itself a vital dimension of the work. León has an ambivalent view of memory: it becomes increasingly painful for her to remember (memory becoming more and more a record of death); but simultaneously memory is her ultimate shelter. However, despite the pain involved in remembering, León cannot evade the telling.

Although it ends up being much more than that, León intended *Memoria de la melancolía* to be, at least initially, a testimony, her stated purpose for writing it being to record the small daily facts that would never make it to the official histories of the war (43). Besides offering her personal testimony, León also exhorts the exiled community to tell their own, irreplaceable stories: "Contad vuestras angustias del destierro. No tengáis vergüenza. Todos las llevamos dentro" (Tell of your anguish in exile. Don't be ashamed. All of us carry it inside.) "Sí, desterrados de España, contad, contad lo que nunca dijeron los periódicos, decid vuestras angustias y lo horrorosa que fue la suerte que os echaron encima. Que recuerden los que olvidaron" (Yes, Spanish exiles, tell, tell what newspapers never said, tell about your anguish and how terrible was the fate they imposed on you. Let those who forgot remember.)[73] Shoshana Felman argues that testimonies have a performative force that takes them beyond the constative: "To *testify*—to *vow to tell*, to *promise* and *produce* one's own speech as material evidence for truth—is to accomplish a *speech act*, rather than to simply formulate a statement." That excess beyond the constative that testimonies possess is characterized by Felman as responsibility: "Since the testimony cannot be simply relayed, repeated, or reported by another without thereby losing its function as a testimony, the burden of the witness . . . is a radically unique, noninterchangeable, and solitary burden. . . To bear witness is *to bear the solitude* of a responsibility, and to *bear the responsibility*, precisely, of that solitude."[74] However, any autobiography partakes of Felman's characterization of testimony. In what they have of *saying*, all personal writings always go beyond the factuality of the *said*; besides, all autobiographies are always acts of responsibility (nobody can respond for one's life other than oneself) that bring into relief the absolute singularity, or irreplaceability, of the subject who tells. Thus the only difference between testimony, in Felman's characterization, and the ethical definition of autobiography proposed here would be one of emphasis but not of nature.[75] Rousseau was right in seeing his *Confessions* as something absolutely unique; he was wrong, however, in thinking that what made them irreplaceable was their content. His book's singularity was in the saying, not in its scandalous revelations or in its novel techniques, of course, but in the fact that only Rousseau could take upon himself the responsibility of telling his life (what each autobiographer does with that responsibility is another issue). Any autobiography is absolutely singular in that only its protagonist can tell it, although the other is always before, beside, and beyond the telling subject. The autobiographies read and reread are not those that have an informative or shocking content (those are read, but rarely more than once), but the ones (Rousseau's and St. Augustine's are the first paradigms) in which the other and the *saying*—the ethical as responsibility—are most prominent. María Zambrano lucidly indicates that the moment one starts "el relato de nuestro ayer que constituye la confesión, en realidad ya la confesión ha logrado su fin" (that account of our past which is a confession, the confession has already accomplished its goal.)[76]

León aptly foregrounds her irreplaceable ethical responsibility in the form of a dialogue with a fictitious reader, as response to another: "Nos están llamando: ¡Eh, váyase! Su papel no da para más. Salga de la escena.

Está concluyéndose el último acto. . . . ¿No ve como bosteza el público? . . . No se enfade, ya me marcho. Pero '¿quién podrá contar esta triste historia' si yo no lo hago?" (They are calling us. Hey!, go away! Your role is over. Leave the stage. The last act is coming to an end. . . . Don't you see the audience is yawning? . . . Don't get upset, I am leaving now. But, "who will tell this sad story" if I don't do it?).[77] The inclusion of answers and objections, the transformation of autobiography into an act of apostrophic interpellation, of dialogical interplay with the reader, exceeds the testimonial itself. As María Zambrano writes, "Toda confesión es hablada, es una larga conversación" (14; every confession is done talking, it is a long conversation).[78] The other, however, has a place not only as an inner (or, in this particular case, an outer) voice that calls for a response, but shapes also León's memory in various ways, thus showing that memory is also, and always, suffused with the ghostly presence of the other.[79] The most common form in which León brings the other to play on her memory is when she summons someone to validate an episode she has just recalled: "¿Recuerdas, Dolores [Ibarruri, 'La Pasionaria']?" (214; Do you remember, Dolores); "¿Te acuerdas, Rafael?" (172; Do you remember, Rafael [Alberti]); "¿Te acuerdas, Luis?" (174; Do you remember, Luis [Buñuel]?). Although in many cases León's interpellation is merely rhetorical, this constant address to others in search of corroboration underscores that memory always participates in the communal.[80] Memory always falters, but not on account of its gaps or repressions, its voluntary or involuntary forgetfulness. On the contrary, memory is always already faulty, it is never self-sufficient, because it is marked by the spectral trace of the other (who, as León does, can be explicitly summoned as witness or addressee of one's memories). Whether it is summoned or not, the other always lurks within memory, as it is clearly, and paradoxically, evidenced in the cases when someone strives to keep some memories secret. Precisely when it attempts to keep the other at bay with secrecy, memory avers that it is commanded by that other.[81]

In her apostrophic "Do you remember . . . ?" León foregrounds this unremitting presence of the other, which the self, due to inadvertence or egotism, frequently fails to acknowledge or detect.[82] And yet, whether one is oblivious or aware, that shadowy presence takes memory beyond the constative and into the ethical. There is not such a thing as a properly personal memory: no one owns his/her memory, because memory is always a response and a responsibility. Memory, however, is not simply marked or haunted by the other, but it is also addressed to the other, it is for the

other. León brings this dimension into relief in her frequent injunctions to
the readers (29, 40, 43, 164, 192, etc.), especially when she suspects they
might be reluctant to hear her stories or the exiles', thus refusing to accept
the responsibility that the testamentary nature of autobiography assigns to
them. That other-addressed quality is especially prominent in her frequent
exhortations to the youth of Spain, an addressee privileged in *Memoria de
la melancolía*. And yet, as already noted, León becomes increasingly and
painfully aware that the continuity she is looking for with her testimony is
endangered precisely by her inability to communicate with the young people of Spain who have renewed the exiles' fight for Spain's freedom. This
fear of not connecting has a concomitant aspect in León's anxiety of being
forgotten, which gradually displaces her narrative from political activism,
testimony, and the preservation of collective memory to an increased concern with the precariousness of her self. This shift from the imposition of
her memory onto others to her plea for remembrance is noticeable in her
address to her children: "Nos aficionamos a gente que se debe morir y a
cosas que se van a quedar. Yo no quedaré, pero cuando yo no recuerde,
recordad vosotros las veces que me levanté de la silla, el café que os
hice. . . . Recordad que mi mano derecha se abrió siempre. . . Cuando pen-
séis en mis pecados, tenéis que sentir la misma piedad que yo por los
vuestros. Cuando yo todo lo olvide y cante como mi abuela con la última
luz de la memoria, perdonadme vosotros, los que os agarrasteis a mi vesti-
do con vuestras manitas tan pequeñas" (169–70; We become fond of people who must perish and to things that remain. I will not remain, but when
I can't remember any longer, remember the times I got up from the chair,
the coffee I prepared for you. . . . Remember that my right hand always
opened itself. . . . When in the future you think about my sins, you should
feel the same forgiveness I felt towards yours. The day I forget everything
and sing like my grandmother with the last light of memory, forgive me,
you that clutched at my dress with your little hands).[83] This fear of being
forgotten reaches its extreme in the terror she feels, when she is already living in Rome, that one day nobody will see her: "Por la calle se da uno cuenta de que las viejas son todas del mismo modelo. Lo difícil es diferenciarse.
A mí me da miedo que llegue un día en que nadie me vea. Sería un purga-
torio eso de andar por la calle sin que ninguna mirada se cruzase con la
mía" (44; Walking through the streets one realizes that all old ladies are cut
from the same pattern. What is difficult is to differentiate yourself. I am
afraid that one day nobody will see me. It would be a purgatory to walk the
streets without any gaze encountering mine).[84]

León's frequent use of apostrophe, her running dialogue with a multitude of readers (identified or generic), underlines the ethical, other-directed nature of autobiography. Who could be, however, the third, the indirect addressee who always lurks behind the ostensible addressee of her apostrophes, of any apostrophe?[85] León's ultimate fear of not being seen (recognized, interpellated) and its obverse, her wish for transcendence, help delineate that unknown superaddressee for whose name one would search in vain in *Memoria de la melancolía*. That addressee, ever-present but never directly acknowledged in León's book, has to be the only one who can guarantee transcendence, the overseer with no oversight, the absolute counterpart to the black hole of transience where León fears all her pleas and invocations might one day disappear swallowed up by a silence that offers no response.

León's imperative need for memory and remembrance, her longing to be seen and acknowledged, runs into a final, terrible irony. According to the testimonies, León ended her days with a total loss of memory, a loss that seems to have been already patent when, finally, she and Alberti were able to return to Spain after Franco's death and the legalization of the Communist Party.[86] After spending years obsessed with remembering and asking people not to forget, gripped later by the fear of being ignored, and always longing to return home, that day in April 1977 León, beyond memory, did not recognize anyone precisely at the moment in which she was finally seen and recognized by all.

JUAN GOYTISOLO
Telling Death and the Nostalgia for Origins

4

In his two autobiographical works, *Coto vedado* and *En los reinos de taifa,* Juan Goytisolo presents his life as a series of sheddings of skin that allows him finally to reach, presumably, an authentic identity that, stifled in the past by social, political, and personal encumbrances, he could reveal and accept only through a prolonged and painful struggle.[1] In a first step Goytisolo broke with his family's asphyxiating morals, which condemned several of his familial predecessors to a life of hypocrisy, dissimulation, capitulation, and even insanity. His discovery of Marxism in the fifties gave him a new vision of his social class, his family, and his country's past and thus facilitated both his repudiation of that world and his political commitment to Leftist ideals that he thought would bring an end to bourgeois political and moral hegemony. Frequent trips to Paris helped him distance himself from the world he abhorred, and he finally settled there to live with Monique Lange, an employee of the prestigious Gallimard publishing house, where Goytisolo began working as a consultant on Spanish literature. Monique Lange soon introduced him to Jean Genet, a decisive figure in Goytisolo's life.

In the early sixties Goytisolo began to feel straitjacketed by the social roles imposed on him by Marxism and by heterosexuality. For him this was a time of profound ambivalence regarding his political commitments and also a period of continuous crisis in his relationship with Monique Lange. His gradual exploration of the Arab world in Paris led him to Mohamed, a Moroccan immigrant with whom he had his first fulfilling homosexual experience. That relationship served also as a springboard for both an acquaintance with the Arab world and his realization that he was "Total, definitiva, irremediablemente homosexual" (totally, definitively, irrevocably homosexual), as he wrote in a letter to Monique (*RT* 240/204). At about the same time, his ideological contradictions and misgivings prompted him to another significant break, this time with the strictures of Marxism and the tenets of literary social realism.

In his two autobiographical books, Goytisolo narrates this process of discovery, unveiling, or (re)construction of his true identity at the expense of his old, unsatisfying one. The uncertainty in the vocabulary used here to describe that development arises from the difficulty of discerning what it is that Goytisolo does in his autobiographical texts or, better still, what those texts actually do.[2] His insistence on seeing his past self as inhabited by a double or impostor and his repeated use of terms such as authenticity to describe what he considers the result of a process of purification or expulsion of his doubles raise many questions about his understanding and figuration of identity. By presenting his life as a struggle for authenticity, Goytisolo resembles most autobiographers: he views his self-writing primarily as a cognitive operation. One has to ask, however, what is really involved in the achievement of authenticity through the liberation/unveiling/assumption of a dormant or repressed identity and in particular what, besides self-awareness, would seem to be required for such achievement.

Against the grain of his convictions regarding the possibility of self-knowledge, Goytisolo explicitly foregrounds his self-consciousness about the conventions and shortcomings of the autobiographical genre. This awareness determines in good measure the way he structures both works, especially *Coto vedado*. And yet his recognition of the traps and limitations of autobiography does not keep him from engaging wholeheartedly in its practice. And what are the consequences of this apparent contradiction (an autobiographer who seems fully aware of the limitations of the genre undertaking a most passionate display of achieved authenticity)? The study of Goytisolo's cognitive thematics shows the importance of a rhetorics of tropes in any autobiographical formulation of self-knowledge. And the exploration of his works' structures and self-reflexivity leads to an examination of his interlocutors and addressees and ultimately into autobiography as ethics and alterity. To put it simply, Goytisolo's will to self-knowledge seems to be undermined by the structural and rhetorical underpinnings and the self-reflexivity of his texts. Although those formal drawbacks do seem to endanger his epistemological project, they actually throw into relief autobiography's ethical

dimension and convincingly display its decisive preeminence in
Goytisolo's project.

Divided into two parts, *Coto vedado* intersperses a chronological narrative with numerous vignettes that interrupt its linear temporal order
at regular intervals. The chronological account starts with an overview
of the lives of Goytisolo's grandparents and ends in 1956, when he settled down in Paris with Monique Lange and made his first visit to the
province of Almería (in southern Spain), a journey of discovery that, as
he asserts at the end of *Coto vedado,* had for him an epiphanic value. In
the first part of this work, Goytisolo tells the story of his maternal and
paternal families, as well as his own, up to the time he was about to
enter the University of Barcelona. The linearity and integrity of this
account is broken periodically by sections in which Goytisolo either
jumps forward in time to illumine the narrated present with later
developments or reflects on the dangers and difficulties of any autobiographical project. Also, in almost every narrative segment, the narrator offers considerations from his perspective at the time of writing,
helping the reader delineate, beneath the events being narrated, a subtext that fitfully tells another story, that of the true identity of
Goytisolo, which he did not fully assume until the mid-sixties. With
retrospective wisdom the narrator calls the reader's attention to the
sporadic details or episodes that in the past already pointed, although
unknowingly for Goytisolo at the time, to his future, authentic identity. This longing for authenticity is not limited to Goytisolo's autobiography. Paul Julian Smith argues that *Makbara* (1980) and *Las virtudes
del pájaro solitario* (1988) "reveal a continuing nostalgia for unmediated authenticity, a *tabula rasa* of social and sexual relations. In the first
text the site of this nostalgia is the desert; in the second it is the forest
glade."[3] One finds a similar nostalgia in his two autobiographical volumes, where the Almería of the fifties, with its sparse landscape and, in
his view, its primitive but genuine people, offers perhaps the best physical and human embodiments of his nostalgia for authenticity.
Accordingly he becomes disenchanted with both people and scenery,
perceiving that the economic development of the early sixties is drasti-
cally changing the physical and human landscapes of that province,
prompting him to renounce to visit it again.[4]

Like any other autobiographer, Goytisolo presents his life as if the
facts themselves already configured it. The peculiarity in his case is that
he reconstructs himself by rescuing from beneath the rubble of his

previous self-constructions another identity that, although it was always there, was not permitted to flourish because of social, political, and personal constrictions. This "other," earlier Goytisolo that he repudiates in his autobiography began his self-inventions by telling alternative familial stories in his childhood and, later on, by imitating wealthy teenagers (*CV* 125/104). Goytisolo calls this inventions "mitomanía" (mythomania; *CV* 90/74). And this, he later realizes, was his way to compensate for the familial traumas and shortcomings that led him at several junctures in his life to the creation of false self-images that evinced his inauthenticity (*CV* 117/98) and gave him a double identity (*CV* 125/104).[5] The first part of *Coto vedado* revolves around these youthful, troubling, and, judged retrospectively, failed attempts to re-create his self. It ends when Goytisolo is ready to abandon his home and the remaining members of his family (his father, grandfather, and the maid Eulalia) in order to open a new chapter in his life.

The second part of *Coto vedado* begins with his entering the university in 1948 and ends with his first trip to Almería in 1956. While the first part offers a searing attack on most of the members of his family's two previous generations and also debunks both the family myths created by his father and his own misguided attempts at self-creation, the book's second part targets not primarily his family, but Goytisolo's false identities during his years at the university and beyond. The epigraph by Montaigne that precedes this second part—"et existe autant de différence de nous à nous-mêmes que de nous à l'autrui" (*CV* 135/113; "and there is as much difference between me and myself as there is between me and the others")—already anticipates that this part of the book will revolve around Goytisolo's self-deceiving stratagems and points to his future awareness of that duplicity. In the period covered by the second part, his "mythomania" will lead him to create new artificial images that prolong his inauthenticity, whether as a flashy freshman who tries to impress his fellow students with his faked superiority (*CV* 146/123) or as cultivation of an external self-fashioning that he associates with being a writer (*CV* 165/140). This theme of the pose-striking writer plays a decisive role in Goytisolo's autobiography, and he finds a good expression of it in the Spanish saying "Genio y figura hasta la sepultura" (airs and genius to the end) to which he adds a rejoinder "cuanto más genio, más figura: cuanto más figura, más genio" ("the more genius, the more airs; the more airs, the more genius").[6] An entire section of *En los reinos de taifa,* "Las chinelas de Empédocles"

(The Slippers of Empedocles), will develop this theme, examining the attitudes of well-known writers from both Spain and other countries, while the following section, "El territorio del poeta" (The Poet's Territory), centered on Genet, forms a positive counterpart to that scorching chapter.

Under the confused, misbegotten attempts at self-creation that the narrator excoriates, in both *Coto vedado* and *En los reinos de taifa* he can spot some inchoate traits that in retrospect he sees as becoming an essential part of his identity. Three strands in particular will be woven into his authentic identity: sexuality, politics, and writing. On each of those fronts, Goytisolo breaks with his past, and those ruptures, narrated in *En los reinos de taifa,* come almost simultaneously: his assumption of his homosexuality; his definite rejection of Marxism as a form of understanding and changing the world; and his transition from being a passive victim of Spain's dictatorship and its cultural/historical constrictions to an aggressive attitude that, presiding over his fiction since *Reivindicación del conde don Julián (Count Julian),* leads him to ransack the cultural and political fabrications of Spain and to adopt the Spanish language as his only and true "fatherland."

This triple dimension of his counterstory explains the composition of *En los reinos de taifa* in seven sections. While in the first one Goytisolo continues the chronological account of *Coto vedado,* extending it from 1956 until 1964, in the remaining six he covers almost the same temporal range as the first one (mid-fifties to mid-sixties). At any rate the six sections continue the same pattern of official story/emerging counterstory centered around the three basic components of Goytisolo's new self-imaging: *politics* (1: "El ladrón de energías" [The Stealer of Strength], 4: "El gato negro de la Rue de Bièvre" [A Black Cat on the Rue de Bièvre], 6: "La máquina del tiempo" [The Time Machine]); *sexuality and love* (5: "Monique"); and *writing* (2: "Las chinelas de Empédocles" [The Slippers of Empedocles]; 3: "El territorio del poeta" [The Poet's Territory]). The seventh section, "No es moro todo lo que reluce" (All That Glitters Isn't Moorish), covers only the few months of his first stay in Morocco (fall of 1965 to January 1966): his arrival and stay in Tangiers; his brief visit to Marrakesh; and the seminal events that took place after he received the news of the death of Eulalia (who had been officially a maid, but actually a surrogate mother for the Goytisolo children), a watershed event that precipitated an identity crisis that had been brewing for several years and that ended with his resolution to engage in a new type of writing that conjoins a reappropriation of Spain's cultural past with his proclamations of a finally accepted homosexuality. Thus ends Goytisolo's autobiography and from that point on, he argues, identity, language, and sexuality will become inseparable in his life.

Of the three strands that he uses to weave his life, the political one revolves around the tight relationship between his self-definition and his representation of Spain (in the double sense of his role as representative of the opposition and of his portrayal of the nation). When he writes about Spain, he is writing also, and above all, about himself, since his understanding of the nation grants that imagined community a reality that allows him to imagine his self in opposition to his construction of the nation. In other words, Goytisolo's self-imaging is a counterimage of the nation, which he holds largely responsible for just about everything that went wrong with him in his early years.[7] When he opened up to Marxism, he also began to shift the blame first from his family to his class, then to Francoist politics, and later to an "official" national self-understanding whose propriety is constructed through repression and exclusion. Goytisolo organizes the political thread of his autobiography as a conflict between a story of his "representativeness" and a counterstory formed by his increasing awareness of signs that cast doubts on the accuracy of his portrayal of the nation and on the legitimacy of his representational rights. This drama is illustrated by several instances in the first section of En los reinos de taifa, but one case will suffice. Rereading his writings of the early sixties about Spain, the narrator finds them aberrant because his proposal that Spain should align itself with the Third World and not with the Common Market seems to him in retrospect to betray a fundamental misunderstanding of the nation, which he now attributes to his propensity to take his wishes for reality (RT 64/54). Goytisolo specifically writes that his misrepresentation of Spain was actually a self-misrepresentation, a compensatory fantasy that denied him true self-knowledge (67/57). Consequently his self-portrayal for that period insists on duplicity, contradictions, moral schizophrenia, irrationality, and imperviousness to the reality of his true self.[8] After its extensive treatment in the first segment of En los reinos de taifa, Goytisolo continues his political account in the third one, devoted to his complex, changing, and eventually disillusioned relationship with Cuba from 1962 to 1974. A similarly disenchanted view of politics impregnates the sixth part, in which the sexually and politically "new" Goytisolo visits Russia in 1965 and examines socialism without "las telarañas de la ideología" (*RT* 255/216; "the cobwebs of ideology").

The narrative thread on sexuality chronicles his discovery of bodily pleasures, which already in his youth "se transformó en uno de los centros reales, por no decir el más real, de mi vida" (*CV* 121/101; "became one of the centers, if not the epicenter, of my life"), starting with his discovery of masturbation and culminating with his first joyful homosexual experiences, which make possible a full understanding of the homoerotic sexual fantasies about rugged, invasive males that had haunted him since his childhood. The narrative of Goytisolo's homosexual awakening starts with a stay in Madrid, while taking care of family business, that brought about an initiation into a nocturnal life of dissipation and also yielded a first, clumsy emergence of his homosexual inclinations, to which he reacts with a swift and falsely comforting self-denial. This narrative line reaches its climax in the fifth part of *En los reinos de taifa,* where Goytisolo offers an account of his consequential and troubled relationship with Monique, as well as of his assumption of homosexuality.

Another story, that of his relations with language and reading, is fitfully developed in a trajectory similar to that of his sexuality. He partially exonerates the otherwise arrogant self of his college years because it now appears to him that his love of reading and his tendency to question his milieu's values have already pointed to an honest, if confused, quest for authenticity. In particular his reading of forbidden books while at the university seems to him in retrospect to have provided a clandestine pleasure that he finds as preparatory to another form of transgression, homosexuality. This fumbling relationship with reading will be the first chapter of a story that ends with the discovery of his unalloyed passion for the Spanish language. This story of reading, writing, and literary models and ideals will develop slowly, through tentative and at times misguided choices that set back his recognition and appropriation of what he calls "una escritura personal y responsable" (*CV* 209/177; "a responsible, personal form of writing"). Judging the attitudes of many writers he personally knew or admired, he assembles them in two contrasting groups: those who live for their external image and have thus betrayed themselves, and those that have been loyal to themselves even under the most trying situations or have created a personal morality that defies the most respectable social values. This segment leads naturally to the next, "El territorio del poeta" (The Poet's Territory), centered around Jean Genet, the moral-literary model par excellence for Goytisolo, whose friendship with the French writer, starting in 1956, had a seminal influence on his life and writings.

Beyond the Ideological: The Attachment to Subjection

In his autobiographical reconstruction, Goytisolo represents himself as being consumed in the mid-sixties by a struggle between his official identities (political, sexual and literary) and compulsions, tendencies, or desires that, although not yet accepted or acknowledged by him, gave rise to a relentless and increasing discomfort that finally shattered his complacent self-representations. In hindsight Goytisolo identifies those disturbing forces as the authentic components of his true self and accuses himself time and again of "insidiosa irracionalidad" (insidious irrationality), of a "falta de una relación limpia contigo mismo" (RT 63/53; "lack of an unsullied relationship with yourself"), of disagreement between his being and his image (RT 86/72), of a "sigilosa conciencia de impostura" (RT 114/97;"furtive awareness of being an impostor").[9] Schizophrenia, Mr. Hyde, "malsín" (the informer) are some of the figures that yield to Goytisolo's self all its radiant truth, once those ghosts are ousted. Once he figures the self as a (metaphorical) space occupied by an unwelcome and treacherous guest, it becomes possible for "cualquier cartógrafo competente y honrado" (RT 216/183; "any honest, competent cartographer") to expel that bogus double. Goytisolo's spatial figuration of identity betrays its rhetorical nature, but the unavoidable rhetoricity of any attempt to locate spatially the self should not be seen as an irredeemable failure. After all the cognitive domain that rhetoric undermines is not the most important one for autobiography (and Goytisolo himself casts doubts upon the representational success of his autobiography). The ethical dimension supersedes not only Goytisolo's epistemic ambitions but also his misgivings about the success of his autobiographical enterprise.

The division and self-estrangement of Goytisolo's recurrent doubleness point to the constitutive splitting of the subject. As explained in the first chapter, Levinas argues that the subject originates as response to the call of the other. In Lacan's terminology, this would correspond to the mirror stage, in which the subject first becomes aware of itself as a reflection of the other. This initial self-division of the subject constitutes the grounds for the subsequent ideological colonization of the subject's body and psyche as subject of the law. In other words, the law colonizes both the mind and the affects, or, as Deleuze and Guattari argue, it produces *corporeal* and *incorporeal* transformations. This two-stage process of identity creation casts light on the self-reconstruction that Goytisolo postulates in his autobiographical account. As Foucault argues, there is always a margin of resistance to the identity imposed by the law, because power is by definition a force pitted against another, resisting force. But it will not suffice for a subject who seeks change to locate the space or nature of that resistance to power; furthermore the possibility of resistance, or even the awareness of its need and nature, does not imply that reconstructing oneself is a simple task, for in order to effect any profound and significant change in one's identity, it is necessary to go beyond the ideological to its very foundation in the affective/imaginary. This is the reason why mere consciousness of the effects of ideology (as proposed, for instance, by classical Marxism) is insufficient to promote any really revolutionary personal change, since such consciousness leaves untouched the terrain of the affects that grounds the discursive. Attending to the issue of resistance to ideology, Judith Butler argues that in Althusser's interpretation of Lacan, the domain of the imaginary, due to its constitutive vacillation, "makes *misrecognition* possible" and thus thwarts ideological interpellation: "the imaginary signifies the impossibility of the discursive—that is, symbolic—constitution of identity. Identity can never be fully totalized by the symbolic, for what it fails to order will emerge within the imaginary as a disorder, a site where identity is contested." However, in this Lacanian/Althusserian formulation, the imaginary "cannot turn back upon the law, demanding or effecting its reformulation. . . . Resistance is thus located in a domain that is virtually powerless to alter the law that it opposes." Butler contends that, in contrast with this Lacanian configuration of identity in which the misadjustment between the symbolic and the imaginary makes unavoidable the appearance of a resistance that is nonetheless beyond the control of a virtually powerless subject, when Foucault effects a shift from a juridical consideration of power to an understanding of power as "a field of productive, regulatory, and contestatory relations," resistance is posited as an effect of power itself. Thus, Butler argues, from a Foucauldian perspective "the symbolic produces the possibility of its own subversions, and these subversions are unanticipated effects of symbolic interpellations."[10] While Butler seems to propose that Foucault's theory of power opens up the possibility for the subject to act on the space of resistance that that same power, by its very nature, inevitably generates, she still remains in the domain of (ideological) consciousness without engaging the affective/imaginary. But a case such as Goytisolo's shows unequivocally that the success of a thorough reconstruction of identity hinges on the possibility of going beyond the discursive in order to alter its very affective foundations.

Therefore it is not enough for a subject intent on reconstructing itself to be conscious of the effects of ideology and to try somehow to reverse them, as the story of Goytisolo's shift to Marxism clearly exemplifies. Becoming acquainted with Marxism in the fifties, Goytisolo opens his eyes to the nature of his social class, "cuya decadencia y precariedad creía ver reflejadas en el declive de la propia familia" (*CV* 199/169; "the decadence and precarious state of which I saw reflected in the decline of my own family"), and feels compelled "por el deseo de hacerme perdonar la mancha original de mi clase y pasado infamante de la familia" (*CV* 218/184; "[by my desire] to atone for the original sin of my class and my family's odious past") by becoming a supporter of the Spanish communist party. With the adoption of Marxist discourse, Goytisolo believes to be in possession of a powerful tool that not only explains his past identity and his family's history but also opens exhilarating vistas into the future. Although Marxism brings some temporary order and clarity to Goytisolo's life, it progressively imprisons him in an ideological determination of his identity that forces him into untruthful, or inauthentic, positions regarding his writing, sexuality, and politics, as the second part of *Coto vedado* and the first section of *En los reinos de taifa* illustrate. In other words, a mere ideological shift leaves unrecognized the deepest pulsions in Goytisolo's being; furthermore his acknowledgement of those impulses leads him beyond simple ideological explanations, thus undermining the explanatory power of ideology and exposing its limitations.

Goytisolo's representation of his life unequivocally shows that the mere self-awareness of ideological interpellations can lead only to an equally ideological response that can be even more restrictive and entrapping than the one it supplants. Neither ideological consciousness nor any response emanating solely from it is sufficient to effect a radical transformation of the subject, which demands going into the terrain of the prediscursive where the grounds for the colonization of the subject's affects are established. In other words, the subject has to revisit the domain of the ethical (or the imaginary, in Lacan's parlance), of the affective attachments of the subject, with all the opportunities, but also the dangers, that such a move entails. Wondering about the subject's passionate attachments to disciplinary subjection, Judith Butler raises fundamental questions concerning the constitution of the subject: "To what extent has the disciplinary apparatus that attempts to produce and totalize identity become an abiding object of passionate attachment? . . . In particular, how are we to understand, not merely the disciplinary production of the subject, but the disciplinary cultivation of *an attachment to subjection?*"[11] Butler's question hits the mark, but she does not go beyond the puzzlement expressed in her question, due to her inability to locate the origins of the (affective) attachment to subjection in the domain of ethical alterity. When Goytisolo effects his ideological shift to Marxism, he seems trapped in the logic of power and has to acknowledge that his position of Marxist resistance not only ends up reproducing power, but also leaves him powerless to control the monstrous doubles engendered by his political position. If Goytisolo's autobiographies illustrate that an ideological shift, no matter how lucid, does not suffice to effect a radical change, they also show that the subject's only hope for a radical transformation resides in the possibility to undo the affective attachments that ground the ideology he is attempting to discard. Goytisolo dramatizes that move in two scenes that he fittingly places in the last section of *En los reinos de taifa,* stressing in that way the occasion and nature of the deep transformation of identity that will provide him with the perspective necessary to narrate his life as a series of failed reconstructions. Failed, that is, except for the last, fateful one.[12]

Goytisolo portrays that last transformation as successful precisely because it does not take place at the level of consciousness, but in the terrain of the prediscursive or the presymbolic. For that reason such transformation will have to involve one's doubles, including the foremost double or image of the self: the body. "In man the relation to one's own body characterizes . . . the restricted, but really irreducible, field of the imaginary," writes Lacan.[13] In the same way that consciousness originates in the call from, and response to, the other that precedes it, the inaugural figuration of the body is also given outside of itself since it first appears as a reflection of/on the other. The body, then, first comes to light as an image, as a projection onto a mirror (real or figural), and

therefore, as Butler suggests, "any sense of bodily contour, as project-
ed, is articulated through a necessary self-division and self-estrangement."[14] The first sense of one's own body can only appear as an
outside projection, as an other body, as a trace of the other. It is this
physical self-division, this seeing oneself outside of oneself, that originates self-reflection. The body allows one to think oneself, but only
because the body appears originally outside, as the body of the other.
The initial external surface that constitutes the body is later disciplined
or structured by the acquisition of language, by its accession to the
symbolic, which will grant the subject the illusion of owning the body.
As Lacan argues, one "thinks as a consequence of the fact that a structure, that of language . . . carves up his body, a structure that has nothing to do with anatomy."[15] The body, then, is formed both at the level
of the ethical and at the level of the political, and its constitution and
fate are tightly wound with those of the subject. In its apparition as an
external other, at the ethical level it provides the model for the ego, but
were it to remain at that stage it would be permanently caught in the
alienating adoration of the other. The advent of the law, of the discursive, liberates the body from its imprisonment in the mirror of the
other, makes the body "ours," and allows us to talk about it, but it
simultaneously introduces another separation, a further form of alterity, since the speech on the body is always indirect, always indebted to
the other. Lacan contends that this twofold alienation of the subject is
already theorized in Freud: "There is the other as imaginary. It's here in
the imaginary relation with the other that . . . self-consciousness is
instituted. . . . The ego isn't even the place, . . . the organizing center of
the subject. It's profoundly dissymmetrical to it." And he continues:
"There is also the other who speaks from my place, apparently, this
other who is within me. This is an other of a totally different nature
from the other, my counterpart."[16]

It seems necessary to warn against an identification of the "body"
with the anatomical, the physiological, the domain of sexual desire, or
any other physical determination, since any of those embodiments is
just one of the multiple possible forms to constitute the body in discourse, and only a naive conception can assume that the body is
exhausted in any material formulation, be it in anatomical terms or in
a physiological tabulation of flows, fluids, or physical feelings and
desires. The body cannot be exhausted in any of its definitions since,
as Butler argues, the body is "that which exceeds and confounds the

injunctions of normalization."[17] Resisting totalization, the body is an elusive referent, the privileged site where the pressures of the Real are manifested; but by the same token it is also a primary locus of contestation where both the workings of power and the resistance to it are particularly evident. The pressure of the Real evinces the constitutive vacillation of the body (and of the self that the body helps to institute), but it should be contended that such vacillation does not imply a constitutive lack or fictionality of the subject (contrary to Lacan's arguments), being on the contrary the ground necessary for freedom (a freedom that claims a harsh price, the price of instability, of vacillation), the possibility of resistance to power, to the symbolic injunctions that attempt to freeze us in a fixed, stable identity. The body is one of the privileged locations where the drama of power and identity permanently unfolds, and only by going beyond any of its insufficient discursive formulations can the terms of that drama be really changed. This is the move that Goytisolo effects after his roaming through the ideological brings him more grief and relief. The Tangiers episodes that close *En los reinos de taifa* teach that the only possibility to really effect a profound transformation of identity is through a bodily ritual, through a hellish, hallucinatory trip to the other side of the discursive that brings about a replacement of the father and an expiation of guilt that amounts to the repayment of a personal and national debt dispensed primarily through an estrangement and punishment of his body. Establishing a close connection between guilt (and its purification) and self-understanding, Goytisolo portrays himself as emerging from these experiences with a new identity that entails a renewed genealogy. Those exemplary episodes show that the ethical/imaginary is not simply overcome by the symbolic/discursive, but lurks as both a danger and a possibility: as a danger of psychosis (in which a substitution of the imaginary for the symbolic would result in an imaginary reinvention of reality), but also as the possibility of resistance, of a refashioning and reinvention of identity.

Self-Fathering and the Nostalgia for Origins

The Tangiers episodes narrated in the seventh and closing section of *En los reinos de taifa* are among a few events that Goytisolo underscores as watershed moments in his autobiographical reconstruction. The first episode takes place during a night in Tangiers in which Goytisolo undergoes considerable verbal, physical, and, seemingly, also sexual abuse from a Moroccan companion. The second chronicles another night in that same town a few weeks later when, after receiving the news of Eulalia's demise, he takes a strong dose of *maashun* and embarks on a long journey through doubleness and death.[18] In different but related ways, those events are portrayed by Goytisolo as bringing about significant breaks and renewals in his life, and accordingly they call attention to the prominence of agon, death, rebirth, and the search for origins in Goytisolo's autobiographical self-figurations.

The significance of the Paris encounter with Mohamed resides in that it brings concinnity between Goytisolo's sexual fantasies and his actual experiences, but also in that it awakens in him the desire to explore the Arab language and culture, an exploration that will ultimately lead him to underscore the Arab influence in Spanish culture. And yet Goytisolo will need two other awakenings before he is presumably able to achieve that self-coincidence that he flaunts in his autobiographies. His self-confrontation reaches a striking climax when, in a long night of drugs and alcohol in which "todo es neblinoso e irreal" (*RT* 302/255; "everything is misty and unreal"), he deliberately provokes a Moroccan friend who has acted as his guide through the city of Tangiers. Instigated by Goytisolo's taunting, the laid-off employee of a Spanish company ends up hitting Goytisolo and ordering him in a brutal manner to lie on the bed of the room they are sharing:

> en el piso al fin, sin saber cómo habéis llegado ni por qué os disputáis, provocación tuya?, como dirá después al enfrentarse a las secuelas de la escena, afán soterrado de atizar su furor hasta sacarle de las casillas?, de alcanzar la cruda verdad de tu acerbo jardín de delicias?, imágenes veladas, opacidad interrumpida por el fucilazo esclarecedor de la violencia, vuestra fulgurante comunicación energética, contundencia del golpe, caída, penosa incorporación, orden brutal de tenderte en la cama, . . . y, al despertar, le ves tumbado en el suelo, inerte, despatarrado, roncando, en medio del interior devastado, ropa esparcida, sillas volcadas, cama sucia y deshecha, ...desorden material y mental, esfuerzo trabajoso de levantarse, ir al baño, mirarse con incredulidad en el espejo y descubrir un rostro que no es el tuyo, transmutado también en el feroz remolino nocturno, incapaz de reflexionar aún y entender qué ha ocurrido.

(finally in the flat, unsure how you have arrived or why you are arguing, did you start it, as he'll say later when facing up to the consequences of the scene, a hidden desire to kindle his fury till you drove him out of his mind? to reach the bitter raw truth in your bitter garden of delights? veiled images, opacity broken by the glaring lightning flash of violence, your stunning communication of energy, the bruising damage of the blow, fall, painfully get up, brutal order to stretch out on the bed . . . and, when you wake up, you can see him there lying on the floor, inert, spread-eagled, snoring in the middle of the ravaged room, clothes scattered everywhere, upturned chairs, dirty, unmade bed, . . . mental and material disorder, painful effort to get up, go to the bathroom, look at yourself incredulously in the mirror and find a face that is not yours, transmuted as well into the fierce whirlwind of the night, still incapable of thought, of understanding what has happened.)

(RT 302–3/255–56; trans. modified)

Awakening to the lamentations and apologies of his companion, Goytisolo dismisses him:

> pero tú quieres estar a solas, digerir lo acaecido, poner tierra por medio, transformar humillación en levadura, furia en apoderamiento: llegar a ese punto de fusión en el que la guerra emprendida contra ti mismo simbólicamente trascienda, augure moral y literariamente una empresa, vindique la razón del percance, del cataclismo buscado y temido: recia imposición del destino cuyo premio será la escritura, el zaratán o la gracia de la creación.

> (but you want to be alone, to digest what has happened, distance yourself, transform humiliation into yeast, rage into power: reach that point of fusion in which the war waged against yourself symbolically transcends, augurs morally and literarily a new departure, vindicates the reason for the mishap, the cataclysm both sought and feared: stern imposition of destiny whose prize will be the written word, the blight or grace of creation.)

(RT 303–4/256; trans. modified)

Thus Goytisolo's narrative of his doubleness reaches its resolution in a blatant search for a masochistic encounter that will mete out a punishment that Goytisolo portrays as purgative and restorative. That Goytisolo considers this incident to be a watershed event seems beyond a doubt considering its lengthy and detailed description, the context in which it happens (Goytisolo's inaugural visit to the country where he will later settle), and its placement in the last section of *En los reinos de taifa*, with its rebirth of the "new" Goytisolo, the one who will soon thereafter write *Reivindicación del conde don Julián*. Why the need for this cathartic masochistic experience? What are the demons Goytisolo is trying to exorcise through the unsuspecting medium of his companion? Why the need to suffer at the hands of another? An inquiry into masochism's reasons can cast light not only on this cathartic scene but also on Goytisolo's insistent denunciation of clan, class, and country, as well as on the dismantlement of his own duplicity.

Although masochism is often considered merely as a sexual preference, it has also been viewed as an ethical practice. According to Deleuze, masochism consists of a ritual in which the masochist, feeling guilty for his resemblance to the father, instructs and provokes a disciplinary agent to dispense punishment, ostensibly to the masochist but in reality to the father who therefore is not the beater but the beaten. A symbolic abolition of a father whom the masochist holds in low regard, the scene of punishment enacts also a ceremony in which the law consequently passes to the hands of the mother, who is thus invested with the power to give birth to a new, ideal ego. Deleuze argues that masochistic practices are essentially a rite of regeneration and rebirth, and for that reason the symbolic annihilation of the ego's unacceptable model signals also the death of the old ego and the rebirth of a new one: "The ego triumphs, and asserts its autonomy in pain, its parthenogenetic rebirth from pain, pain being experienced as inflicted upon the superego."[19]

Interpreting the provoked incident in terms akin to those proposed by Deleuze in his elucidation of masochism, Goytisolo himself construes it as an empowering ferment in his war against himself, as a new moral and literary beginning. By letting himself be abused, Goytisolo is punishing a father that he repeatedly depicts in his autobiographical works as a weak and morally unacceptable model. The ritualistic obliteration of the father brings with it the opportunity of a new beginning, of a refashioning of the self along new genealogical lines. The substitution of the mother for the father that Goytisolo carries out symbolically in the masochistic episode offers the key to Goytisolo's replacement of his biological origins with alternative genealogies and rebirths from the beginning of *Coto vedado*. Although Goytisolo starts his autobiography by satirizing the typical autobiographer's genealogical obsession, the presentation of his own lineage fulfills an essential role in his narrative: it allows him not only to disown his father's exploitative, slave-owning lineage and all that it stands for, but to propose an alternative female ancestry. Goytisolo explains his guilt as a residue left by Catholic morality. And yet perhaps such guilt should instead be attributed to the shame provoked by a defective paternal model, whose rejection he has been effecting since his childhood (see *CV* 58/48 and 72/59). His downright repudiation of the institution of the family is counterbalanced by an ensuing celebratory rescue of his female ancestors from the shadows to which they were relegated by patriarchal norms. This vindication is effected through ungrounded interpretations of their characters and lives, based solely on pictures, anecdotal details, or even Goytisolo's willful surmises. Goytisolo himself admits as much when he writes that, once healed of his father's genealogical dreams that he once shared, he prefers to invent a fantastic Venusian ancestry (*CV* 43/34).[20]

Departing from a complete rejection of his paternal lineage, *Coto vedado* is permeated by a true obsession and even nostalgia for origins, which is revealed by Goytisolo's constant references to births and rebirths. Over and over Goytisolo creates for himself new genealogies or interprets events and scenes in terms not simply of new beginnings but of true rebirths and baptisms, starting with his alternative female ancestry. Later on, the Civil War will displace the mother as Goytisolo's true originator:

> *No obstante, en la medida en que la querencia relativa a tu madre se había eclipsado con ella, puedes decir que, en estricto rigor, más que hijo suyo, de la desconocida que es y será para ti, lo eres de la guerra civil, su mesianismo, crueldad, su saña : del cúmulo desdichado de circunstancias que sacaron a luz la verdadera entraña del país y te infundieron el deseo juvenil de alejarte de él para siempre.*
>
> *(However, to the extent that the affection for your mother vanished with her, you can say quite rigorously that rather than her son, the son of a woman who is and always will be unknown to*

you, you are a son of the civil war, its Messianism, cruelty, and anger: of the unhappy accumulation of circumstances that brought into the open the real essence of the country and filled you with a youthful desire to abandon it forever.)

(CV 66/54; trans. modified)

At another moment, Goytisolo submits that one more originating point was his discovery of Islam, whose role in his life he considers preordained by the stories of Muslim cruelty narrated in his childhood by an old maid, to whom fate granted an "papel iniciático, bautismal" (*CV* 74/61; "initiatory, baptismal role"). This preparatory but deformed view of the Arab world will be later transmuted into a closer approach to that world in his first trip to Almería: "*Baño lustral, deslumbramiento epifánico . . . : afecto instintivo, espontáneo a un paisaje huérfano y suntuoso, nítida asunción del goce identificatorio, fulgurante anágnorisis de tu encuadre espacial : afinidad, inmediatez, concomitancia con una tierra casi africana que confiere al viaje el aura iniciática de una segunda, demorada natividad*" (*CV* 275/233–34; "Purifying bath, epiphanic fascination . . . : an instinctive, spontaneous affection for the sumptuous, orphaned landscape, sharp acknowledgement of the enjoyment of your identification, blinding recognition of your spatial frame: affinity, immediacy, harmony with an almost African land that endows the journey with the initiating aura of a second, deferred nativity"). Still other episodes that Goytisolo interprets in terms of rebirth are his first visit to the Arab cafes and the peripheral neighborhoods of Paris (*CV* 243/205), as well as the new period in his life that starts with his full acceptance of his homosexuality (*RT* 248/210).[21] Goytisolo's ultimate attempt at self-restoration took place after he was mauled by a bull in the fair of Elche de la Sierra, an episode that, bringing home the specter of death, spurred in Goytisolo the urge to restore his life by preserving it in writing. The proximity of death induced the need for life-writing, an impulse that transformed Goytisolo from a son in constant search of rebirth and reconstruction into a (metaphoric) mother that engendered her/his own story.

The full consequences of the masochistic Tangiers episode are made explicit by Goytisolo in an account, pervaded by ruination and rebirth, in which he conflates the personal with the political, the linguistic, and the historical. Leaving aside the questions raised by such conflation and concentrating instead on the overall pattern of Goytisolo's narrative, one can ascertain that the violence inflicted on him by his Moroccan friend transcends the merely episodic and personal and becomes instead for Goytisolo a revelatory experience:

> . . . Encerrado en tu habitación del hotel, . . . vivías momentos de soledad, exaltación y de rabia, consciente de haber roto la corteza de tu centro ardiente, llegado a la entraña de la que brota a borbollones el magma de escorias, materias abrasadas. La brusca y violenta jubilación, el nítido ramalazo destructor presentidos desde la infancia habían dejado de ser una visión sigilosa, acechante para hacerse reales: fuerza ligada a tu vivencia peculiar del sexo, gravitación animal de los cuerpos que debías asumir e integrar en tu conjunto textual. . . .
>
> A diferencia de lo acaecido en Madrid años atrás, la velada en la que te emborrachaste con Lucho, el descalabro moral se ha convertido en una fuente vital de conocimiento. Más allá de la esfera personal, diafaniza y revela los mecanismos latentes en la sociedad, exhuma y rescata de lo medular la energía que propulsará la vandálica invasión que proyectas: esa obra no escrita aún en nuestra lengua, contra ella, a mayor gloria de ella, destrucción y homenaje. . . . Resoluciones en serie forjadas vertiginosamente . . . : calar en la historia auténtica del país del que te sentías inexorablemente proscrito; embeberte en el baño lustral de sus clásicos . . . ; poner el acervo humanístico de la época–lingüística, poética, historiografía–al servicio de dicha empresa; llegar a las raíces de la muerte civil que te ha tocado vivir; sacar a luz demonios y miedos agazapados en lo hondo de tu conciencia. Días, horas, instantes privilegiados, . . . sed de venganza contra esos molinos o gigantes llamados religión-patria-familia-pasado-niñez. El dispositivo mental puesto en marcha por el vejamen de tu cancerbero es alambicado y proliferante. . . .

> (. . . Closeted in your hotel room . . . you experienced moments of solitude, elation, and madness, conscious you had broken the cortex round your burning center, reached the depths from which bubbled, poured out, the magma of filth, burnt matter. The sudden, violent exhilaration, the

bright, destructive lash glimpsed from childhood had ceased
to be a secretive, lurking vision, and had become real: a force
tied to your peculiar experience of sex, the animal gravita-
tion of bodies that you had to experience and integrate in
the body of your text. . . .

Unlike what happened in Madrid years before, that evening
you got drunk with Lucho, moral disaster has become a vital
source of self-knowledge. Beyond the personal sphere, it
reveals, renders diaphanous the latent mechanisms within
society, exhumes and rescues from the bone marrow the
energy that will propel the devastating invasion you propose: that work not yet written in our language, against it,
to its greater glory, to destroy and pay homage. . . . Strings of
resolutions forged dizzily. . . : penetrate the real history of
the country from which you felt inexorably proscribed;
immersion in a lustral bath of its classics . . . ; place all the
knowledge offered by today's humanities—linguistics, poetics, historiography—at the disposal of such an enterprise;
reach down to the roots of the civil death you have had to
live through; bring out into the light the demons and fears
crouching in the depths of your consciousness. Days, hours,
privileged moments, . . . thirst for revenge on those wind-
mills or giants by the name of religion-fatherland-family-
past-childhood. The mental spring set off by the affront of
your guard proliferates in complex ways. . . .)

(RT 304–5/257–58; trans. modified)

There is a striking disproportion here between what seems an innocu-
ous (if violent) private episode and Goytisolo's reaction to it. A literal
reading (a dispute between friends that turns violent) would not do
justice to it, since Goytisolo has to withdraw to Marrakesh (curiously
the same location where he is writing *En los reinos de taifa*) to unveil its
full consequences. Goytisolo magnifies that experience because the
violence literally inflicted upon him, symbolically destroys the father,
leaving also open to obliteration all he stands for, as Goytisolo makes
explicit by hyphenating "religion-fatherland-family-past-childhood"
when he lists the targets of his program for destruction. The ritualistic
annihilation of the father leaves him an orphan, thus imposing on him
the need to rewrite a new genealogy. That "descalabro moral" (moral

disaster) becomes for Goytisolo "una fuente vital de conocimiento" (a vital source of self-knowledge), not because it grants him access to a full self-understanding but because the symbolic elimination of the father frees him to attempt a reconstruction of his identity, which he will do in at least three different, complementary ways: by substituting his paternal genealogy with a maternal/female one; by replacing/rewriting the national and literary history of Spain; and by erecting a new superego, a new personal/literary lineage that he embodies in writers such as Beckett, Lezama Lima or Cernuda, and, above all, Blanco White and Genet.[22] Goytisolo transforms the guilt he suffers for having an improper father into responsibility for his own life, and thus his masochistic experience transcends the anecdotal and the sexual to become instead an ethical episode because it burdens Goytisolo with the duty of responding (to his alternative superegos) for the re-construction of his life, and thus for his autobiographical self-interpretation. And one truly responds only to the other, which in Goytisolo's case will be embodied preeminently in Genet.[23]

In a most fitting coincidence, shortly after the masochistic episode, Goytisolo received the news of Eulalia's death, which plunged him into another "disaster" whose narrative tinges his life again with profound ethical resonances. Goytisolo underscores the significance of that death by providing two strategically placed accounts of his reaction to it. Its largest development appears jointly with his account of the deaths of his father and grandfather at the end of the first part of *Coto vedado*. The placement there of his account of the three demises is fully appropriate because the three deaths bring closure to Goytisolo's narrative of family life. Consequently, in the second part of that book Goytisolo can fittingly displace the responsibility for his life's falseness from his family to himself, since once he has squared off the family accounts he is forced to face himself. A new narrative of Eulalia's death concludes *En los reinos de taifa*, bringing closure to another chapter of Goytisolo's life and simultaneously signaling a final rebirth of both his self and his writing. As already noted, after receiving the news Goytisolo takes a strong dose of maashun and embarks on what he describes as "la noche más larga de tu vida" (*CV* 132/110; "the longest night in your life"), spending twenty hours in bed immersed in dreams (in which he visits the three dead ones: Eulalia, his father, and his grandfather), dreams that he slowly reconstructs on the following day. As with the previous masochistic episode, this night is marked by death, guilt, and responsibility.[24]

Lacan asserts that "what is foreclosed in the symbolic reappears in the real," and here the real takes the form of a dream in which Goytisolo pays visits to his dead father and grandfather.[25] This scene brings closure to *En los reinos de taifa* not simply because it fits chronologically but above all because the symbolic elimination of the father in the masochistic episode promotes his reappearance as hallucination (one of the possibilities for the real to manifest itself) in a dream sequence in which, since Goytisolo has finally assumed responsibility for his life(story), he can face the (dead) father without guilt because he is *"muerto y los dos lo sabéis. Sin embargo os saludáis, cambiáis unas cuantas palabras. Ningún dolor de tu parte, ningún remordimiento. Su presencia es grata, suave : irradia una balsámica impresión de sosiego, dulzura, apacibilidad"* (CV 132/111; "dead and you both know. However, you greet each other and exchange a few words. No pain on your part, no remorse. His presence is pleasing, gentle: he radiates a soothing impression of quiet, sweetness, peace").[26]

The ethical renaissance that is portrayed by Goytisolo through the significant Tangiers episodes is a *textual* rebirth, not a real-life one (whether such an almost instant rebirth is possible or not in real life is a totally different issue). As stated before, a deep self-reconstruction can only be promoted through an immersion in the ethical prediscursive, and this is what Goytisolo is doing through his magnification of the Tangiers events. In other words it is impossible to ascertain whether Goytisolo's changes in identity occurred precisely in the way he narrates them; but by the same token he can narrate them only as a sudden transformation achieved in the domain of the ethical. There is no other way for an autobiographer to represent such a drastic conversion than as a punctual event, because that is imposed by the laws of self-representation. The Pauline fall from the horse and the Augustinian "tolle, lege" bear witness to the constraints faced by autobiographers when they try to represent as a sudden event the experience of seeing the light.

The Hermeneutics of Guilt

Guilt permeates Goytisolo's autobiographies, and culpability drifts back and forth incessantly between himself and a multitude of others (family, social class, country). Goytisolo's insistent accusations can be interpreted, along with Lacan, in terms of desire and betrayal: "In the last analysis, what a subject really feels guilty about when he manifests guilt at bottom always has to do with. . . the extent to which he has given ground relative to his desire."[27] Lacan argues that this giving ground "is always accompanied in the destiny of the subject by some betrayal. . . Either the subject betrays his own way, betrays himself, and the result is significant for him, or, more simply, he tolerates the fact that someone with whom he has more or less vowed to do something betrays his hope." Betrayal, which Lacan qualifies as "contempt for the other and for oneself,"[28] structures in complex ways Goytisolo's self-figurations, both in its old (false) manifestations and in its new ("authentic") ones. Goytisolo's autobiographical acts bring to the fore-front the intricate connections between guilt, responsibility, betrayal and autobiographical self-construction, and that is precisely what makes them such formidable and provocative works. An ethical inter-pretation of autobiography revolves around the nature and degree, meaning and implications of taking upon oneself, or ascribing to some-thing/someone else, responsibility for one's life. By foregrounding guilt and betrayal, Goytisolo raises this fundamental issue and constrains the reader to examine the extent of the responsibility Goytisolo takes for his life and how that assumption shapes his self-interpretation. Therefore, the ultimate conundrum of Goytisolo's autobiographies hinges on ascertaining the hermeneutical implications of the ways in which he responds for his life or abdicates that responsibility.

We know that Goytisolo accuses himself of self-betrayal in his youth for having succumbed to what he calls "mythomania;" later, in his Marxist, Parisian period, that disloyalty takes the form of a political, literary and sexual identity that bring him power, renown and a new family life with Monique Lange, but that he ultimately judges as men-dacious and duplicitous, as the first and fifth sections of *En los reinos de taifa* (centered on his political activities and on his life with Monique, respectively) amply demonstrate. Waiting for an apocalyptic resolution of his problems, in the early sixties Goytisolo comes to the realization that Spain's material progress will make revolution impossi-ble. Furthermore, he soon has to admit that his former representation of the country's future (which, as was previously indicated, he saw not in its alignment with the industrial nations but in its identification with the Third World) was "aberrante" (a real aberration), and consequent-ly he realized that his "visión apocalíptica de las cosas" (apocalyptic vision of life) led him to avoid "el debate contigo y con tu verdad" (*RT* 64/54, 65/55; trans. modified; "the debate with yourself and your truth"). His political reawakening throughout the sixties culminated in his renunciation of the right to "represent" the country and in his vindication of a postnational personal/literary (for him indistinguishable) identity.[29] Goytisolo presumes to get out of the vicious circle of his deluded literary and political self-definitions simply by abandoning his defense of literary social realism and by abjuring politics as a defining referent of his identity, by abandoning what he calls "nacionalismo anacrónico" (anachronistic nationalism): "El acto de desprenderse de unas señas de identidad opresivas y estétiles, abría el camino a un espacio literario plural, sin fronteras: prohibidos por el franquismo, mis libros podían asilarse en México o Buenos Aires. En adelante el idioma y sólo el idioma sería mi patria auténtica" (*RT* 72/60–61; "The act of casting off oppressive, sterile identity markers opened the way to a plural literary space that had no frontiers; banned by Francoism, my books could seek refuge in Mexico or Buenos Aires. From now on, the language and only the language would be my real country"). His resolution to become stateless and his exaltation of exile were also decisively fostered by the continuous attacks and insults that he received in the Spanish press (starting around 1961), first for his antiregime activities and later for his new books (see especially *RT* 47–61/39–51), which were forbidden in Spain for several years. In good measure Goytisolo redefined his self as an answer to the injuries inflicted on him by the fatherland and its representatives, as a response to the injurious speech that tried to blow him out of existence by censoring his being and his writings. Despite its obliterating intentions, injurious speech is still a contorted form of recognition, an attempt at disqualification that still has to address—and so recognize—the subject that it tries to set amiss. In the injurious disfiguration, the power of the injurious party engenders a resistance that empowers the injured. And the range of that resistance can go from a response in kind to a reconsideration and a relocation of one's self, the latter being Goytisolo's response.[30]

Accordingly, Goytisolo's professed indifference towards Spain (81/68) runs counter to his autobiographical self-definition. For one, he alleges that the political ostracism and the literary censorship that he suffered fomented his resolution "de ser quien eres, de afirmar tu verdad y escala de valores frente a las normas y ritos de la tribu" (*RT* 81/68; "to be yourself, to defend your truth and scale of values against the norms and rituals of the tribe"); moreover, his adoption of language as his true fatherland compels him to a political reading of Spanish literary history and thus reintroduces the national into his self-portrayal.[31] John Guillory argues that "[i]n the early modern period, the great vernacular literary works of the nation-states were taught in such a way as to constitute retroactively a pre-national 'West' (usually classical rather than medieval), a continuity intended to cover over the traumatic break of early modern societies with traditional feudal cultures."[32] Goytisolo's revision of Spain's literary tradition (in the line opened by Américo Castro and continued by Hispanists like Stephen Gilman, Márquez Villanueva and Luce López-Baralt) reconstructs a pre-modern (and thus pre-nationalist) tradition presumedly characterized by an intercultural exchange that was erased by subsequent Spanish nationalist agendas grounded in ideals of racial purity and cultural uniformity.[33] Goytisolo's profession of "Mudejarism," however, rests simply on a displacement of his focus of attention from the representation of Spain's present to a representation of its past, and the latter supposes a re-emergence of the national/political self-definition that he had supposedly forsaken. Goytisolo criticizes the chronic tendency to look for an immutable essence of Spain (a trend he sees continued in today's Spanish regional nationalisms), responsible in his opinion for the cleansing of everything not considered "genuinely" Spanish, which led to the dismantlement of the rich, bastardized, hybrid culture of Medieval and Renaissance Spain.[34] Despite Goytisolo's rejection of nationalism in its narrow contemporary form, he stills defines his literature (and himself) in reference to an understanding of the nation, albeit in its (debatable and arguably idealistic) past configuration.[35] Even in his post-national self-definition, and for all his awareness of the shortcomings of epistemic autobiography, Goytisolo cannot forgo the pull to enunciate the truth, and he seems to fit the description, proposed by Said, of the intellectual as an exile (real or metaphoric) with "a vocation for the art of representing" a view in public, against power, dogma and orthodoxy and in defense of "the weaker, the less well represented, the forgotten or ignored," an activity that involves "passionate engagement, risk, exposure, commitment to principles, vulnerability in debating and being involved in wordly causes."[36]

Still, it is legitimate to ask whether in his new role as an "exilic intellectual" (to use Said's term), Goytisolo abandons a nationality-defined identity and becomes a postnational subject. Does he relinquish national identity without a remnant, without replacing it with something curiously similar? Notice, to begin with, that when he declares his allegiance to the Spanish language, Goytisolo cannot refrain from depicting it as his "true fatherland." When he renounces a nationalist self-definition in favor of a literary lineage, Goytisolo reverts in fact to the political, since all he does is reverse some of the basic mechanisms of national construction. According to Renan, "the essence of a nation is that all individuals have many things in common, and also that they have forgotten many things."[37] Goytisolo's literary and personal revision necessarily disturbs this politics of silence and produces alternative senses of national literary tradition. When, in his attempt at self-reconstruction he substitutes a linguistic sense of identity for a nationalist one and, concomitantly, stops representing Spain's present in favor of portraying its past, he is searching in history for clues to his predicament as well as for figures that can help him reach self-understanding. Benedict Anderson shows how Michelet stipulated that the duty of the French historian was to rescue from oblivion the dead whose sacrifices "made possible the rupture of 1789 and the self-conscious appearance of the French nation."[38] If the meaning of a nation rests on its dead, any alternative history will have to choose its own dead, to replace the official dead with forgotten ones, and this is precisely what Goytisolo does. By vindicating figures such as Blanco White, whom the official culture consigned to an interested oblivion, and by identifying with him to the point of seeing himself as a reincarnation of the self-exiled Spanish priest; by portraying him as a victim of intolerance and orthodoxy—actually by misrepresenting him, and Goytisolo is aware of that misrepresentation—Goytisolo is rescuing from oblivion an alternative nation while simultaneously, in identifying himself with Blanco White, he finds confirmation of the appropriateness of his self-construction.[39] But although such construction is effected against the grain of the nation and outside its frontiers, it cannot occur without reference to the national. In Goytisolo's case the national is not only the springboard of his autobiographical telling but also the referential telos of his presumedly post-national self-definition.

The Hermeneutics of Betrayal

It has been suggested that "affective peaks of collective belonging" to the nation are not possible without the possibility of sacrifice for the fatherland: "It is during war that the nation is imagined as a community embodying ultimate values."[40] It could be argued that this war could be for the nation but also against the unsatisfactory nation; hence, betrayal of the fatherland would be the exact opposite of nationalist sacrifice. Goytisolo closes *En los reinos de taifa,* and announces the future direction of his fiction, with an identification with count Julian, the preeminent Spanish traitor.[41] One can thus surmise that his conclusions about the masochist night ("Más allá de la esfera personal, diafaniza y revela los mecanismos latentes en la sociedad, exhuma y rescata de lo medular la energía que propulsará la vandálica invasión que proyectas" (*RT* 304/257; "Beyond the personal sphere, it reveals, renders diaphanous the latent mechanisms within society, exhumes and rescues from the bone marrow the energy that will propel the devastating invasion you propose") have to be reinterpreted to mean that what is really disclosed in that scene is the machinery behind his vindication of treason and in particular the allotment of guilt that comes with that betrayal.

If the masochistic episode punishes the father (who, moreover, stands also for his class and his nation) because his insufficiencies amount to a betrayal of the son, in the maashun night that feeling of having been betrayed is turned around and converted into political counter-treason. With that reversal the father is finally exempted of a culpability that Goytisolo, ultimately and exclusively, projects over a country that he represents as not measuring up to his expectations, be it because of a repression that muffled dissidence and difference or because its progress preempts a revolution capable of redeeming the individual.

Lest this assessment be taken as a moral indictment of Goytisolo's autobiographical reconstruction (which it is not), it should be rephrased as a question about the implications of responding with betrayal to having been betrayed. Goytisolo borrows the theme of betrayal from his interpretation of Genet's life, whom he exalts as the embodiment of the values Goytisolo aspires to profess.[42] An examination of his portrayal of Genet can help shed light on the shaky and shady terrain that connects betrayal, self-interpretation, and responsibility. "He denied materialism, the machinery of career, the obligations of sustained friendship, even the vanity of artistic achievement, in order to render his life exemplary," writes Edmund White by way of a general assessment of Genet.[43] Goytisolo attests to the allure of that exemplarity when he states that Genet has been his

> única influencia adulta en el plano estrictamente moral.
> Genet me enseñó a desprenderme poco a poco de mi vanidad
> primeriza, el oportunismo político, el deseo de figurar en la

vida literariosocial para centrarme en algo más hondo y difícil: la conquista de una expresión literaria propia, mi auténticidad subjetiva. Sin él, sin su ejemplo, no habría tenido tal vez la fuerza de romper con la escala de valores consensuada a derecha e izquierda por mis paisanos, aceptar con orgullo el previsible rechazo y aislamiento, escribir cuanto he escrito a partir de *Don Julián*.

(only adult influence on the strictly moral plane. Genet taught me to cast off my early vanity, political opportunism, my desire to cut a figure in the life of literary society, to center in on something deeper and more difficult: the conquest of my own literary expression, my subjective authenticity. Without him, without his example, I would perhaps not have had the strength to break away from the hierarchy of values accepted on the right and the left by my compatriots, to accept proudly my predictable rejection and isolation, to write all I have written from the time of *Conde Julián*.)

(RT 153/128; trans. modified)[44]

And yet Goytisolo's specific evaluation of Genet's life raises thorny issues. In Goytisolo's view, Genet "no cesa de cobrarse la deuda que, desde la concepción en el vientre de su madre, la sociedad ha contraído con él; de resarcirse, ahora que es respetado y famoso, de las miserias e injusticias sufridas en su niñez y juventud" (*RT* 131/109–10; "continually exacted payment for the debt that society had contracted with him ever since his conception in his mother's womb; now that he was respected and famous, he made up for the unhappiness and injustice suffered as a child and youth"). By interpreting Genet's behavior as an act of retribution against a world that in the past deprived him of everything, Goytisolo seems to reduce Genet's demeanor to a reactive series of vengeances. But based on the testimonies adduced by Edmund White in his biography (among them Goytisolo's *En los reinos de taifa*) and on his general portrait of the French writer, it could be argued that Genet does something very different from what Goytisolo purports: rather than taking vengeance on the world, he seems on the contrary to ignore it, to respond to it with a counter moral that would arbitrarily undermine established values. Being beyond vengeance is what explains Genet's unpredictable, and thus uninterpretable, behavior, as

Goytisolo unwittingly asserts: "su moral se sitúa a un nivel diferente. Una vez en éste, su conducta será, al contrario, modelo de escrúpulo, de rigor. Pero, y esto sólo lo advertiré más tarde, su nivel varía. La entrega absoluta a la amistad no excluye así el germen de una posible e inopinada traición" (133/111; "his morality worked at a different level. Once at this level, his behavior would be on the contrary a model of scrupulous rigor. But the level varied—and I noticed this only later. His absolute surrender to friendship did not exclude the seed of possible, unexpected betrayal"). It would seem that Genet's unreliable moral rigor—fidelity could instantly become betrayal—would explain the lack of remorse that Goytisolo attributes to him; however, that innocence would be at odds with a constant claim of retribution of societal debts and with the assignment of guilt that it entails. When he is reaching the end of his lengthy and passionate vindication of Blanco White, Goytisolo admits that when he was writing about the exiled Spanish priest he was actually writing about himself.[45] It could be argued that when he is speaking about Genet, Goytisolo is actually speaking about himself, the only difference being that while he totally identifies with Blanco White (to the point of characterizing that identity as a reincarnation, *RT* 81/69), Genet (*his interpretation of Genet,* that is) stands as a moral paragon that he aspires to reach. Betrayed by the father, who for that reason is masochistically eliminated, evicted as an unworthy superego, Goytisolo finds a replacement in "Genet," who in this way not only acts as model but also as ultimate addressee of Goytisolo's autobiographical narrative.

A Future, but No Becoming

Before exploring the imperative to tell others/to tell oneself and the complex narrative strategies that such an imperative imposes, as well as its rhetorical/ethical implications, one needs to go back to the epistemic dimension foregrounded by Goytisolo. In its yearning for self-knowledge and in its desire to control self-representation, autobiography betrays its unavoidable insufficiencies, which the most lucid autobiographers (Goytisolo among them) thematize as self-consciousness about the limitations of the genre. However, autobiography's epistemic limitations do not doom it to failure, because the manifestations of an ethical imperative burst through, and ultimately supersede, not only the pretensions of self-knowledge but also the autobiographers' self-conscious misgivings and even their ironic denials.

Lacan writes: "I think that throughout this historical period the desire of man, which has been felt, anesthetized, put to sleep by moralists, domesticated by educators, betrayed by the academies, has quite simply taken refuge or been repressed in that most subtle and blindest of passions, as the story of Oedipus shows, the passion for knowledge."[46] At first sight (considered exclusively from a cognitive point of view), autobiography is an "exemplary" actualization of this passion for (self)-knowledge since the laws of the genre constrain it to be a discourse of truth and sincerity no matter how clever or ironic the autobiographer. Goytisolo's representation of his life as an ascension to authenticity demands of necessity the exclusion of all the pulsions that in his autobiographical formulation could unsettle his epistemic insights, his self-figuration as authenticity, by not fitting under those codes. While in his fiction Goytisolo submits himself to the flows of desire, to a constant game of unstable, unsettled, and unsettling identities exposed to constant refiguration, in his autobiography he brings to the surface of his text exclusively those pulsions that disturbed him in the past to rationalize what he deems to be his former irrationality. But by the same token he cannot admit being haunted by new ones. Jo Labanyi argues that in his fiction Goytisolo creates a monologic discourse in which all voices are the author's own, while in his autobiography he dissects the self "to see what it is made of," and she concludes: "For Goytisolo fiction is the projection of the self as *alter ego*, whereas autobiography is a critical medium that requires the author to take the self to pieces and see what it is made of."[47] Undeniably Goytisolo's autobiography rests heavily on the display of the contradictions and discontinuities of his self, but of *his old self*. No such questioning of his present self is to be found in it, his only questioning of the present revolving around the impossibility to *represent* the self and the past in writing. It is only because he has achieved certainties about his present self that Goytisolo can unmask his contradictions in the past.

In his paradigmatically self-reflective autobiography, Barthes writes: "What I write about myself is never *the last word*: the more 'sincere' I am, the more interpretable I am, under the eye of other examples than those of the old authors, who believed they were required to submit themselves to but one law: *authenticity*."[48] By making authenticity one of the basic guideposts of his autobiography, Goytisolo is compelled to overinterpret both his past and his present identities. In this light his insistent self-accusations and the obsession with the adjudication of culpability form a tight network of causalities that could be seen as an involuntary attempt to preempt further interpretation. Goytisolo opens his past to his own criticism but simultaneously forecloses any revision of his narrating voice and its epistemic certainties. It is in this regard to interpretation that autobiographical narrative strategies show they are not merely techniques but form part of the story. Although some of them (those that try to enforce the genre's epistemic value) aim at closing off interpretation, as saying to another, the storytelling opens it up. More than any other genre, autobiography foregrounds its addressees, and in Goytisolo's case the privileged addressee, the one that, provoking "afán irresistible de sinceridad" (an irresistible desire for sincerity), stands behind the overpowering need to tell is Genet. In his reverential view of the French writer, Goytisolo stresses that his exemplarity resides in the unsettling and even self-destructive forces that he unleashed: "Conocer íntimamente a Genet es una aventura de la que nadie puede salir indemne. Provoca, según los casos, la rebeldía, una toma de conciencia, afán irresistible de sinceridad, la ruptura con viejos sentimientos y afectos, desarraigo, un vacío angustioso, incluso la muerte física" (*RT* 152/128; trans. modified; "To know Genet intimately is an adventure from which no one could emerge unharmed. Depending on one's case, he provokes rebellion, self-awareness, an irresistible desire for sincerity, the break from old feelings and attachments, disarray, an anguished void, even physical death").

Brad Epps has addressed the limits of Goytisolo's self-writing, arguing that in their linearity, their avoidance of metaphoricity and their strict demarcation between the word and the world, the text and the flesh, Goytisolo's autobiographical texts resist Genet's exemplarity:

> . . . Goytisolo's commitment to the autobiographical project—
> opening as it does with genealogical reflections and familial
> documents—places him on guard against the exuberant
> metaphoricity that, through the influence of Genet, has pur-
> portedly come to imbue his writing since *Don Julian.*
> Striving to distance itself from fiction in order to approxi-
> mate reality, autobiography must also, in Goytisolo's case,
> distance itself from onanistic ornamentation. But in so
> doing, autobiography paradoxically distances itself from the
> most touching way in which reality, however fleetingly, may

(re)appear in representation, the one way in which the flesh of the anonymous reader may (re)vitalize the words of the writer.[49]

Epps conflates onanism and ornamentation and sets Genet's *Journal du voleur* as an example because it can move the reader to onanism, while Goytisolo explicitly recoils in *En los reinos de taifa* from such a "touching" connection between word and world. That possible form of performativity of the autobiographical text is by no means the only fleeting way in which the text can exert its performativity nor is it arguably the most touching one. Autobiographical performativity is not just chance or choice but an ethical inexorability. Epps perceptively points out Goytisolo's rigidification of the autobiographical text in contrast with the textual freedom of the novels he writes at the same time; however, the restrictions imposed on Goytisolo's text by that cognitive desire are ultimately counterbalanced by their touching ethical import.[50]

Caught in the Mirror: The Paradox of Textual Self-Reflexion

While autobiography must reject the threat of shapelessness and unfigurable pulsions, in some of its modern manifestations it is also haunted from the inside by an inexorable sincerity that is not thematic but formal, that is, the ironic textual self-reflexivity that, especially in contemporary texts, mimics and mocks the autobiographer's self-reflections. Textual irony always lurks as a possibility in autobiography, and it will appear in Goytisolo in the form of intermittent but numerous textual self-reflexions that will regularly puncture or cast doubts on the illusion of reaching the truth.[51] The representational goals of autobiography, argues Paul Jay, are disrupted by the problems inherent in transposing the psychological subject into a literary one. While in premodern works, such as St. Augustine's *Confessions* or Wordsworth's *Prelude,* form (narrative strategies) undermines content (the truth), modern authors such as Valéry or Barthes, suggests Jay, have an awareness of the compositional problems of autobiography that leads them to reject the idea of a unified and coherent subject and converts their autobiographies into self-reflexive works that dispense with chronological narration and biographical materials in favor of "fragmented discursive forms that seek by their fragmentation to mirror what modern criticism has come to call . . . 'the divided self.'" Jay calls that maneuver not antimimetic but "mimetic in a new way," and he sees it, quoting Barthes, as a reflection of a "'new knowledge' of the subject."[52] If Barthes writes his autobiography as fragments placed in theme-determined alphabetical order instead of the more typical chronological sequence of facts, it is because the idea of the fragmentation of the subject, assumes Jay, guides his narrative. Mimesis as form would follow the guide of "philosophical certainties," and this conclusion would be in agreement with Jay's fundamental premise that the form of autobiography "reflects and reifies" (27) the changing philosophical, epistemological, theological, or psychological conceptions of the subject. But as seems inevitable in any consideration of autobiography, Jay ends up raising the subject of truth when he wonders whether that type of autobiography "can be more truthful about the self than a narrative mode," since perhaps Barthes and Valéry "have simply found ways to register more carefully and self-consciously the unavoidable ironies of self-representation that always render suspect its value as truth."[53] Jay wants to preserve some truth-content for autobiography, the difference between his approach and a content-based one being that he does not look for the truth in facts but in form, and especially in its ironic, self-reflexive manifestations. Practitioners and critics of autobiography might have become more ironic (or cynical), but they are not yet ready to discard all forms of truth. By flaunting his self-consciousness, Barthes pretends to dispense with the idea of autobiography while at the same time writing one, and Jay views that maneuver as a higher, more contemporary form of truth. As long as writers and critics alike continue to conceive autobiography as primarily an epistemic genre, no matter their degree of ironic determination, they will be caught in the typical predicaments generated by that view and will fail to perceive a possible way out of their epistemic dilemmas: autobiography's ethical dimension.

James Fernández has observed that despite the textual self-awareness of Goytisolo's autobiographical texts, they end up offering a fairly conventional and coherent narrative.[54] Put otherwise, Goytisolo is highly aware of the shortcomings of representation, and although his autobiography revolves around his restless questioning of the *represented* former self, it does not extend to the *representing* current self. The paragraph that closes *En los reinos de taifa* provides stark evidence of this selective doubting:

La infranqueable distancia del hecho a lo escrito, las leyes y exigencias del texto narrativo transmutarán insidiosamente fidelidad a lo real en ejercicio artístico, propósito de sinceridad en virtuosismo, rigor moral en estética. Ninguna posibilidad de escapar al dilema: reconstruir el pasado será siempre una forma segura de traicionarlo en cuanto se le dota de posterior coherencia, se le amaña en artera continuidad argumental. Dejar la pluma e interrumpir el relato para amenguar prudentemente los daños: el silencio y sólo el silencio mantendrá intacta una pura y estéril ilusión de verdad.

(The unbridgeable distance between act and written word, the laws and requirements of the narrative text will insidiously transmute faithfulness to reality into artistic exercise, attempted sincerity into virtuosity, moral rigor into aesthetics. No possibility of escape from the dilemma; the reconstruction of the past will always be certain betrayal as far as it is endowed with later coherence, stiffened with clever continuity of plot. Put your pen down, break off the narrative, prudently limit the damage: silence, silence alone will keep intact a pure sterile illusion of truth.)

(309/261)

The most conspicuous paradox here comes from the fact that this paragraph closes a narrative of awakening and enlightenment, liberation and lucidity that sheds light on a past of darkness and self-deceit, the representation of which Goytisolo proclaims impossible only after writing some five hundred pages pursuing a truth whose existence he never denies, as attested by this paragraph's emphasis on faithfulness to reality and betrayal of the past. The relevant issue here is not to outsmart Goytisolo, to recriminate him for his blindness and contradictions, but to wonder what motivates his paradoxical writing, what force stands behind and beyond both the impossible truth and the aesthetics that Goytisolo postulates as the ultimate obstacle to its achievement. In other words the crux here is to explain why Goytisolo cannot avoid autobiographical writing, cannot evade the call to telling the impossible truth, why he cannot, in fact, avoid or evade telling.[55]

Telling: Death and the Other

The watershed experiences of Tangiers are simultaneously truth-making and story-making events since they not only give Goytisolo access to a new form of self-understanding that is also a program of future action, but also grant him renewed insights into his past, allowing him to make out of it an ordered, teleological narrative that develops around the basic theme of two Goytisolos, the impostor and the authentic one that, smothered underneath the first, is finally able to come to the surface and assert himself. The elements of the story are there (the before and the after that would make a neat narrative of self-transformation), but the urgency to tell the story is still lacking.

This need emerges only when Goytisolo comes to terms with the possibility of his own death. From beginning to end Goytisolo's autobiography is traversed by death, whether real or symbolic: premature death of the mother; "death" in life of his dearest familial predecessors (mostly women); double death of the father (real and ritual); death of the grandfather; and, finally and crucially, Eulalia's demise, which impels Goytisolo to come to terms with the death of the other, to assume responsibility for it. Another death, that of the dictator Franco, prompts Goytisolo to write an article, "In memoriam F.F.B. 1892–1975)" that "sería (sin saberlo tú entonces) la almendra o germen de esta incursión en el campo de minas de la autobiografía" (RT 83/70; "would be [though you were unaware of it at the time] the seed or kernel of this incursion into the minefield of autobiography"). Cristina Moreiras interprets Franco's death as the "escena fundacional" (foundational scene) of Goytisolo's autobiography since in her opinion it gives origin to an autobiographical project that would strive to bury the past and set off a program of self-definition liberated from the constrictions of dictatorship.[56] However, Franco and his death, for all of Goytisolo's vehement reaction to both, have only a relative value in his autobiographical enterprise.[57] As Cristina Moreiras notes, Goytisolo's autobiographical impulse had already began with his novel Señas de identidad (written in the early sixties, around the time of the Tangiers episodes). For all his towering and prolonged presence in the life of all Spaniards and for all of Goytisolo's fervorously inimical feelings toward him, Franco does not play a particularly important explanatory role in a detailed examination of Goytisolo's autobiography. In a telling contrast, Franco's death is dealt with on one page of En los reinos de taifa

(83/70), while the Tangiers episodes not only go on for an entire chapter, but Goytisolo significantly chooses to end that book narrating
them. It would seem that those are the events that ultimately trigger
Goytisolo's urgent need to reconstruct his identity (a project that was
initially fueled in decisive ways by Monique and especially by Genet).

If the Tangiers episodes, permeated by death, awaken in Goytisolo
the need for self-reconfiguration, the impulse to actually *write* about
that process comes also from death but not from the death of Franco.
Precisely because it emerges from Goytisolo's intimations of death and
not from the death of the dictator, Goytisolo's autobiography over-
comes the moral level of vengeance and regains the ethical domain of
exposure to the other; and instead of being an exercise in mourning for
the death of Franco, Goytisolo's autobiographies are more like an exercise in anticipated melancholy for his own eventual demise. The fact
that autobiography is always addressed to the other implies a fundamental distinction between *private* self-reconstruction and *public* exposure in writing. Goytisolo traces the need to put his life in writing back
to two experiences in his life that, bringing death to his vicinity, force
him to face his *"conciencia de una irremediable caducidad"* whose signs
"[i]mperceptiblemente . . . se acumulan" (CV 25/18; trans. modified;
"awareness of inevitable extinction," "[i]mperceptibly . . . accumu-
late"), writes Goytisolo in the first pages of *Coto vedado*. From the start,
then, Goytisolo foregrounds the warnings of death as the springboard
that launches the telling of his life story, and he illustrates his case with
the recounting of a traffic accident in France that left him badly shak-
en and especially with the incident (in the town fair of Elche de la
Sierra) in which a stray bull dragged and mauled him, Goytisolo being
saved only by the timely intervention of his Arab companion. Back in
their hotel room and discomfited by the experience, Goytisolo feels the
urgency to tell:

> *Como la madre frustada que despúes de un aborto involun-*
> *tario busca con impaciencia, a fin de superar el trauma, la*
> *forma y ocasión apropiadas a lograr un nuevo embarazo, sen-*
> *tir aflorar bruscamente, en el dormitorio de la habitacion en*
> *donde os reponéis del percance, la violenta pulsión de la escri-*
> *tura tras largos meses de esterilidad sosegada, urgencia y*
> *necesidad de escribir, expresarte, no permitir que cuanto amas,*
> *tu pasado, experiencia, emociones, lo que eres y has sido*

desaparezcan contigo, resolución de luchar con uñas y dientes contra el olvido, . . . súbita y reiterada acumulación de recuerdos, . . . ebriedad de ver, tocar, oír, oler, palpar, evocar lo sucedido, la Historia, las historias, el encadenamiento de hechos, imponderables, circunstancias que te han convertido en este cuerpo maltrecho tumbado bocarriba sobre la cama de la escueta habitación en que te alojas, instante revivido ahora, a vuela pluma, cuando casi dos años más tarde empiezas a ordenar tus sentimientos e impresiones, plasmarlos en la página en blanco, vueltratás sincopado, a bandazos, sujeto a los meandros de la memoria, imperativo de dar cuenta, a los demás y a ti mismo, de lo que fuiste y no eres, de quien pudiste ser y no has sido, de precisar, corregir, completar la realidad elaborada en tus sucesivas ficciones, este único libro, el Libro que desde hace veinte años no has cesado de crear y recrear y, según adviertes invariablemente al cabo de cada uno de sus capítulos, todavía no has escrito.

(Just like a frustrated mother after an unwelcome miscarriage wishes to overcome her trauma and impatiently searches for a suitable opportunity to become pregnant again, you suddenly feel in the bedroom where you are recovering from the blow the violent urge to write rise up after months of sterility, the urgency and need to write, express yourself, not to allow all that you love, your past experience, emotions, what you are and have been, to disappear with you, determination to fight tooth and claw against oblivion, . . . sudden, repeated floods of memories, . . . an intoxication with seeing, touching, hearing, smelling, stroking, evoking the past, History, histories, the linking of facts, imponderables, circumstances that have changed you into this misused body stretched out on your back on the bed in the narrow room where you are staying, a relived moment, now almost two years later, quickly written down when you begin to order your impressions and feelings, shape them on the blank page, rhythmic reminiscences, like waves breaking, subject to your wandering memory, imperative to tell others and yourself what you were and are not, whom you might have been and have not become, to clarify, correct, complete the reality

elaborated in your successive fictions, the single book, the
Book you have been creating and recreating for twenty years
and as you invariably note, at the end of each of its chapters,
that you still have not written.)

(*CV* 28–29/21; trans. modified)

There are events that escape categorization under a narrative of truth,
while simultaneously standing at the origin of a truth that is neither
formal nor referential. Usually a result of chance, those events shatter
all forms of complacency and shake the subject. In Goytisolo's case life-
shaking chance irrupts in the two accidents that make him suddenly
face the idea of death, prompting him to write his autobiography.
Chance works its way into his life, manifesting itself in moments that,
while resisting inclusion in a teleological narrative, are nevertheless
crucial points in the subject's story.

Autobiographers are compelled to face in one way or another the
impossibility of bringing closure to any autobiographical text. All the
reasons commonly adduced (the necessary incompleteness of a life
at the moment of writing, the pitfalls and shortcomings of memory, the
incommensurability between life and language, the inevitable disfiguration brought about by the rhetorical workings of language) share a
concern with cognitive closure, and in this death-driven paragraph
Goytisolo gathers some of those pressing and troubling issues raised by
autobiographical practice. Goytisolo seems to yearn for a complete
reminiscence while simultaneously conceding its impossibility; however, his lamentations for the inherent imperfections of memory (a
topic he broaches repeatedly in his two autobiographical works) prevent him from acknowledging that only a defective memory allows for
self-reconstruction: perfect recollection would be self-smothering and
would not leave room for self-recreation. However, the impossibility of
autobiographical closure originates in the ethical configuration of identity that makes the self responsible to/for the other that precedes it.
Being a privileged form of response to the other, autobiography con-
tinuously defers to the other the moment of truth and interpretation,
and thus its patent epistemic shortcomings are a consequence of the
ethical dimension of the self. No matter its degree of fidelity or reliabil-
ity, personal memory, one's own remembrances, are not self-sufficient.
Their ultimate and peculiar truth resides in the ethical injunction to
tell others, to respond for one's own truth, which only an incomplete

memory makes possible. Incomplete memory is thus not a hindrance but an absolute necessity: a perfect memory would leave room only for the either/or of veracity or deceitfulness, and the responsibility of/for self-interpretation would be ridiculously curtailed to a binary choice. In the final analysis, then, autobiography's impossible closure, brought about by the limitations of language and memory, is precisely what opens it, as saying, to an alterity that has always been there *before* the subject.

Although Goytisolo must tell after facing death, although death is at the origins of telling, the others are the inescapable telos of telling: "*imperativo de contarle a los otros y a ti mismo*" ("imperative to tell others and yourself"). If we interpret "Genet" as a progenitor of Goytisolo's struggle for authenticity as well as a figure who stands for the ultimate addressee of his autobiography, one may finally be able to understand authenticity not as a hokey or hackneyed concept—equivalent to a hard-won self-coincidence, to being finally what one truly is—but as an acceptance to respond for one's life before the other.[58] The ethical manifests itself also formally in Goytisolo's frequent use of the second person. His employment of the third narrative person, although not common in autobiography, has illustrious antecedents, with *The Education of Henry Adams* as its first prominent instance. Far from being an exotic narrative technique in autobiography, the third person is arguably the natural form of autobiographical accounts because of the distance it marks between the narrator and the "character." In works such as Goytisolo's, which narrate the overcoming of false identities, the use of the third person seems especially called for, and Goytisolo clearly employs it to signal his estrangement from his old selves. Goytisolo's frequent use of the second person, however, appears to be a more striking feature, but it is arguably as intrinsic to autobiography as the third person. While the latter imposes an evaluating detachment between the two sides involved, the second person shows explicitly that autobiography is an apostrophic exercise, an inconclusive dialogue between two sides of the subject. But apostrophe (the main structural figure in autobiography, as suggested in the first chapter) does not involve only the two people engaged in its open-ended dialogue; it puts in play a triad, whose third member, while apparently absent, is actually the real addressee of the narrative voice and as such has decisive consequences for the interpretation of the auto-biographical text because that addressee is the force compelling the subject to face itself, to examine itself: thus the appropriate use of the second person. As an indirect form of invoking the absent other, the second person foregrounds the saying of the text at the expense of the said, and through its remittance outside both the text and the self in it reconfigured, the ethical suspends and supersedes the text's cognitive values, its truth-seeking goals. The second person transfers the final word to the other and thus shows that autobiography is an exposure to the other that puts its meanings in perpetual abeyance, even (and perhaps more so) when it is presented as narcissistic self-exhibition. This autobiographical exposure to the other is beyond truth because it entails that in the end one abrogates the right to one's truth. As such it is also the supreme form of authenticity, not one that concerns itself with self-coincidence, with oneself, but one that consists in exposing oneself to the judgement of another, in giving up one's rights to personal truth.[59]

This form of authenticity as self-renunciation is marvelously thematized in Goytisolo's autobiography in an abstract, disquisitory scene that does not reproduce any factual occurrence in Goytisolo's life but that, notwithstanding, condenses magnificently the ethical import of his autobiography. That scene appears in the first textually self-reflexive vignette in *Coto vedado,* and in it Goytisolo already anticipates the program of his autobiography (the unmasking of doubleness and the goal of authenticity). Although he also displays his awareness of the ultimate cognitive failure of any autobiographical account, ultimately he posits that such hindrance is superseded by the imperative need to tell one's life:

Conciencia de la total inanidad de la empresa : amalgama de sus motivaciones e incapacidad de determinar con claridad su objetivo y presunto destinatario: sustituto laico del sacramento de la confesión? : necesidad inconsciente de autojustificarse? : de dar un testimonio que nadie te solicita? : testimonio de quién, para quién? : para ti, los demás, tus amigos, los enemigos? : deseos de hacerse comprender

The anticipation of epistemic failure and the obscurity of the purpose of autobiographical writing leads inevitably to the unquestionable fact that despite those uncertainties one still feels compelled to tell (someone), and his awareness of such imperative forces him to wonder about the identity of so compelling an addressee and about the motivations of the telling. It should be

mejor? : despertar sentimientos de afecto o piedad? : sentirse acompañado del futuro lector? : luchar contra el olvido del tiempo? : puro y simple afán de exhibicionismo? : imposibilidad de responder a estas preguntas y acometer sin embargo la tarea, el cotidiano martirio de enfrentarse a la página, de poner toda la vida en el tablero, la innombrable realidad material de tu cuerpo.

clear by now that the questions Goytisolo asks go the heart of autobiography as ethical writing. It really does not matter whether one knows or not with certainty the motivations or addressees privileged by any given autobiography, the important fact being, as Goytisolo foregrounds, that autobiography demands to be written and is always written for another.

(Awareness of the complete inanity of the enterprise: amalgam of its motivations, and inability to make up your mind about its goals and would-be addressee: a lay substitute for the sacrament of confession?: an unconscious desire to justify yourself?: to offer a testimony that nobody asks you for?: a testimony of whom, for whom?: for you, for the others, your friends, enemies?: the wish to make yourself better understood?: to awaken feelings of affection or pity?: to feel yourself accompanied by future readers?: to struggle against the oblivion of time?: purely and simply an exhibitionist impulse?: impossible to answer these questions and yet attack the task, the daily torture of confronting the page, putting your life on the drawing board, the unnameable material reality of your body.)

(CV 40/31)

As could be expected, in this nonnarrative aside the theme of the double and its overcoming makes an appearance, but in this passage it does not manifest itself as Goytisolo's consciousness of having overcome his false identities, but as an illustration of Goytisolo's decision to expose himself to the reader, not as cognitive overcoming of duplicity but as ethical display that accomplishes a form of authenticity that resides in the mere exposure and not in any achieved self-coincidence. This explains that the utmost example of that exposure that Goytisolo can offer will be "the unnameable material reality of

your body, not the one hidden by masks and disguises in daily ritual
farce," but

el otro, el que dentro de horas, días, semanas, despatarrado, combado, de hinojos, inerme como un feto, repetirá los gestos y ademanes de succión, la alimentación visceral, polimorfa del remoto claustro materno, verdad silenciosa, proscrita, privada del poder de la palabra, eso yo-otro escamoteado al prójimo y a sí mismos por quienes aspiran al oropel de la fama, portavoces del poder futuro razón dogma o ideología, sin arrestos para sacar a luz en público las pequeñas o grandes codicias, miserias, deslealtades. . . .

Goytisolo exposes his body in a fellatio position as a paradigm of the highest form of exposure to the other, and in (and because of) its defenseless muteness, the body condenses the ethical impulse of Goytisolo's autobiography. But the unnameable body is also the body before the discursive/symbolic: the original/originating image of the self in the mirror of the other; and finally, in its ethical exemplarity, Goytisolo's mute body becomes the mirror in which the others/readers are forced to reflect and thus rethink themselves.

(the other one, which within hours, days, weeks, his legs
wide open, bent, on its knees, defenseless like a fetus, will
repeat the sucking gestures and mannerisms, the internal
polymorph feeding of the remote maternal cloister, the
silent, proscribed truth, deprived of the power of speech,
that other ego whisked out of the sight of their neighbor or
of themselves by those aspiring to the tinsel of fame, spokes-
men for future power reason dogma ideology, not daring to
bring into public gaze their great or small covetousness, misery, disloyalties. . . .)

(*CV* 40/31; trans. modified)

The displayed body turns out to be also the inverted image, the
negative of the "genio y figura" theme that Goytisolo's develops in
"Las chinelas de Empédocles" section of *En los reinos de taifa*, and
therefore exemplifies the fundamental norm of Goytisolo's autobiographical writing: "*centrarte en lo más duro y difícil de expresar, lo que
no has dicho todavía a nadie, recuerdo odiosamente vil o humillante, el*

trago más amargo de tu vida : hallar en la resistencia interior a desnudarlo el canon moral de tu escritura" (CV 41/32; "to concentrate on what is the most painful and difficult to express, what you haven't yet said to anybody, an odiously vile or humiliating memory, the bitterest blow in your life: to find in the internal resistance to laying it bare the moral canon of your writing").[60] While these lines sound like an extreme rehashing of the old theme of sincerity, the moral canon that Goytisolo imposes on himself does not entail any cognitive dimension but demands only the assumption of the complete responsibility that comes with/from absolute exposure, the penalty of doing otherwise consisting in being *"lamentablemente infiel a ti mismo y a los demás"* (41/32; "pitifully unfaithful to yourself and to the others"). This passage illustrates also that all the epistemic shortcomings of autobiography do not imply the end of autobiography because they are superseded by its other-directed nature (autobiography's true end). The inexorability of having to write, and to write for the other, entails furthermore that the primordial form of rhetoric in action in autobiography is not that of tropes (that attempts to pass as knowledge) but one more akin to the other brand (rhetoric as persuasion), not so much because of its persuasive goals but due solely to the necessary relationality of autobiographical writing, the need for that type of writing to be addressed to someone: rhetoric as faulty knowledge is not undermined but superseded by autobiography as performance. Goytisolo's autobiographical writings, and in particular this paradigmatic passage that displays the body as a mirror, foreground magnificently the fact that in autobiography, ultimately, the saying, exposure, and ethics, overshadow the said, memory, and self-knowledge.

JORGE SEMPRÚN
Radical Evil and the Secrets of Fraternity

5

orge Semprún's internment in the concentration camp of Buchenwald has marked profoundly his literary creation,which centers obsessively on that experience and has culminated in *L'écriture ou la vie* (*Literature or Life*), an autobiographical work that appeared in French in 1994 and that was followed promptly by its Spanish translation (*La escritura o la vida*) in 1995. *L'écriture ou la vie* differs from most accounts of the concentration camps in that it does not want to be a personal testimony; instead it deals primarily with the consequences of survival (the "life" in the title) and self-reflexively with the perils and possibilities involved in writing about the camps ("literature"). Literature and life fuse and feud in this book, which narrates three episodes of their entangled alliance: literature as frame of reference to comprehend the trauma of the internment; writing as a threat to survival after that experience; and the self-reflexive story of the generation of *L'écriture ou la vie* as a conciliation between self-writing and the memory of death.

The grandson of Antonio Maura (Spain's prime minister at the beginning of the century), Jorge Semprún (Madrid, 1923) has lived outside Spain since July 1936, when the outbreak of the Spanish Civil War prevented his vacationing family from returning to Madrid from a seaside resort in northern Spain. His family settled first in The Hague, where his father was representative of the Spanish Republic, but in 1939 Semprún moved to Paris to study, and he has since lived there for the most part. He has written some of his works in Spanish, but most of them were written in French. Enlisted in the French Resistance, he was caught by the Gestapo in November 1943 and was interned in Buchenwald until the camp was liberated by the Allied forces in April 1945. Buchenwald takes center stage in three of his autobiographical novels, and it is also present in different ways in several other of his works. His first novel, *Le grand voyage* (1963; The Long Voyage) focuses on the transportation of French prisoners to Buchenwald. *Quel beau dimanche* (1980; What a Beautiful Sunday!) concentrates on a Sunday at Buchenwald in order to portray the complexity of life at the camp. Depicting the problems of reintegration to civil life of a former camp inmate, *L'Évanouissement* (1967; The Blackout) anticipates an important concern of *L'écriture ou la vie*, the travails of survival and self-reconstruction. In two other works the camp appears only in the background, but its memory haunts one of the main characters. In *La montagne blanche* (1980; The White Mountain) Jorge Larrea (an alter ego of Semprún, who used that name as a pseudonym while he was a member of the clandestine Spanish Communist Party) ends up killing himself, tormented by certain memories (the crematorium's chimney, the smoke, the smell of burning flesh). And finally a character in *Netchaïev est de retour . . .* (1987; Netchaïev Has Returned) cannot forget the desolate gaze of a prisoner (Semprún) he encounters at the gate of the recently liberated Buchenwald. This same scene opens *L'écriture ou la vie*.[1]

To date he has written four works that are directly autobiographical, two of them in Spanish. In *Autobiografía de Federico Sánchez* (1977; The Autobiography of Federico Sánchez) he chronicles his years as a member of the Communist Party, particularly his clandestine stays in Spain from the mid-fifties until his expulsion from the party in 1964, while in *Federico Sánchez se despide de ustedes* (1993; Federico Sanchez Bids Farewell) he offers an account of his years as Spanish minister of culture (1988–1991) with the Socialist government of Felipe González. In *Adieu, vive clarté . . .* (1998; Goodbye, Light of my Youth . . .) he revisits his childhood, his adolescence in exile, his first intellectual influences, and his discovery of love. Besides his literary production he wrote the scripts for Alain Resnais's film on the Spanish Civil War, *La guerre est finie* (1966), for his *Stavisky* (1974), and also for Costa-Gavras's *Z* (1969) and *L'Aveu* (1970).

The Holocaust has traditionally been characterized as a limit-experience that defies comprehension and challenges the imagination, rendering inappropriate all traditional narrative and historical models and showing the limitations of language. "The Shoah carries an excess," writes Saul Friedlander, who rejects the model of "catastrophe and redemption" used by many Jewish historians to bring "hasty ideological closure" to the Holocaust.[2] Or, in the words of Geoffrey Hartman, the Final Solution "threatens to remain an open grave, an open wound in consciousness" that forces one to "reflect on the limits of representation."[3]

As a matter of fact, in this respect professional critics and thinkers seem unable to go beyond the first official reactions of prominent military officers and politicians. "The things I saw beggar description," writes Eisenhower on April 15, 1945, after visiting the concentration camp at Ohrdruf, while on his way to inspect Buchenwald, which he describes a few days later as a place of "indescribable horror."[4] And on the same day, April 19, Winston Churchill remarked in a speech to the British parliament that "No words can express the horror" of the camps.[5] One has to wonder why so many historians and critics still profess the same representational impotence proclaimed by politicians more than fifty years ago. Is it really the case that language and the imagination betray their limits when confronted with the horror of the Nazi's programmatic destruction? Could it be that what is at stake is not simply a problem of representation, but perhaps some of the most fundamental beliefs and values regarding our conception of reality, selfhood, morality, and art?

A good starting point for an elucidation of the most troubling aspects of the Holocaust is the polemic between "literalists" such as Lawrence Langer and those interpreters whom he calls "exemplarists." According to Langer, critics such as Todorov refuse to keep the "literal memory" of the suffering of victims and survivors of the Holocaust, preferring to adopt an exemplarist position that, focusing on the testimonies of acts of generosity and solidarity in the concentration camps, extracts principles from which to derive a hopeful lesson for the future. Langer finds this attempt troublesome because it neutralizes "the depressing fact of mass murder," postulating instead that the history of the Holocaust should be the sum of all the stories of torture and death one can rescue from oblivion through the testimonies of witnesses.[6] It is doubtful, however, that this literal memory of the horrors of the Holocaust advocated by Langer is a more fitting, or even a more faithful, representation of the events. Although in different ways, Langer's literalism and Todorov's exaltation are blinkered interpretations. As such they exclude as much as they explain.

"Literalist discourse about the Holocaust . . . leads nowhere but back into the pit of destruction. At least it has the grace to acknowledge that we learn nothing from the misery it finds there," writes Langer, for whom "the Holocaust experience challenged the redemptive value of all moral, community, and religious systems of belief." It would seem that Langer is intent on drawing an unsparing conclusion, but his literalist reading is actually based on the realization that the Holocaust does not admit a moral reading. He confesses that when he hears Holocaust stories, "it violates my sense of how life should and might be lived," a moral scandal to which he adds his outraged frustration at crimes that will go unpunished and perhaps even unrepented.[7] Moral outrage and a sense of unfulfillable justice drive Langer's admonition to remain faithful to the letter of testimonies of unassuaged cruelty and horrendous death, and that same morality prevents him from drawing the peremptory lessons of the disaster.

Contrary to Langer's belief, one can extract considerable learning from the Holocaust, but only if one is willing to be, at least initially, much more radically pessimistic than he is. In order to take an unblinkered look at the horror one has to start by dispensing not only with all sorts of comforts and consolations, but also with all types of lamentations and moral indignations. Having no sway in the hell of the camps, moral values such as the ones proffered by Langer are hermeneutically ineffective because an event such as the Holocaust demands that one bracket received ideas about history, morality, and representation.

Excesses

Hayden White contends that history was constituted as a discipline by relegating a dimension, which he calls the historical sublime, that presents a spectacle of confusion, uncertainty, moral anarchy, chaos, and terror: "The sublimity of the spectacle of history had to be transcended if it was to serve as an object of knowledge and deprived of the terror it induced as a 'panorama of sin and suffering' [Hegel]." The repression of the sublime, asserts White, resulted in a practice of history as realistic narrative, a model that, still prevalent today, he would like to see replaced by "a recovery of the historical sublime."[8] And yet, when faced with that opportunity, he recoils from it. Shying away from viewing the Holocaust as a case of the historical sublime, White argues that the typical conundrums associated with the representation of that event are the result of an excessive allegiance "to a realism that is inadequate to the representation of events, such as the Holocaust, which are themselves 'modernist' in nature." For White the

problem is simply that a new type of event like the Holocaust requires
a new mode of representation: "In point of fact I do not think that the
Holocaust, Final Solution, Shoah, Churban, or German genocide of the
Jews is any more unrepresentable than any other event in human history. It is only that its representation, whether in history or in fiction,
requires the kind of style, the modernist style, that was developed in
order to represent the kind of experiences which social modernism
made possible."[9]

White's modernist proposal is nothing more than a rehashing of realism, and he admits as much when he writes that "[m]odernism is still
concerned to represent reality 'realistically,' and it still identifies reality
with history."[10] While Langer would let the facts speak for themselves,
White argues for a change of style, an adjustment that would leave
intact the historian's ability to know and represent reality. But White's
new realism, his equation between modernist reality and modernist
style, is as problematic and limiting as Langer's own version of realism
(his enraged literalism). However, an extreme experience such as the
Final Solution prevents any realistic representation, historical or artistic, from achieving closure, and furthermore it exposes the shortcomings of the moral and epistemological certainties that undergird those
representations.

The Holocaust resists a realist representation not because it is a new,
unique monstrosity, but only because its sheer magnitude foregrounds
the historical sublime in a most unequivocal way. The manifestations
of the sublime in history could be formulated also as an irruption of the
Real into the fabric of reality. As delineated in the first chapter, there is
a need to distinguish between reality as a construction effected by discourses (or in Lacanian terms as the domain of the symbolic) and the
Real. Reality is constructed by imposing order on, or foreclosing, a
presymbolic domain, the Real, which nonetheless can return and upset
social constructions. Without a Real that escapes all discursive or symbolic formations, there would be no space of freedom where the subject could resist, contest, or alter the discursive formations that at any
given moment constitute reality. This possibility of agency, however, is
counterbalanced by the less savory possibility of the tumultuous return
of the Real. As seen in the chapter on María Teresa León, Žižek interprets the Real as the intrinsic instabilities that underlie, and are contained by, any social formations. In periods of social, political, or
economic turmoil, that excess that underlies and threatens all social

orders is made to be embodied in people whose difference makes them an easy target for victimization and scapegoating.

Lyotard calls that excess "the jews," without capitalizing the word, so that it is not confused with just one of its common subgroups (the Jews). Arguing that "the jews" resist the spirit of a Western world that is obsessed with foundational thinking, he adds: "'The jews' are the irremissible in the West's movement of remission and pardon. . . . 'The jews', never at home wherever they are, cannot be integrated, converted, or expelled." They are "an immanent terror, not identified as such, unrepresentable, . . . an unconscious affect" that undergirds Western thought. The sublime is for Lyotard another manifestation of this terror, being an excess that resists representation (although the discipline of aesthetics attempts to domesticate it). Yet, although unrepresentable, although unable to conform, in any manifestation of the sublime "something, at least, remains there, ignored by imagination, spread in the mind as both pleasure and pain—something Burke called terror, precisely, terror of a 'there is nothing,' which threatens without making itself known, which does not 'realize' itself."[11]

It could be argued that a history blind to the return of the Real, a history whose object of inquiry and type of representation are not obvious or objective but are generated instead by a wishful moral and political vision, is self-defeating when confronted with events such as the Holocaust, which cannot be comprehended unless one assumes that there was much more going on in it than the extermination of a people. A view of the Holocaust as one instance of the manifestation of that originary terror, of the return of the Real any society has to repress to constitute itself, in no way justifies Nazism's barbaric deeds or devalues the suffering of the people killed or terrorized by it. By the same token, however, any attempt to comprehend the Holocaust without paying heed to a formulation of the sublime will end up repeating the same self-defeating, pious pattern of blindness, be it a literalist version, an exemplarist one, or any other within the range encompassed by those two extremes. A view of the Holocaust as a case of the historical sublime offers neither justification nor consolation nor redemption. It is an unsparing look that demolishes all cognitive and moral certitudes, but only to reveal humanity's ethical foundations. This revelation offers no assurances that the horror will not return (it will, it constantly does: Cambodia, Bosnia, Rwanda . . .), but it affords the lucidity that, even in the most cruel case of ethnic

cleansing or scapegoating, the torturers (and the victims) are haunted by the ethical.

Viewing the Holocaust as a case of the historical sublime explains
the dimensions of purification, carnivalization, "sacrificialism, regen-
erative violence, and victimization or scapegoating" that LaCapra sees
in it.[12] It was not simply a matter of extermination but a ritual that gave
the Nazis the elated feeling of complete control over the excess that for
them embodied the threat of disruption of their planned society. One
can thus understand that Finkielkraut denounces as obsolete the characterization of the Nazis as decadent, perverse, or primitive monsters,
proposing instead to portray them as dispassionate technicians:
"National Socialism transferred into the realm of crime a rationality
hitherto reserved for the industrial sphere. . . . They were the heroes of
maximum efficiency and of absolute indifference. . . . It would certainly have been reassuring to be able to attribute this crime without prece-
dent to human beasts, to the violently insane or to fanatics, but in
reality the most merciless inhumanity emanated from the most ordi-
nary humanity."[13] Without the technological advancements of the century, the mass destruction perpetrated by the Nazis could not reach its
horrific level of efficiency. However, Finkielkraut's instrumental explanation confuses the means of destruction with its motivation. The
Final Solution was an attempt to get rid of the "excess" that over-
flowed, and thus threatened, the Nazi order. It was something that
exceeded reason (National Socialism's reason, that is), and not an
excessive rationality, that made the Final Solution unavoidable for the
program of National Socialism.

The view of the Holocaust as an instance of the sublime also helps
one to understand Semprún's obsession with radical Evil in *L'écriture ou
la vie*. Radical Evil functions in Semprún's narrative as a theme that he
explicitly foregrounds at crucial points in his account by referring to
the philosophical works where this problem is broached, Kant's
Religion within the Limits of Reason Alone and Schelling's *On Human
Freedom*. Kant's (and Schelling's) conception of radical Evil has nothing
to do with the modern concept of diabolical evil, which for Kant cannot exist since nobody can live totally against the law.[14] Although
Semprún invokes Kant to explain that Evil is not inhuman, but rather
it lies at the very foundation of the human, his conception of radical
Evil is closer to Schelling's reasoning, for whom only if the subject is
grounded in darkness can it have reality and freedom, that is, freedom

to perform good or evil deeds. "Le Mal n'est past l'inhumain, bien sûr.
. . . Ou alors c'est l'inhumain chez l'homme" ("Evil is not what is inhuman, of course. . . . Or else it's what is inhuman in man"), and thus its
experience is possible anywhere, but in a place such as Buchenwald it
is massive"), asserts Semprún (99/88), who concludes, "de cette
expérience du Mal, l'essentiel est qu'elle aura été vécue comme expérience de la mort" (99/88–89; "the essential thing about this experience
of Evil is that it will turn out to have been lived as the experience of
death").[15]

Semprún's formulation of radical Evil might seem close to the reasoning of the universalists who, in their interpretation of the
Holocaust, maintain that evil is universal and thus that anyone in the
same situation might have done the same. There is, however, an essential difference, in that radical Evil posits a space of freedom that can
also be the source of disorder. Universalists such as Todorov are rightly taken to task by Langer because they introduce the possibility of
moral relativism. But this has nothing to do with radical Evil, which
does not belong to the realm of morality but to that of ethics; more
explicitly, moral relativism refers to the sphere of action, while radical
Evil refers to the constitution of the subject. As Copjec explains, for
Kant radical Evil means simply that the only thing of which the subject can be sure is of its guilt (and not of any cognitive or moral certitude). The subject is always guilty, independently of its actions, its
deeds and misdeeds, and this guilty conscience founds the subject. In
other words it is possible (although unlikely) that not everyone will
have to face a situation of moral relativism or the possibility of acting
immorally, but radical Evil is universal because the subject itself
would not exist outside it. Comparing Lacan and Kant, Copjec concludes: "In Lacan's translation, the status of the subject becomes, with
Kant, ethical rather than ontological; the subject can only be supposed
on the basis of moral conscience."[16] As was pointed out in the first
chapter, Lacan's and Levinas's formulations of the constitution of the
subject are very close, the main difference between them being that
while Lacan sees guilt at the origin of the subject, Levinas talks about
responsibility. But both formulations presuppose an other that precedes the subject, which is founded as an answer to the other's requi-
sition. Whether one chooses to speak of guilt or prefers to talk about
responsibility, the bottom line is that the subject originates burdened
with a debt and a duty.

The concept of radical Evil formulates at the moral level what the theories of the Real do at an epistemological level. Reality as discursive construction has to be undergirded by a Real that offers a space of resistance and agency for the subject. Similarly, if moral law were not accompanied by the possibility of radical Evil, freedom could not be conceived. And in both cases the same instance that grants the possibility of social action and moral freedom looms simultaneously as a possible source of inordinate disruption of moral and social order.

The experience of the camps is so harrowing because all the moral and social discourses brought by the inmates from the outside world are woefully ineffectual in the camps, and that realization struck the prisoners from the first moment of their arrival. The enormity of the Holocaust, the horror it elicits as a case of the historical sublime, results in a traumatic breakdown. Cathy Caruth describes trauma as "an overwhelming experience of sudden or catastrophic events," whose tremendous impact converts them into partially unassimilated or "missed" experiences that are not fully mastered by the person who endures them. Their radical incomprehensibility prevents the subject from assimilating them or even registering them, which often provokes a delayed reaction, known as traumatic repetition, in which the traumatic event "returns to haunt the survivor later on."[17] The subject might relive obsessively and uncontrollably the traumatic experience because, being beyond comprehension, it is internalized by the subject without mediation. As Friedlander writes, in "the extreme character of the events and the indeterminacy surrounding their historical significance," the Holocaust remains "an unmastered past."[18]

A traumatic experience shakes all certainties about reality, personal identity, and representation. The foremost traumatic experience in the camp is the constant exposure to death, which brings with it the realization of death's radical incomprehensibility. A traumatic event such as the concentration camps questions an epistemological model of the subject and posits the need for an ethical consideration of subjectivity. Furthermore, if the subject does not "know" what happened, if understanding is always delayed, the representation of a traumatic experience becomes highly problematic, and it certainly cannot be a plain account of facts that, by the very definition of trauma, escape the understanding of the witness. Therefore any account of trauma casts doubts on referentiality and makes suspect any realistic narrative. As with any autobiographical narrative, but only more so, an account of a traumatic event requires not only a narrator but demands also a true listener, thus evincing another dimension of the ethical.

The Nightmare of Reality

Survivors describe as horrifying not only their experience in the camps but also, and even especially, life after their release. One of the effects of the internment is the production of a deep fissure in the experience of time, according to Lawrence Langer, who distinguishes between chronological time (everyday, normal time) and what he calls durational time, which is a new time generated by the experience of the camps. While chronological time is a time of hope, of redemption and consolation, of reason and logic, of communality and continuity, argues Langer, durational time signals an unbridgeable temporal discontinuity that mires the subject in a past of such intensity that its constant memory defeats the passage and continuity of time.[19] It could be said that the traumatic aftermath of the camp experience consists in producing two levels of reality that remain separated and vie for supremacy after the liberation. Once released, survivors not only have to suffer the painful resurfacing of durational reality into their everyday lives, but are often forced to conclude that their perception of chronological, normal reality has been changed forever. In its fierce intensity and permanence, durational reality shakes all epistemological certainties about everyday reality. The standard reference in this respect is Primo Levi's revelation at the end of *The Reawakening* that after his return home "a dream full of horror has still not ceased to visit me, at sometimes frequent, sometimes longer, intervals." Levi continues with a detailed description of the dream, which is reproduced here for the relevance it has for an interpretation of *L'écriture ou la vie:*

> It is a dream within a dream, varied in detail, one in substance. I am sitting at a table with my family, or with friends, or at work, or in the green countryside; in short, in a peaceful relaxed environment, apparently without tension or affliction; yet I feel a deep and subtle anguish, the definite sensation of an impending threat. And in fact, as the dream proceeds, slowly or brutally, each time in a different way, everything collapses and disintegrates around me, the scenery, the walls, the people, while the anguish becomes more intense and more precise. Now everything

has changed to chaos; I am alone in the center of a grey and turbid nothing, and now, I *know* what this thing means, and I also know that I have always known it; I am in the Lager once more, and nothing is true outside the Lager. All the rest was a brief pause, a deception of the senses, a dream; my family, nature in flower, my home. Now this inner dream, this dream of peace, is over, and in the outer dream, which continues, gelid, a well-known voice resounds: a single word, not imperious, but brief and subdued. It is the dawn command of Auschwitz, a foreign word, feared and expected: get up, *"Wstawàch."*[20]

The Reawakening is an unfortunate and inaccurate translation of the Italian *La tregua* (The Truce), because the English term has redemptive connotations that are totally absent from the Italian title, used by Levi to refer to the period between his liberation from Auschwitz in January 1945 and his arrival in his native Turin in October of the same year. The disorganization of the evacuation process forced Levi to travel aimlessly through Poland and Russia before he was returned to Italy. However, he describes that period as a truce because it postponed having to face his reintegration to his former reality with the burden of "a year of ferocious memories" that has left him "emptied and defenseless" (206). The venom of Auschwitz that Levi feels running through his veins refers not only to the traumatic experience of the camp itself, but especially to the dire consequences Auschwitz has for life after the camp. Trauma fills reality with epistemological uncertainty and existential uneasiness.

Semprún draws heavily on Levi's image of a dream within a dream, transforming it into the well-known literary *topos* of life as a dream, a meaning that is not necessarily present in Levi's image. Semprún, however, will take Levi's image one step further in the account of his own dream, a recurrent nightmare he had after being freed. In it Semprún hears an imperious, resonant voice saying the words *"Krematorium, ausmachen,"* an order, heard repeatedly at Buchenwald, to shut down the crematorium so that the incoming Allied planes could not see at night the flames belching out of the chimney:

> Cette voix enflait, devenait bientôt assourdissante. Je me révellais alors en sursaut. Mon cœur battait follement, j'avais l'impression d'avoir crié.

Main non, Odile dormait à mes côtés, paisiblement.

Je me redressais dans le lit, moite de sueur. J'entendais le souffle régulier de mon amie. J'allumais une lampe de chevet. J'écartais le drap, je regardais son corps nu. Une peur abominable m'étreignait, malgré la certitude déchirante de sa beauté. Toute cette vie n'était qu'un rêve, n'était qu'illusion. J'avais beau effleurer le corps d'Odile, la courbe de sa hanche, la grâce de sa nuque, ce n'était qu'un rêve. La vie, les arbres dans la nuit, les musiques du «Petit Schubert» n'étaient qu'un rêve. Tout était un rêve depuis que j'avais quitté Buchenwald, la forêt de hêtres sur l'Ettersberg, ultime realité .

(The voice swelled, soon grew deafening, then jolted me awake. My heart was pounding; I had the impression I'd cried out:

But no, Odile was sleeping peacefully at my side.

I sat up in bed, damp with sweat. I could hear Odile breathing evenly. I turned on a bedside lamp. I threw off the sheet, looked at her naked body. A ghastly fear gripped me, despite the piercing certainty of her beauty. All this life was only a dream. An illusion. Even though I might lightly caress Odile's body, the curve of her hip, her delicate nape—it was only a dream. Life, the trees in the night, the music at Le Petit Schubert: only a dream. It had all been a dream ever since I'd left Buchenwald, the beech wood on the Ettersberg, the ultimate reality.)

(164/154; see also 21–22/12)

In Levi's account the dream of the Lager ends up invading and erasing the scene of family life that frames it, but Levi says nothing about the reality of the vigil. In Semprún's retelling, however, what is effaced is not the dream that frames another dream but daily reality itself (which is the frame of his dream):

C'est vrai que tout devient chaotique, quand cette angoisse réapparaît. On se retrouve au centre d'un tourbillon de néant, d'une nébuleuse de vide, grisâtre et trouble. On sait désormais ce que cela signifie. On sait qu'on l'a toujours su. Toujours, sous la surface chatoyante de la vie quotidienne, ce savoir terrible. À portée de la main, cette certitude : rien n'est vrai que le camp, tout le reste n'aura été qu'un rêve, despuis lors. Rien n'est vrai que la fumée du crématoire de Buchenwald, l'odeur de chair brûlée, la faim, les appels sous la neige, les bastonnades, la mort de Maurice Halbwachs et de Diego Morales, la puanteur fraternelle des latrines du Petit Camp.

(It's true that everything becomes chaotic, when that anguish reappears. You find yourself in the middle of a whirlwind of nothingness, a nebulous void, murky and gray-ish. From that moment on, you know what this means. You know that you have always known. Always, beneath the glit-tering surface of daily life, this terrible knowledge. Close at hand, this certainty: nothing is true except the camp, all the rest is but a dream, now and forever. Nothing is real but the smoke from the crematory of Buchenwald, the smell of burned flesh, the hunger, the roll calls in the snow, the beat-ings, the deaths of Maurice Halbwachs and Diego Morales, the fraternal stench of the latrines in the Little Camp.)

(245–46/236)

Semprún's rewriting of Levi is not, or not only, an ingenious exercise of literary one-upmanship on Semprún's part, but a way of stressing the loss of an ontological foundation of reality that survivors endure after the camp. As Langer writes, the survivor lives "a parallel existence. He switches from one to the other without synchronization because he is reporting not a *sequence* but a *simultaneity*."[21] Semprún adds a new dimension to that formulation, because for him it is not simply a mat-ter of parallel worlds but of the destructive effects one of them, the memory of the camp, has over the other: "Deux univers, deux vies. Et je n'aurais su dire, sur le moment, laquelle était la vraie, laquelle un rêve" (244/234; "Two worlds, two lives. And at the time I could not have said which was the real one, which the dream").

By affirming that reality is a dream and that Buchenwald is the true reality, Semprún is also identifying the obstacles faced by anyone who attempts to represent a traumatic experience. A faithful account of the horrors endured cannot do justice to an event that, because it is impos-sible to master, invalidates any sense of certainty about itself and about the reality that frames it. Infected with epistemological uncertainty, a faithful, factual account is clearly insufficient to represent an event that has such dire consequences. Literature, with its well-worn *topos* of life as dream, offers a precarious consolation, but it rescues representation from its complete dissolution. This palliative, however, should not disguise the fact that no representation, realist or modernist, can offer any cognitive certitude. But then again the writing of the Holocaust is not just about accurate, constative representations.

The Fall

It could be said that the uncertainty about reality generated by the camps was an unintended institutional effect, given that no one was expected to survive. The camps, however, were not simply places for systematic, efficient destruction. As an institution the camps aimed first of all at dehumanizing the inmates before destroying many of them. Although "the transformation from human beings into animals" was not, as Levi argues, "planned or formulated in so many words at any level of the Nazi hierarchy," such dehumanization was the resulting effect.[22] Levi notes that one of the most striking features of the camps was their "widespread useless violence, as an end in itself, with the sole purpose of inflicting pain, occasionally having a purpose, yet always redundant, always disproportionate to the purpose itself."[23] This disproportion, this excess beyond usefulness, was one of the ways of pushing the inmates to the limits of the human. After that they could be gassed and cremated as inanimate objects. And if they were not destined for destruction or if by chance they survived, the camps worked to ensure another type of destruction, one that would insidiously gnaw forever at the survivors: shame.

The need to make the victim fit the crime, to discipline the inmates until they conformed to the model—to make the human inhuman—was the camps' main institutional import. The idea was not simply to punish, exploit, or exterminate, but to make the inmates infrahuman: thus the "useless violence," the random cruelty, the ineffectual work, the senseless sport exercises. Before physical destruction there was destruction as human beings, making the inmates perform acts that would devalue them in their own eyes so as to make them confirm with their own actions the social stigma that led to their internment and shaming them to a point of nonreturn. By interning them they were excluded from the sociopolitical order; by debasing them and making them debase themselves, they were made to contravene the ethical. The inmates were pushed to choose between the others and themselves, to abjure all responsibility toward the others, to negate them as other. They were regressed to the domain of the ethical, so that they would deny it, thus ensuring that the living hell of shame would burn forever, even outside the camp, were they to survive. Some survivors might or might not have felt guilt for having lived in the "grey zone" (Levi's term) of collaboration with the system of the camps; arguably all of them felt shame. Shame for the loss of dignity, but above all retrospective shame derived from "having failed in terms of human solidarity," a fault that "almost everybody" incurred.[24] As Levi writes woefully: "whoever waits for his neighbor to die in order to take his piece of bread is, albeit guiltless, further from the model of thinking man than the most primitive pygmy or the most vicious sadist."[25] This inconsolable shame is the best proof of the success achieved by the camps as institutions. And they did it primarily by pushing the inmates to the limits of the human, by shaking their very foundations as subjects, by pushing them to decline all responsibility for their neighbor.

The camps left the survivors mired in an epistemological uncertainty and convulsed by ethical failure. As a consequence, once out of the camp they have the unenviable double task of restoring solidity to reality and reconstructing themselves. One of the main stories of L'écriture ou la vie is precisely an account of Semprún's reinvention of himself as an individual, which he happens to perform in conjunction with a philosophical re-creation of the subject. If L'écriture ou la vie can be called a testimony at all, it is the testimony of a thorough self-reconstruction and not merely a restoration, effected with the complete awareness that nothing can be as it was before the camp. However, the loss of reality and the discovery of radical Evil do not necessarily lead to a negative outcome, because in his voyage through death Semprún discovers also the ethical foundations of the subject. Semprún's rebuilding of himself, and of the subject in general, is narrated in three reconstruction scenes. In the first two Semprún reinvents a phenomenological subject that proves to be insufficient; ultimately he will ground himself on the terrain of the ethical. Semprún's narrative of Buchenwald resembles a new "discourse of the method," in that his autobiographical account, like Descartes's, is also a tale of the foundation of a new philosophical subject. However, instead of starting with a certainty about himself, Semprún departs from the ultimate reality of radical Evil, from the experience of death.

In Semprún's case it all begins with trauma, and the key will be to understand it, to comprehend what was going on at the camp, so that the event can be stored in oblivion and thus be safely remembered. This project is articulated in one of the two epigraphs of *L'écriture ou la vie,* a quote from Maurice Blanchot that illustrates the paradoxical interplay of memory and forgetfulness: "Qui veut se souvenir doit se confier à l'oubli, à ce risque qu'est l'oubli absolu et à ce beau hasard que devient alors le souvenir" ("Whoever wishes to remember must trust to oblivion, to the risk entailed in forgetting absolutely, and to this wonderful accident that memory then becomes.") It is necessary to forget not only to be able to live but also to be able to remember. In the camps trauma originates mainly in pervasive death: death in the gas chambers, but also by malnutrition, disease, or accident. Death of others, but also the constant, incomprehensible possibility of one's death, the constant threat of leaving the camp "through the chimney," as the inmates were constantly reminded. Paradoxically trauma is less about the possibility of dying in the camp than about the inability to fathom one's death: thus the mere fact of being alive becomes a real mystery. Philosophy ground zero. As Cathy Caruth writes: "For consciousness, the act of survival, as the experience of trauma, is the repeated confrontation with the necessity and impossibility of grasping the threat to one's own life. It is because the mind cannot confront the possibility of its death directly that survival becomes for the human being, paradoxically, an endless testimony to the impossibility of living."[26] As a consequence traumatic repetition, the uncontrolled return of an undigested experience, is an attempt to make sense of survival: "Repetition . . . is not simply the attempt to grasp that one has almost died but, more fundamentally and enigmatically, the very attempt *to claim one's own survival.* . . . the endless attempt to assume one's survival as one's own."[27]

Semprún confronts for the first time the horrid enigma of being alive when, standing guard at the main gate of Buchenwald the day after its liberation, he sees himself reflected in the gaze of three Allied military officers. This is precisely how *L'écriture ou la vie* begins:

> Ils sont en face de moi, l'œil rond, et je me vois soudain
> dans ce regard d'effroi: leur épouvante.
>
> Depuis deux ans, je vivais sans visage. Nul miroir, à
> Buchenwald. Je voyais mon corps, sa maigreur croissante,

une fois par semaine, aux douches. Pas de visage, sur ce
corps dérisoire. . . .

. . . . . .

Ils me regardent, l'œil affolé, rempli d'horreur.

(They stand amazed before me, and suddenly, in that terror-
stricken gaze, I see myself—in their horror.
  For two years, I had lived without a face. No mirrors, in
Buchenwald. I saw my body, its increasing emaciation, once
a week, in the shower. Faceless, that absurd body. . . .

. . . . . .

They stare at me, wild-eyed with panic.)

(13/3)

After rejecting different possibilities for their horrified stare (Semprún's
close-cropped hair, his outfit, his thinness), he concludes:

C'est de l'épouvante que je lis dans leurs yeux.
  Il ne reste que mon regard, j'en conclus, qui puisse autant
les intriguer. C'est l'horreur de mon regard que révèle le leur,
horrifié. Si leurs yeux sont un miroir, enfin, je dois avoir un
regard fou, dévasté.

(What I read in their eyes is fear.
  It must be my gaze, I conclude, that they find so riveting.
It's the horror of my gaze that I see reflected in their own.
And if their eyes are a mirror, then mine must look like those
of a madman.)

(14/4)

Recognizing himself in the other's eyes is a first step in Semprún's
self-reconstruction, but the horror he discovers in that gaze shows him
the precariousness of the ground he must build on:

Je compris soudain qu'ils avaient raison de s'effrayer, ces
militaires, d'éviter mon regard. Car je n'avais pas vraiment
survécu à la mort, je ne l'avais pas évitée. Je n'y avais pas

échappé. Je l'avais parcourue, plutôt, d'un bout à l'autre. J'en
avais parcouru les chemins, m'y étais perdu et retrouvé, con-
trée immense où ruisselle l'absence. J'étais un revenant, en
somme

(I have abruptly understood that these soldiers are right to
be afraid, to avoid looking into my eyes. Because I have not
really survived death. I have not avoided it. I have not
escaped it. I have, instead, crossed through it, from one end
to the other. I have wandered along its paths, losing and
finding my way in this immense land streaming with
absence. All things considered, I am a ghost.)

(24/15)

Semprún's account deals primarily with the enigma of survival,
and consequently it revolves around the uncertainty involved in
passages and in particular in the transit between a before and an
after, reality and dream, sleep and awakening, memory and forgetting, loss and recovery. The gaze of the three officers reveals to
Semprún what he has become—a man returned from the dead, but
instead of fostering a reencounter with himself, that first reconstruction scene results only in the blurring of the border between
life and death. Far from reaffirming his survival, Semprún's first reencounter with the outside inaugurates an unsettling and pervasive
uncertainty.

The second scene of self-reconstruction also involves transits, in
this case the transition between sleep and awakening, and the result
is as discomfiting as it was in the confrontation with the three officers. This second attempt at figuring reconstruction involves another gaze, but this encounter differs considerably from the first. In this
scene Semprún narrates his fall, in a small station north of Paris,
from a crowded commuter train that stopped abruptly. Having lost
consciousness, he later wakes up to the realization that he is lacking both language and a sense of self (as with the camp, the passage
from a before to an after, with a blank in the middle, involves loss
of reality and of self). At this point all there is is a collection of
unnameable objects in the room. It is as if he had awakened not
from sleep but from nothingness given that, contrary to what happens when one wakes up from sleep, there is no world he can go
back to:

Mais je ne sortais pas du sommeil, je sortais du néant.

Ainsi, soudain, il y a eu des objets. Il n'y avait jamais rien eu avant. Il n'y aurait peut-être rien après: la question ne se posait pas, de toute façon. Il y avait simplement des objets non identifiés, non encore nommés, peut-être innommables. . . .

Il n'y avait aucune possibilité de dire «je», à ce moment-là, originaire en quelque sorte. Je n'existais pas: il, ce «je», ce sujet qui aurait regardé, n'existait pas encore. Il y avait le monde, un fragment infime de monde qui se faisait visible, c'était tout. Mon regard n'a surgi qu'ensuite. C'est la visibilité du monde qui m'a rendu voyant.

(But I was not emerging from sleep, I was emerging from nothingness.

And so, suddenly, there were objects. There had never been anything before *them*. Perhaps there would be nothing after them, either; the question did not arise, in any case. There were simply unidentifiable objects as yet unnamed, perhaps unnameable. . . .

There was no possibility of saying "I" in that instant, which was primordial, in a way. I did not exist: he, this "I," this subject who would have been looking, did not yet exist. There was the world, a minute fragment of the world making itself visible: that was all. Only then could I look at it. It was the visibility of the world that allowed me to see.)

(223-24/213-14)

The perception of this reality composed of nameless objects provokes in him an extraordinary happiness, but it comes to an end when he is addressed with words he is able to understand. He sits up painfully and faces the doctor who has just spoken to him:

. . . Je voyais un homme, vêtu d'une blouse blanche, qui m'observait attentivement.

C'est à cet instant prècis que j'avais commencé à exister. Que j'avais recommencé à savoir que c'était mon regard qui contemplait le monde, alentour: . . . Je suis redevenu «moi» à cet instant précis, sous le regard attentif de cet homme.

Avant, il y avait des objets visibles: ils l'etaient pour ma vision, désormais, pour moi.

(. . . I saw a man wearing a white coat, observing me carefully.

It's at this precise moment that I began to exist. That I began to realize once more that it was my gaze that contemplated the world around me. . . . I became "me" at his very instant, beneath the watchful eye of that man. Before, there had been visible objects: from now on they were visible in my sight, for me.)

(224-25/214)

As in the encounter with the three officers, a gaze makes Semprún into a subject, although still an incomplete one because, up to this point, Semprún is merely an entity differentiated from the world, but lacks a specific identity. As should be obvious by now, Semprún re-creates his awakening through a well-known phenomenological discourse along the line of thinkers such as Sartre and Merleau-Ponty. Undoubtedly Semprún's philosophy-infused account might be charged with being arranged to make a point and not sticking to the facts, but then one would miss the crucial role literary self-consciousness has in this auto-biographical account.[28]

At any rate, up to this point in his awakening, Semprún has gained only differentiated existence. In Lacanian parlance (another phe-nomenological view), this would be equivalent to the sense of detached existence reached by the infant at the mirror stage. In order to reach full identity, the child still needs to gain access to the sym-bolic, and this step entails a foreclosing of drives that threaten social order, their commitment to forgetfulness. A bargain is struck by which memory and identity are established at the cost of oblivion. In Semprún's awakening, however, the opposite happens, and his bid for self-reconstruction fails because, instead of commitment to obliv-ion, there is an overflow of undesirable memories. Told that he fell from a train, along comes the memory of another crowded train and also of another "fall," the descent from the transport train to the plat-form at Buchenwald. At this point his memory returns, and he acquires sudden, painful acknowledgment of having a past and with it an identity:

C'était ainsi, dans l'éclat de ce souvenir brutalement resurgi, que j'avais su qui j'étais, d'où je venais, où j'allais réellement. C'était à ce souvenir que se ressourçait ma vie retrouvée, au sortir du néant. Au sortir de l'amnésie provisoire mais absolue qu'avait provoquée ma chute sur le ballast de la voie ferrée. C'était ainsi, par le retour de ce souvenir, du malheur de vivre, que j'avais été chassé du bonheur fou de l'oubli.

(That was how I found out, in the abrupt flash of this resurgent memory, who I was, where I'd come from, where I was really going. This memory was the source of my recovered life, as I emerged from the void. From the temporary but complete amnesia caused by my fall onto the track bed.
That was how—by the return of this memory, of the sorrow of living—I was driven from the mad bliss of oblivion.)[29]

(229/219)

The unremitting permanence of trauma blocks memory into an eternal present, makes the past immemorial, disrupts the precarious balance between memory and oblivion that allows for the flow of time. As Langer observes, durational time "is a constantly re-experienced time, [it] threatens the chronology of experienced time."[30] Hence durational time cannot be foreclosed, cannot be converted into a past, cannot be inserted into a temporal continuity, and traumatic memory becomes a timeless, uninhabitable present. The key for self-reconstruction, therefore, will be to recover the ability to forget. The narratives of sleep and awakening, loss and restitution, expatriation and return, lack here their customary positive signification. As the child must leave behind the world of undifferentiated drives, Semprún needs to repress the sublime horror of the camp, the realm of the Real:

Grâce à Lorène, qui n'en savait rien, qui n'en a jamais rien su, j'étais revenu dans la vie. C'est-à-dire dans l'oubli: la vie était à ce prix. Oubli délibéré, systématique, de l'experience du camp. Oubli de l'écriture, également. Il n'était pas question, en effet, d'écrire quoi que se fût d'autre. Il aurait été dérisoire, peut-être même ignoble, d'écrire n'importe quoi en contournant cette expérience.
Il me fallait choisir entre l'écriture et la vie, j'avais choisi celle-ci. J'avais choisi une longue cure d'aphasie, d'amnésie délibérée, pour survivre.

(Thanks to Lorène, who had no idea of this, who never knew anything about it, I came back to life. In other words, to oblivion: that was the price of life. A deliberate, systematic forgetting of the experience of the camp. Of writing, as well. There was no question, in fact, of writing anything else. It would have been absurd, perhaps even ignoble, to write anything at all that would pass over that experience in silence.

I had to choose between literature and life; I chose life. I chose a long cure of aphasia, of voluntary amnesia, in order to survive.)

(205/195–96)

And yet, there is no forgetting permanently the irremissible experience of the camp, and Semprún's final attempt at self-reconstruction is grounded on that inescapable but most elusive reference. After a period of latency, of mulling over the initially unmediated trauma, Semprún finds a way to incorporate death into the very fabric of the human and thus into his self-reconstruction. Literature is the primary means of self-recovery, and an ethical redefinition of the subject brings light to death, although not consolation or redemption.

Dying with the Other

As previously noted, trauma is about the mystery of survival. Therefore it is about the mystery of death, and nowhere is death's nonsense more apparent than in the camps. At bottom the question concerns the impossibility of imagining one's death, and the other's death is the occurrence that sets off this concern. Survival is paradoxically problematical because, Caruth contends, the mind cannot comprehend the possibility of its own death. Only the other dies, only the death of the other can be grasped, or at least witnessed. One of the themes running through *L'écriture ou la vie* is a dictum by Wittgenstein, "Der Tod is kein Ereignis des Lebens. Den Tod erlebt man nicht," which could be translated as "Death is not an event of life. Death cannot be lived." In *L'Évanouissement,* Semprún had already engaged in an exegesis of this statement (which had attracted his attention at the age of eighteen), and in *L'écriture ou la vie* he proposes a reformulation:

En fait, pour être rigoureux, l'énoncé de Wittgenstein devrait s'écrire ainsi: «*Mein Tod ist kein ereignis meines*

Lebens. Meinen Tod erlebe ich nicht.» C'ést-a-dire: *ma* mort
n'est pas un événement de *ma* vie. Je ne vivrai pas *ma* mort.
C'est tout, ça ne vas bien loin.

(In fact, to be rigorous, Wittgenstein's pronouncement
ought to be phrased like this: "*Mein Tod ist kein Ereignis
meines Lebens. Meinen Tod erlebe ich night.*" In other words:
my death is not an event in *my* life. I will not live *my* death.
That's it, and it's not much.)[31]

(182/171)

The realization that "la mort ne peut-elle être une expérience vécue"
(182/171; "death cannot be a lived experience") or "une expérience de
la conscience pure, du *cogito*" ("an experience of pure consciousness,
of the *cogito*") seems "d'une extrême pauvreté spirituelle" ("spiritually
quite meager") to Semprún, who also dismisses as rather trivial
Heidegger's famous characterization of *Dasein* as "Sein zum Tode"
(being-towards-death). As a matter of fact Semprún goes beyond
rejecting Wittgenstein and Heidegger, and reformulates their assertions
about death. Wittgenstein's dictum might dazzle in its imperative negativity, but it applies only to the terrain of the cognitive; similarly
Heidegger's assertion partakes of an ontological search for the meaning
of death. However, neither cognition nor ontology are for Semprún the
proper spaces of death.[32]

Semprun's autobiographical reconstruction hinges on the possibility
of ascribing meaning to the traumatic experience of rampant and
apparently senseless death. Not surprisingly Semprún's interpretation
of the mystery of death is identical to the one mapped out in the first
chapter of this book as response to the cognitive obstacles faced by
autobiographical writing, because he ends up making sense of death on
the terrain of the ethical. The key is to realize that autobiography is far
from being only a cognitive operation, a re-creation of the past. It will
always attempt, and fail, to do that, because one can never know oneself. But this cognitive failure in no way entails the failure of a genre
that is as much about ethics as it is about cognition. And as an ethical
act, as response to the other, autobiography does not fail or succeed.
Similarly one will never know anything about death, but one can
respond to the death of the other.

Semprún reformulates Wittgenstein precisely by displacing his
deathly conundrum from the terrain of cognition to the realm of ethics,

thus extracting from the trauma of survival the only possible lesson about death: death is always the other's death, a realization that is pregnant with consequences. Semprún is a witness, but not one that must go into the world and bear testimony to the atrocious in order to preclude that it happen again (actually, it might, and probably will, according to Semprún's formulation of radical Evil). As testimony *L'écriture ou la vie* does not proffer a moral or political admonition but proposes only an ethical elucidation of death, although not necessarily a comforting one.

As stated earlier, Semprún's phenomenological awakening after his fall started with his awareness of being situated in a world of objects, and only when he was addressed did he recover language, have access to memory, and become a subject. And yet that reconstruction was a failed one because along with memory came the trauma of an unmastered past permeated by death. Only by achieving an interpretation of death (which is not the same as making sense of it) can Semprún conciliate memory and oblivion, being and death, literature and life. He responds to Wittgenstein and Heidegger with a formulation strikingly close to the thinking of Levinas, for whom the highest form of responsibility is precisely "being answerable for the death of the other," which for him means "not let[ting] him die alone."[33] Responding to the death of Morales (a Spanish Republican interned in Buchenwald) and in all probability consciously echoing Levinas, Semprún answers Wittgenstein:

> Il continue de mourir, il continue de pénétrer dans l'éternité de la mort. C'est alors que je me souviens de Ludwig Wittgenstein. «La mort n'est pas un événement de la vie. La mort ne peut être vécue», avait écrit ce con de Wittgenstein. J'avais vécu la mort de Morales, pourtant, j'étais en train de la vivre. Comme j'avais, un an auparavant, vécu la mort de Halbwachs. Et n'avais-je pas vécu de même la mort du jeune soldat allemand qui chantait *La Paloma*? La mort que je lui avais donnée? N'avais-je pas vécu l'horreur, la compassion, de toutes ces morts? De toute la mort? La fraternité aussi qu'elle mettait en jeu?

> (He continues dying, he continues entering the eternity of death. That's when I remember Ludwig Wittgenstein. "Death is not an event of life. Death cannot be lived," this idiot

Wittgenstein had written. Yet I have lived the death of Morales, I am living it now. The way I had lived the death of Halbwachs a year earlier. And hadn't I likewise lived the death of the young German soldier who sang "La Paloma"? The death I had given him? Hadn't I lived the horror, the compassion, of all those deaths? Of all death? And the fraternal kinship of men before death?)[34]

(202/192–93)

While, according to Heidegger, *Dasein* is a "Sein zum Tode" (being-towards-death), for Semprún the human is "*Mit-sein-zum-Tode*" (100/89), which could be translated as "dying together" or "fraternity in death"; or, as Semprún puts it, with an unlikely amalgam of Baudelaire and Levinas, "D'être pour la mort avec les autres: les copains, les inconnus, mes semblables, mes frères: l'Autre, le prochain" (166/155; "being *for* death with the other—pals, strangers: the Other, my fellow man"). In other words: "Celle-ci était substance de notre fraternité, clé de notre destin, signe d'appartenance à la communauté des vivants. Nous vivions ensemble cette expérience de la mort, cette compassion. Notre être était défini par cela: être avec l'autre dans la mort qui s'avançait" (34/24; "Death was the substance of our brotherhood, the key to our destiny, the sign of our membership in the community of the living. Together we lived that experience of death, that compassion. This defined our being: to be with one another as death advanced upon us").[35]

Dying with the other can be seen as an existential response but also as an ethical interpretation. Given the atmosphere of lack of solidarity prevalent in the camps according to Levi, perhaps Semprún did not experience, at the moment when they died, Halbwachs's and Morales's deaths "Comme un morceau de pain: signe de fraternité" (27/17; "like a piece of bread: a sign of brotherhood"), but that does not detract from his ethical interpretation. Whether that response took place in the immediacy of death or much later in retrospect does not change anything since autobiography is not simply an account of facts, which, anyway, never exist in themselves. At any rate the ethical dimensions of the other's death are not exhausted with fraternity in death, but they extend to the very foundations of the subject. *L'écriture ou la vie* is not a literal memory of the facts, but an *ethical* memory instead.

In Caruth's view Lacan provides an ethical, not an epistemological, foundation for the subject based precisely on "the necessity and impossibility of responding to another's death," that is, on what the subject cannot grasp in the death of the other.[36] This reading of Lacan requires a further reinterpretation of the mirror stage (a theory proposed very early in Lacan's career) because the image in the mirror whose recognition allows the subject to be initially founded as a separate entity is not the infant's or that of some other live person, but always a "dead" or absent one. This entails a displacement of the mirror stage from epistemological grounds to ethical ones because in this view the subject does not originate burdened with a cognitive predicament (never to be able to know itself) but, more primordially, weighted down with an ethical obligation (to respond to the other's death), a daunting obligation that forces the subject to face the other's death and thus the mystery of its own life.

One's death cannot be imagined, and this radical challenge to the imagination gains urgency in a place such as Buchenwald, where death is the order of the day. Being unimaginable, death marks the cognitive boundaries of selfhood, but simultaneously that same limitation makes the other's death more compelling for the subject. What death closes cognitively (self-knowledge, the ultimate fate of the self), it opens ethically in two different although interrelated senses: one responds to the death of the other (with ethical compassion), but one should also see that the disappearance of the other (even before the other dies), determines one's own self-imaging, one's identity. The anticipated mourning for the other mediates one's sense of being and one's relationship with others, as Derrida suggests:

> The "me" or the us . . . arise and are delimited in the way that they are only through this experience of the other, and of the other as other who can die, leaving in me or in us this memory of the other. This terrible solitude which is mine or ours at the death of the other is what constitutes that relationship to self which we call "me," "us," "between us," "subjectivity," "intersubjectivity," "memory." The *possibility* of death "happens," so to speak, "before" these different instances, and makes them possible. Or, more precisely, the possibility of the death of the other *as* mine or ours in-forms any relation to the other and the finitude of memory.[37]

Death resonates in *L'écriture ou la vie* with several meanings. In his 1992 visit to Buchenwald, Semprún unveils for us (325/305) what he calls "les mystères de Buchenwald" ("the mysteries of Buchenwald"): the experience of death yielded for him "les secrets de la fraternité" ("the secrets of fraternity") but also imposed on him the contemplation, "face à face" ("face to face"), of "l'horreur rayonnante du Mal absolu" ("the radiant horror of absolute Evil"). Death's double face (death's double lesson) is articulated in Malraux's epigraph to *L'écriture ou la vie:* " . . . je cherche la région cruciale de l'âme où le Mal absolu s'oppose à la fraternité" ("I seek the crucial region of the soul where absolute Evil contends with fraternity").[38] Or as Levinas writes: "It is this attention to the suffering of the other that, through the cruelties of our century (despite these cruelties, because of these cruelties) can be affirmed as the very nexus of human subjectivity."[39] This is not a consolatory interpretation (it leaves the horror, and its renewed possibilities, intact), nor is it a fatalistic one, because the vilest abjections cannot erase ethics. They are immoral and can even pervert the victim's morality, but they could never uproot the very foundation of the human. This untouchability of ethics does not erase the suffering of the victims, but it offers the ultimate basis for political hope, even in the midst of the most inconsolable events. Contrary to Langer, it would seem possible to learn something from the misery.

Living to Tell about It

One of the most conspicuous aspects of Holocaust accounts is the burden of unbelievability they carry since they began to be divulged or, more precisely, since they began to be imagined in the camps. Primo Levi opens *The Drowned and the Saved* by making the observation that it was common for inmates to dream of returning home, but only to find that their friends and relatives did not give credence or importance to the accounts of their ordeals. Levi comments that indeed the SS members themselves realized that such was the magnitude of the horror in the camps that they were sure nobody in the outside world would find credible the stories of the survivors (if anyone survived, that is).

The Holocaust is unthinkable and thus also unbelievable. Consequently whoever writes about it faces three dilemmas: the first could be called an epistemological quandary, and it concerns the type of representation demanded by an unthinkable event; the second one is an ethical dilemma, and it regards the type of listener required by an unbelievable story; and the third conundrum, an existential one, revolves around the consequences for the writer of the act of telling. These three aspects commingle in the notion of testimony, provided that it is not conceived as merely a constative report. Even though *L'écriture ou la vie* is a personal testimony and a philosophical disquisition about the camps, it is as much a reflection on how to narrate Buchenwald as it is an account of Semprún's experiences and thoughts. Perhaps the greatest singularity of *L'écriture ou la vie* resides in its self-reflexivity, in its thematization of the dilemmas faced by the writer of the Final Solution.

Death is a radically incomprehensible event, and as such it is the supreme challenge to any representation and indeed to any figuration or even any language. Therefore a chronological or straightforward account cannot do justice to a death-pervaded, traumatic experience such as the one endured at the camps. This issue has been repeatedly broached by critics and historians, but the alternatives they propose are imprecise at best. Langer suggests that only "a mythic narrative" would be appropriate for such unbearable event.[40] Writing about the film *Shoah*, Pierre Vidal-Naquet questions the appropriateness of a historiography of "causes and effects" to represent the Holocaust, enjoining the historian "to be both a scholar and an artist" and proposing a Proustian model of time lost and time recovered.[41] These proposals are fairly vague, but nonetheless they reveal that a mere report of the facts will fall short of doing justice to the event, a conviction vigorously maintained by Semprún.

L'écriture ou la vie devotes considerable space to a discussion of the kind of narrative demanded by the Buchenwald experience. With this in mind, Semprún assesses accounts of the other camps he has personally heard (Mauthausen, Auschwitz; 248–49/239–40; 58–61/48–51), concluding that only through artifice will a narrator achieve the essential condition demanded by such an unbelievable account: to be listened to. This is the conclusion reached by a group of inmates the day after the liberation of Buchenwald.[42] Although it might sound improbable that such a conversation would be held at that moment, exchanges of that type could easily have been sparked by the arrival on April 16 of an intelligence team composed of five members of the Psychological Warfare Division, sent to Buchenwald with the mission to compile a report on the recently liberated camp. Assisted in their writing by ten prisoners especially qualified for the task and having based its work on extensive interviews with some inmates and on written accounts provided by many others, by May 11 the team had put together *The Buchenwald Report*.[43] From the day of its liberation Buchenwald was the center of an Allied campaign to divulge the atrocities of the camps, which led to numerous visits in April and May of 1945 by prominent military officers, politicians, journalists, and even a film crew headed by Billy Wilder. Doubtless the representation of Buchenwald was a pressing issue from the beginning, given the unbelievability of the atrocities committed in the camps.

Actually in December 1945 Semprún watched a documentary on Buchenwald (in all likelihood the one directed by Wilder). Even though its images grant reality to his experience, certifying that it was not a dream, there is a disturbing difference, observes Semprún, between the lived experience and the film images. Only through artifice can such an unbelievable experience be made to look real: "Il aurait fallu, en somme, traiter la réalité documentaire comme une matière de fiction" (211/201; "One would have had to treat the documentary reality, in short, like the material of fiction").[44]

Although some readers may raise doubts about the facticity or the accuracy of certain scenes and even characters in *L'écriture ou la vie*, words such as *artifice* and *literary* here do not mean false, invented, or anything of that order. By using those terms Semprún is highlighting the fact that the rapport between narrator and addressee is one of the most crucial aspects of any account of the Holocaust. In the first place the narrative must attract the attention of the listener or the reader (a need poignantly illustrated by Levi with the dream of the inmates whose stories went unheeded); but even more relevant is that the rapport the narrator manages to establish with the addressee is as important as the facts. Semprún foregrounds this relevance of the addressee right at the start of his highly self-conscious narrative. Dismissing as lazy the commonplace argument about the ineffability of events like the Holocaust, he states: "On peut toujours tout dire, le langage contient tout" (23/13; "You can always say everything: language contains everything").[45] And he adds, foregrounding the first and foremost obstacle any narrative of the Holocaust faces:

> Me peut-on tout entendre, tout imaginer? Le pourrat-on? En auront-ils la patience, la passion, la compassion, la rigueur nécessaires? La doute me vient, dès ce premier instant, cette

première rencontre avec des hommes d'avant, du dehors–
vennus de la vie–, à voir le regard épouvanté, presque hostile,
méfiant du moins, des trois officiers.
Ils sont silencieux, ils évitent de me regarder .

(But can people hear everything, imagine everything? Will
they be able to understand? Will they have the necessary
patience, passion, compassion, and fortitude? I begin to
doubt it, in that first moment, that first meeting with men
from *before,* from the *outside,* emissaries from life—when I
see the stunned, almost hostile, and certainly suspicious
look in the eyes of the three officers.
They're speechless, unable to face me.)[46]

(24/14)

To be able to say everything does not mean that a merely constative
language exhausts an event, especially when it is a manifestation of
the historical sublime: a story of trauma cannot be simply constative
because the first thing trauma puts in doubt is the concept of fact and
the idea of history. In this vein Semprún argues that no historical
reconstruction will ever reach the essential truth, which is the same as
saying that the narrator cannot be a detached, faceless entity. As
Shoshana Felman argues, testimony is not simply constative but also
performative, because the witness is "also, the one who *begets* . . . the
truth, through the speech process of the testimony."[47] Even though
L'écriture ou la vie is not properly a testimony, as Semprún insists, it
partakes of the performative, begetting dimension foregrounded by
Felman. But going beyond that, Semprún's book discloses also the
interpretive tools used by the author for the truth it constructs. Not
surprisingly that disclosure works also in the narrative as another
argument that lends credibility to the interpretations it makes possible.

To opt for a fictive account and to discard as insufficient a historical
one means also to expand the notion of fact. As Nelly Furman writes,
Shoah is so successful because "Lanzmann's film forces us first of all to
hear, to listen," therefore challenging "our notions of facts" and "our
understanding of history."[48] This is also one of the goals sought by
L'écriture ou la vie, and it is implied in Semprún's assertion that the
camp experience is inexhaustible (236/226). This statement is not in

contradiction with Semprún's belief that "You can always say everything": one can say everything one has to say, but no single narrative can exhaust a sublime, traumatic event such as the Holocaust. This entails that if the narrative of a traumatic event projects an interpretation, as Semprún's does, the explanation must do justice to the event, but simultaneously it must be open-ended—it must not aspire to be all-encompassing. Semprún's answer to this double-bind is to interpret Buchenwald as a struggle between radical Evil and fraternity. In this way he transcends the facts, or, better still, he shows that there is more than meets the eye in any fact, thus showing that Langer's literalism is not only untenable but also lacking.

For an event to be inexhaustible implies also that the recollection (or fidelity) to what the witness thought or felt at the moment of enduring the experience does not provide an adequate explanation. Semprún's proposal is that the mediation of literature offers the best access to a comprehension of Buchenwald. First of all this underscores the importance of the narrative act itself. In this respect, as already pointed out, it is imperative for the narrator to establish an adequate rapport with the addressee, and thus another aspect of this issue, the perils of narrating the traumatic in the first person, is a dilemma contained in the title L'écriture ou la vie.

Semprún maintains the open-ended richness of the event through a thick narrative. Instead of offering a multitude of details, he focuses on specific moments, places, or scenes, and, through a narrative structured as a musical piece in which themes and leitmotifs reappear intermittently, he extracts from each of those chosen scenes such a wealth of connections, ramifications, and connotations that the narrative is forced to embark on countless digressions although it ends up returning to the point of departure. In this way Buchenwald is also Weimar, Goethe's town, and Semprún does not miss the opportunity to counterpoise a foundational moment of Western culture (the peripatetic conversations between Goethe and Eckermann through the outskirts of Weimar, exactly in the same area where Buchenwald is located) with one of the most horrid outcomes of the same culture (the camps). Also in this way Buchenwald is connected to other camps such as Ravensbrück, where Milena Jesenská died. Milena happened to be engaged to Kafka, a name properly invoked in a narrative of the camps because he was masterful at disclosing the horror of contemporary life. And Prague is the city of Kafka, but it is also the place where Semprún was summoned by the leaders of the Spanish Communist Party in 1964 to be expelled from the Party. On his way to Prague, Semprún happened to buy Kafka's letters to Milena. A fact, a place, a moment, is never exhausted by the merely constative.

A fact is not just a fact; an autobiographical account of Buchenwald cannot be just a catalog of faithful details, according to Semprún; it must strive instead to establish a potentially endless web of connections and resonances that force the narrative to veer from a linear path, in order to escape the constrictions of time and space. One can say everything, but one will never exhaust an event. And for Semprún literature not only offers the most adequate narrative strategies to capture the attention of its addressees and to unveil the inexhaustible richness of Buchenwald; literature can also be the best *interpreter* of the events that happened there, that continued to happen, as a matter of fact, even after Buchenwald, because what took place there cannot be pinned to a time and a place but is carried on by the former inmates. Andrés Soria argues that the book's numerous quotes represent an attempt "to remove literature from its paper jail and insert it in life" (this author's translation), but just the opposite happens: in Semprún's book literature is used primarily as a tool to comprehend life; furthermore, as the disjunction of the title reveals, literature and life cannot be separated in a narrative of trauma.[49] For Semprún literature and literary figures are not a luxury in need of rescue or redemption; on the contrary they are for him the most effective way to map out the past, thus making it inhabitable again for the self.

Light in Darkness: the Brother

Worth exploration is the role played in the connection between literature and life by three writers—Malraux, Magny and Levi—who, as Soria observes, orient Semprún's writing in *L'écriture ou la vie*.[50] Each one of these writers presides over one of the book's three parts, which are laid out as "scenes of reading" and dialogue, with Semprún playing the role of disciple or apprentice. And each one of those scenes results in a lesson on life and writing. The first part takes place between April 12 and May 1, 1945, and develops under the auspices of Malraux, from whom Semprún borrows a statement to use as a philosophical explanation for Buchenwald (the confrontation between radical Evil and fraternity). It is worth noticing that in all three parts of the book, the main narrative takes place *after* the time of Semprún's internment in

Buchenwald although his crisscrossing account goes back and forth in time and space and thus frequently returns to the months of confinement. In this way Semprún emphasizes that his narrative is an interpretation of Buchenwald, not a chronicle, thus further justifying the mediating role of literature.

The philosophical justification and implications of Semprún's choice of Malraux as overseer for the first part of *L'écriture ou la vie* have already been noted, but the interlocutor that Semprún privileges in this part to discuss the ideas of Malraux, Wittgenstein, Heidegger, and others is also highly significant. He is Lt. Walter Rosenfeld, a member of the team preparing the report on Buchenwald. Semprún initially meets with him as do all the inmates that have had administrative responsibilities in Buchenwald because they were familiar with the organization of the camp.[51]

In many ways Rosenfeld works as an alter ego for Semprún. He has left his country of origin but has returned to fight the Nazis, in the same way that Semprún was, as an underground leader of the Spanish Communist Party, to return to Spain in the late fifties to fight against Franco. Being Jewish, Rosenfeld adds weight to the philosophical arguments adduced by Semprún who, as a political prisoner, never had to suffer the most extreme rigors endured by Jewish inmates.[52] Semprún and Rosenfeld are in perfect agreement in their discussions of mostly German authors (Kant, Schelling, Wittgenstein, Heidegger, Brecht), and together they visit Goethe's house in Weimer (fittingly, on April 23), the key figure to illustrate the tragic contrast between the rich culture and the political aberrations of modern Germany, a conflict expressed also in a poem by Brecht favored by Rosenfeld and Semprún: "*O Deutschland, bleiche Mutter!*" (Oh Germany, pale mother!).

In all, the first part is one of clarity amid the horror in that a carefully argued philosophical disquisition offers an explanation for the contrasting poles of cruelty and fraternity around which Semprún develops his narrative. It is also fitting that a "renegade" German is the main figure used by Semprún to carry out in this part the dialogical structure present throughout the book. And perhaps even more to the point, the theme of brotherhood finds a correspondence in a person such as Rosenfeld, who clearly functions as a brotherly figure for Semprún. Similarly, although this part follows the lead of Malraux, the French writer is presented also more as an equal than as an imposing master.

Listening to the Mother

If Malraux stands as an equal, the critic Claude-Edmonde Magny presides over the second part of *L'écriture ou la vie* as a sheltering figure but also as a teacher of hard lessons. This part covers the first months of Semprún's readjustment to normal life after his liberation, and it focuses on the disjunction between writing and life that gives its title to the book. As happens in the first part, this one is spun out of a fundamental dialogue, has literature at its center, and depicts another scene of teaching. In the months following his liberation from Buchenwald, Semprún frequently went to Magny's house, usually in the early morning hours, seeking refuge from his memories. It is there that the scene of teaching that anchors this second part takes place, one in which Magny reads to Semprún her *Lettre sur le pouvoir d'écrire* (Letter on the Power of Writing), published in 1947 but written (addressing "Mon cher Jorge" [Semprún]) in 1943.[53] If Malraux offers the consolation of philosophical understanding, Magny serves as an illustration of the fact that rational elucidation of a traumatic event is not enough to assuage its memory. Magny reads from her *Lettre sur le pouvoir d'écrire*: "Je n'ai pas voulu dire autre chose que ceci: c'est que la littérature est possible seulement au terme d'une première ascèse et comme résultat de cet exercice par quoi l'individu transforme et assimile ses souvenirs douloureux, en même temps qu'il se construit sa personnalité" (172/161–62; "What I wanted to say is this: literature is possible only at the end of a first period of rigorous self-discipline and as a result of that exercise through which the individual transforms and assimilates his painful memories, at the same time constructing a personality for himself" [Semprún quotes literally, but he writes "sa personnalité" while Magny's text [p. 20] reads "une personnalité"]). This is Magny's main precept, and it happens also to be Semprún's program of reconstruction after Buchenwald. Magny reads her *Lettre sur le pouvoir d'écrire* to Semprún in the early morning of August 5, 1945. With fitting timing later on that same day Semprún falls from a train, and that episode, already mentioned, starts his work on balancing memory and oblivion in his project of self-reinvention. That on the following day, as Semprún points out several times, the first atomic bomb exploded in Hiroshima (a new face of the horror) adds further urgency to Semprún's need for oblivion. If the epigraph with Malraux's quotation presides over the first part, the second epigraph (Blanchot's citation about the work of oblivion) guides the second part, in whose final section

Semprún narrates how he made the decision to choose life over literature/death in December 1945. That decision also entails distancing himself from Magny, who advocates the confluence of literature and life:

> Il me fallait choisir entre l'écriture et la vie, j'avais choisi celle-ci. J'avais choisi une longue cure d'aphasie, d'amnésie délibérée, pour survivre. Et c'était dans ce travail de retour à la vie, de deuil de l'écriture, que je m'étais éloigné de Claude-Edmonde Magny, c'est facile à comprendre. Sa *Lettre sur le pouvoir d'écrire* qui m'accompagnait partout, depuis 1947, même dans mes voyages clandestins, était le seul lien, énigmatique, fragile, avec celui que j'aurais voulu être, un écrivain.

> (I had to choose between literature and life; I chose life. I chose a long cure of aphasia, of voluntary amnesia, in order to survive. And during this work of returning to life, this period of mourning for writing, I grew apart from Claude-Edmonde Magny. Her *Lettre sur le pouvoir d'ecrire,* which had accompanied me everywhere since 1947, even on my clandestine journeys, was the only link, an enigmatic, fragile bond with the person I would have liked to be: a writer.)

> (205/196)

Rewriting the Father

Not surprisingly, the third part focuses primarily on the genesis and writing of *L'écriture ou la vie* itself, and in it Semprún invokes the exemplary advocacy of Primo Levi. While Semprún portrays Malraux as an equal and puts Magny in the role of protector, his relationship with Levi is the most convoluted of the three. It would not be an exaggeration to say that if Malraux is the brother and Magny the mother, Levi plays the role of the father. And mixing fathers and writing makes for a tangled tale.

Universally acclaimed as one of the greatest writers on the Holocaust, Levi is an unavoidable predecessor that anyone who writes about that event must confront. The issue then becomes how to write in the wake of such an imposing epitome without appearing to be repetitive or irrelevant. Wisely Semprún adopts the role of dutiful son but also that of continuator. Faced with the quandary of how, after Levi, to write an autobiography involving the camps, Semprún responds not by correcting or deviating from the master's lessons, but by completing him, taking up where Levi left off.

Semprún claims his place in Levi's writing genealogy in various ways, but first of all through a remarkable temporal coincidence. As he does in the first two parts of the book, Semprún builds the third one around some significant scenes that he takes as home base from which to engage in digressions but always returning to the primary scene. On April 11, 1987,the anniversary of the liberation of Buchenwald in 1945, Semprún was working on a scene of his novel *Netchaïev est de retour* . . . in which three military officers (one of them is Roger Marroux, a central character in the novel) arrive at the gate of Buchenwald on the day of its liberation. Marroux feels trapped by the devastated gaze of the inmate guarding the gate, and Semprún writes in *L'écriture ou la vie:* "Ainsi, le 11 avril 1987, jour anniversaire de la libération de Buchenwald, j'avais fini par me rencontrer à nouveau. Par retrouver une part essentielle de moi, de ma mémoire, que j'avais été, que j'étais toujours obligé de refouler, de tenir en lisière, pour pouvoir continuer à vivre" (238/228–29; "And so, on April 11, 1987, on the anniversary of the liberation of Buchenwald, I'd wound up meeting myself once again. Recovering an essential part of myself, of my memory, which I had been—and was still—obliged to repress, to restrain, in order to go on living"). At that moment Semprún's writing of *Netchaïev est de retour* . . . slips from the third person to the first, and Semprún knows that he has written the first scene of a new book (of the book he has wanted to write since 1945, it should be added). It is in this section of *L'écriture ou la vie* that he quotes Levi's poignant "È un sogno entro un altro sogno . . ." (244/235; "It is a dream within a dream")—and only at the end of the section does Semprún reveal that the first piece of news he heard on the radio the following day was about the death of Primo Levi (256/247): *L'écriture ou la vie* is thus born on the very day that Levi dies. This stunning temporal coincidence might raise suspicions (as does the coordination of the scene of reading at Magny's house and Semprún's significant accident later on the same day). But even if Semprún is taking liberties with time (and he might not be doing it, anyway), collapsing time (say, months into one day) is another way to resort to literature (to literary license) to accomplish what Semprún intends: to portray *L'écriture ou la vie* as a rightful and worthy continuation of Levi's books.

The contemporaneity of Levi's death and *L'écriture ou la vie*'s birth is just one of the ways Semprún uses to claim his originality without renouncing his literary patrimony. Indeed *L'écriture ou la vie* covers the same territory as Levi's three nonfiction books on the concentration camps, but it goes further. As Levi does in *Survival in Auschwitz*, Semprún offers an account about life in the camp (that is what he does primarily in the first part of *L'écriture ou la vie*), although he focuses more on philosophical comprehension than on factual testimony. While Levi devoted *The Reawakening* to the time of truce (February through October 1945) between his liberation and his uneasy return to his former life, Semprún centered the second part of his book also on the months (May through December 1945) immediately after his liberation, a period that reaches closure when Semprún, opting for life against literature, grants himself a truce that will end in the early sixties. And to Levi's thoughts on the Holocaust in *The Drowned and the Saved*, Semprún responds by making them an integral, if not the most important, part of his book. But Semprún goes further, must go further, in order to stake out his own territory.

He accomplishes this goal through an amplification and a rectification of Levi. Semprún makes a claim for his writing uniqueness by adding, and foregrounding, a self-reflexive dimension, by elaborating on the type of writing demanded by an autobiographical account of the Holocaust. And he further claims his personal territory through a correction of the predecessor: to Levi's insistence on shame and selfishness, Semprún responds with his thematic emphasis on the inevitability of Evil and the equally unavoidable but corrective counterpart of brotherhood. Where Levi sees degradation inflicted by useless cruelty and shame provoked by one's own ignoble behavior, Semprún shows the grandeur of fraternity, the unremitting responsibility for the predicament of the other (with a difference in emphasis not unlike the one that separates Levinas from Lacan). He corrects Levi with the assistance of Magny and Malraux: with support from the mother and the brother, he gently corrects and continues the labor of the father.

Another way to articulate his singularity as a writer, which resonates in the title of Semprún's book, is by stating that his case "avait eté différente" ("had been different") from Levi's: "Si l'écriture arrachait Primo Levi au passé, si elle apaisait sa mémoire . . . , elle me replongeait moi-même dans la mort, m'y submergeait" (259/250; "While writing

may have torn Primo Levi from the past, assuaging the pain of memory . . . , it thrust me back into death, drowning me in it"). Semprún
draws this distinction toward the end of this section, titled "Le jour de
la mort de Primo Levi" (The Day of Primo Levi's Death), which is the
"scene of reading" of his book's third part. Here Semprún combines
deference with difference, interweaving his reading of Levi with the
story of his own writing. He pays his respects to the master in a
detailed description of the time (1963), place (a private library in
Milan), and reaction to his first encounter with Levi's writing (*The
Reawakening*), but he ends the section by stating: "Quelques mois plut
tôt, j'avais publié *Le grand voyage*" (246/237; "A few months earlier, I'd
published *Le grand voyage*"), a story about the transportation of French
prisoners to Buchenwald, which was his first novel and signaled the
end of his own time of truce.

Around the death and writings of Levi, Semprún spins the story of
his birth as a writer (*Le grand voyage*) and of the birth of his self writing (*L'écriture ou la vie*), which is also a rebirth, a reencounter at the
gates of Buchenwald with the self he had decided to abandon in order
to survive. Fittingly the next, and final, two sections of his book are
devoted respectively to *Le grand voyage* and to his new voyage to
Buchenwald in 1992, a trip that closes the book. It also brings closure
to his reading of Magny because in the camp he finally assumes the
teachings of her *Lettre sur le pouvoir d'ecrire:* "L'écriture, si elle prétend
être davantage qu'un jeu, ou un enjeu, n'est qu'un long, interminable
travail d'ascèse, une façon de se déprendre de soi en prenant sur soi: en
devenant soi-même parce qu'on aura reconnu, mis au monde l'autre
qu'on est toujours" (314/295; "writing, if it claims to be more than a
game, or a gamble, is but a long, endless labor of ascesis, a way of casting off one's self by keeping a firm hold on oneself. Becoming oneself
through recognizing and bringing into the world that *other* one always
is"). The fact that Semprún articulates that alterity in *L'écriture ou la vie*
through a thematic insistence on fraternity and solidarity is a most fitting disclosure of that originary ethical responsibility for the other that
underlies morality and politics and survives their servitudes.

CONCLUSION
Spanish Autobiography and the Burdens of History

This book's subtitle, "Replacing the Subject in Modern Spain," alludes to the ethical replacement of the subject suggested by Levinas, in whose view the subject is not a self-founded entity but instead is primarily a responsibility toward the other. This ethical origination of the subject sets the affective foundations for the intervention of the political (or the symbolic, or the discursive, however one wants to call it), which displaces the ethical but without ever erasing it. An examination of autobiography must pay attention to the complex interplay among the cognitive, the political, the ethical, and the rhetorical. Therefore the replacement of the subject in autobiography, entailed by the attention to the ethical, also makes necessary a re-placement of the subject of autobiography.

The four autobiographers studied in this book view their lives as stories of self replacement. Driven to exile or self-exile, shaken by momentous events, they feel compelled to reassess themselves, performing it through narratives that, while foregrounding primarily cognitive processes, bear evidence to the unequivocal dimensions of the ethical involved in self-knowledge. Forced to re-place themselves and to replace their selves, it is not surprising that their stories are ultimately narratives of self reparation, although in two different senses: reparation as restoration and renewal of the self (Blanco White and Goytisolo), and reparation of the self as compensation for a loss (León, Semprún). Accordingly they tell two different types of history. Blanco White and Goytisolo view their lives as the story of an insufficiency, while León and Semprún conceive them as a story of loss and fall. And they do not tell about a time of reparation that has reached an end, but the reparation continues in the act of telling itself. Even when they conceive their autobiography as a narrative of achieved self-knowledge, it is also, and always, an endless ethical response.

Goytisolo's and Blanco White's life stories display a process of reconstruction of a deficient self. Viewing their past as an insufficiency, they tell about their struggle to unconceal what they perceive as being their true, or authentic, identity, stifled in the past by institutional constrictions (religious, political, social, familial). Their process of self reparation entails a renunciation of homeland, family, and community of peers (the church in Blanco's case; Spanish writers and later Marxist comrades in Goytisolo's). Blanco narrates his deliverance from asphyxiating orthodoxy, self-alienation, and the disorder of feelings and his access to freedom of thought, true Christianity, and self-knowledge. This cognitive story of liberation is told and retold, written and rewritten, but always as dialogue, address, or response. In a way all his autobiographies are confessions that tell the story of how he won the right to write his own confessional script and to choose a confessor of his choice (God as the spirit that dwells within, which is also a faultless reader). Therefore his is not a story of self-knowledge, but ultimately the search for the purely ethical, a pursuit that leads him to isolation, blindness to the political, and even intolerance.

Blanco White's disenchantment with Anglicanism is parallel to Goytisolo's disillusionment with Marxism. While Blanco White's story illustrates the inescapability of the ethical but shows simultaneously that one cannot live immured in the ethical, Goytisolo's narrative exemplifies the fact that a mere replacement of ideologies is not enough to effect profound changes in one's subjectivity. After Marxism fails to do that for him, Goytisolo goes beyond ideological determinations and into the very domain of the ethical, where he effects a ritualistic replacement of the father by the mother. Only after he does that can he redefine himself through his insertion into new communities (primarily linguistic, cultural, and sexual) composed of rebellious, marginalized, or exiled predecessors that constitute for him a new genealogy. Abjuring "anachronistic nationalism," he ends his autobiography by announcing the project of a (literary) destruction of the nation. To replace it, he builds an antination constituted of writers (Hita, Rojas, Blanco White, Cernuda) emblematic of marginalized cultures or sexualities. And while Blanco's narrative is in the end a search for a worthy addressee for the self, Goytisolo's story of redress and reconstruction tells about his discovery of the other (represented primarily by Genet) before whom he ultimately assumes responsibility for his life and for the telling of it. As must always be the case, in both narratives the other is absent or dead, devoid of presence. Blanco White's and Goytisolo's cognitive stories of self restoration are simultaneously an acknowledgment of alterity, of an other to whom their accounts are addressed. The prosopopoeiac restoration of the past cannot be extricated from the apostrophic address to the other.

León and Semprún narrate stories of redress for a past they view as loss and fall. *Memoria de la melancolía* is León's account of her life as continuous severance and uprootedness; it is also the story of a momentary restoration of her self in the plenitude of solidarity (the Spanish Civil War) that ends up bringing about a new expulsion and with it the definitive fall into melancholy, into a sense of irreparable dispossession. León's telling of the story (her last attempt at redress) is also the construction of a new, promised homeland that should eventually replace the Spain that sent her into exile. In Semprún's case it all begins with the loss of home. The family's home in Madrid, to which he would never return after the Civil War started while his family was in northern Spain, appears in several of his autobiographical works, hauntingly emblematized by a sea of ghostly white sheets used to cover the furniture during the family's summer absence. Actually the story of his losses begins with the death of the mother in his childhood, narrated in *Adieu, vive clarté.* . . . The exile imposed by Spanish history finds new chapters in Buchenwald's fall and his expulsion from the Communist Party of Spain. To his fate of errancy he will respond by redefining himself as a postnational subject, as one who has both many nations and none at all. His liberation from Buchenwald is paradoxically constructed as another expulsion, this time from a true homeland whose members are bonded by fraternity in death. With this gesture the political is replaced by the ethical; solidarity becomes fraternity. Furthermore *L'écriture ou la vie* illustrates that self-knowledge is bound to the death of the other, a discovery that becomes the foundation of Semprún's restored subjectivity after Buchenwald.

While it thematizes in a conscious manner that cognitive restoration is an ethical enterprise, Semprún's story of redress shows also that one cannot remain in the ethical, that one must go again into the world, which Semprún does by imposing upon himself the task of forgetting Buchenwald. As noted, León's solidarity is fundamentally ethical, and as such it attempts to assuage the deficiencies of the political (divisiveness on the Republican side; the civil war itself). Semprún's and León's narratives of loss are haunted by the remains and remembrances of paradise (ruinous Spain, the smoke of the crematorium). Remains of the past, but also remembrances of transience: to fight against them, León will elaborate her allegory of return and restoration of the ruins while Semprún finds in literature scripts for his narrative of loss and excess.

In the four cases a process of cognition, of reparation or reconstruction of self, ends up revealing the ethical and its complex interrelations with cognitive strategies and political positions. Furthermore, as act, as *saying,* their autobiographies foreground addressees to whom the autobiographers ultimately tell their lives, to whom they have chosen to respond. In this way the restitution of the self ends up becoming the acknowledgement of a debt. It is not by chance that these four autobiographers are exiles who reconstruct their selves in a contentious relationship with the nation and its history. Expelled from the homeland, or compelled to abandon it, they write their autobiographies outside of Spain, but also out of Spain and its past, looking past Spain, rejecting or redefining it, constructing alternative histories, building new communities, and accounting for themselves to predecessors of their choice.

The scarcity of autobiography in Spain has been a much-discussed issue. Recent research has unearthed a sizeable body of autobiographical writings published in modern Spain; however, this relative abundance should not mask the fact that few of them are compelling nor do they often veer from trite memoiristic models. The question should thus be rephrased, and, instead of wondering about the genre's scarcity, one should ask why the most searching autobiographies in nineteenth- and twentieth-century Spain have been written by exiles. Perhaps it is a matter of history, but it is also one of interlocutors. A matter of historical responsibility, in sum.

As explanation for the deficiencies of modern Spanish autobiography, it has been argued that Spaniards are not inclined to confess, are reserved about matters of private life, or are people of absolutes who lack psychological nuances. Although such generalizations may arguably contain some truth, those essentialist explanations are not an answer; they are just effects whose causes have to be found in the peculiar history of Spain. Instead of examining the question of Spanish autobiography in terms of the self and its presumed qualities, it has to be done questioning the history that has produced those subjectivities. And part and parcel of that historical determination of the Spanish self is the type of interlocutors that tradition imposes on Spanish autobiographers. Autobiography is always about the other. And in Spain it is also about the other's history and about another history.

Autobiography is closely linked to Spanish history throughout most of the nineteenth century and in many periods of the twentieth. This happened especially in the first years of the post-Franco era, which were marked by an enormous proliferation of memoirs of people who had been implicated in the regime and were attempting to justify or rectify the historical record. Toward the end of the nineteenth century, history ceases to be necessarily the frame of reference, and autobiographers begin to consider their lives instead in the context of a community of peers (most frequently the literary world). But even in this case it is also a matter of constructing a different version of the "national." Cases in point are two other exiles, Rosa Chacel and María Zambrano, who wrote their autobiographies to legitimize their right of inclusion in a literary community that traditionally had excluded women.

Spanish autobiographers frequently view autobiography as a matter of good or bad memory (the words *memory* and *oblivion* appear in many titles) or of unrestrained or controlled remembrance (depending on the writer's sense of privacy or respect), but they rarely view it as a conflictive memory. In Spain autobiography is often about a self that regulates how much it is convenient or appropriate to say; but it is usually a self assured of itself, rarely one that sees itself as a problem. Spanish autobiographers usually opt for a logic of memory or oblivion, of veracity or deceitfulness, of disclosure or reservation, but they rarely acknowledge the other's silent request for acknowledgement. Self-display or self-defense, but seldom an answer to the other's injunction, Spanish autobiography is infrequently conceived as responsibility, in the admirable way carried out by Blanco White and Goytisolo, by León and Semprún. And refusal to take responsibility entails the predominance of formulaic autobiographical narrative in which history is simply a background that at most must be retouched and protagonized by a self that refuses to explore what it has of incertitude and debt, by a self that does not take risks, that does not expose itself.

If the most compelling Spanish autobiographies have been written against the grain of the nation, against Spain's past and past Spains, the issue must be the national subject and its history. This is more pressing now than ever, when Spain has finally shaken off the perennial burden of backwardness, and it revels in its much-delayed incorporation into the community of modern nations. But becoming a modern country is not simply a matter of formal democracy and per capita income, advancements that cannot erase overnight a long past of racial and religious uniformity and intolerance, political authoritarianism, and overbearing social, educational, and cultural institutions. These are the very foundations of Spain as a political entity, they are the burdens of its history, the insidious and still lasting effects of its past, and they cannot be expunged with a mere wishful act of collective oblivion. This is why, in the time of the global village, Spain is still a village-nation.

Social coercion does not promote responsibility. Autobiography is not a matter of saying everything, of merciless judgments, or of humiliating disclosures. Although Goytisolo makes it a personal rule to unveil the most shameful acts or desires, his autobiographical writings are not provocative because of what he discloses, but for the act and the manner of disclosure. They command admirative attention not for what he exposes, but because of the act of self-exposure. Exposing the self is also a form of deposing it, of renouncing its otherwise precarious truth, of addressing the other. Conversely readers have to make themselves worthy of the legacy, have to respond for the other that subjects become the minute they submit themselves to the autobiographical. Writing autobiography, but also reading it, is an ethical engagement because what starts as an author's response ends up becoming the reader's responsibility.

NOTES

Chapter One: Before Reference

1. "Conditions and Limits of Autobiography," trans. James Olney, *Autobiography: Essays Theoretical and Critical,* ed. Olney (Princeton, N.J.: Princeton University Press, 1980), 44 (originally published in French in 1956). Among the critics who emphasized the importance of the present are Barrett J. Mandel, "Full of Life Now," and James Olney, "Some Versions of Memory/Some Versions of *Bios:* The Ontology of Autobiography"; both articles are included in *Autobiography,* ed. James Olney, 49–72 and 236–67, respectively. Critics are neither the only ones nor probably the first to stress the importance of the present in personal narratives. In his "autobiography" Roland Barthes avers to write "without my ever knowing whether it is about my past or my present that I am speaking." In *Roland Barthes by Roland Barthes,* trans. Richard Howard (New York: Hill and Wang, 1977), 142.

2. See, for instance, James Olney's *Metaphors of Self* (Princeton, N.J.; Princeton University Press, 1972); and also his "Autobiography and the Cultural Moment: A Thematic, Historical, and Bibliographical Introduction," *Autobiography: Essays Theoretical and Critical,* 24.

3. Paul John Eakin, *Fictions in Autobiography: Studies in the Art of Self-Invention* (Princeton, N.J.: Princeton University Press, 1985), 213. Eakin elaborates his theories in chapter 4, "Self-Invention in Autobiography: The Moment of Language," 181–278. In a more recent book, *Touching the World: Reference in Autobiography* (Princeton, N.J.: Princeton University Press, 1992), Eakin insists on the referential aspects of the genre, reacting against the proponents of autobiography as a pure textual construct without ties to reality. See especially his discussion of *Roland Barthes by Roland Barthes* (4–23).

4. Elizabeth Bruss, *Autobiographical Acts: The Changing Situation of a Literary Genre* (Baltimore, Md.: Johns Hopkins University Press, 1976); Philippe Lejeune, *On Autobiography,* ed. Paul John Eakin, trans. Katherine Leary (Minneapolis: University of Minnesota Press,

1989), 3–30. In "Full of Life Now," 54–55, Mandel also refers to the crucial role of the reader in relation to autobiographical "truth." In "Autobiography as De-Facement," *The Rhetoric of Romanticism* (New York: Columbia University Press, 1984), Paul de Man charged that critics such as Lejeune, who sustain that "the identity of autobiography is not only representational and cognitive but contractual, grounded not in tropes but in speech acts," convert the reader into a "policing power" or "transcendental authority" (71–72).

5. In "The [Female] Subject in Critical Venues: Poetics, Politics, Autobiographical Practices," *a/b: Auto/Biography Studies* 6.1 (1991): 109–30, Sidonie Smith offers an informative overview of feminist theories of autobiography.

6. Sidonie Smith, *A Poetics of Women's Autobiography: Marginality and the Fiction of Self-Representation* (Bloomington: Indiana University Press, 1987). An excellent discursive analysis of female personal writings can be found in Biddy Martin, "Lesbian Identity and Autobiographical Difference[s]," *Life/Lines: Theorizing Women's Autobiography,* ed. Bella Brodzki and Celeste Schenck (Ithaca, N.Y.: Cornell University Press, 1988), 77–103. Admonishing against the exclusive use of essentialist or totalizing categories such as gender differences or race in the elaboration of a personal or political definition of women, Martin explores the intricate and sometimes contradictory interaction among race, gender, sexual preference, community, the body, culture, and language in the construction of identity in lesbian autobiographies. Another subtle discursive analysis can be found in Felicity A. Nussbaum, "Eighteenth-Century Women's Autobiographical Commonplaces," *The Private Self: Theory and Practice of Women's Autobiographical Writings,* ed. Shari Benstock (Chapel Hill: University of North Carolina Press, 1988), 147–76, where she examines how Hester Thrale, writing in the eighteenth century, defines herself in her diaries after various discourses (law, medicine, education), creating a space for herself in which she accepts but simultaneously undermines the cultural bearings that shape her identity.

7. As a matter of fact, the "fictionality" of autobiography has at least three different meanings in Smith's book, given that she makes at least three different assertions in this respect: all autobiographies

are fictional; only those of pre–twentieth century women are; only those by "phallic women" are. This fictionality has strong connections with the issue of essentialism in characterizations of women's identities, a danger against which Smith warns but to which she is not immune in her theorization of female autobiography.

8. Obviously the issue of the nature of discursive attachments relates to the question of ideology, a matter broached in the chapter on María Teresa León.

9. Susan Stanford Friedman, "Women's Autobiographical Selves: Theory and Practice," *The Private Self: Theory and Practice of Women's Autobiographical Writings*, 34. In "Mothers, Displacement, and Language in the Autobiographies of Nathalie Sarraute and Christa Wolf," *Life/Lines: Theorizing Women's Autobiography*, 243–59, Bella Brodzki calls attention to "the theoretical and political consequences of idealizing the maternal as a category even as each of us negotiates her way within a specific and complex mother-daughter configuration" (247). A direct questioning of Sidonie Smith's poetics of women's autobiography, and of her use of Chodorow's ideas in particular, can be found in C. Margot Hennessy's examination of an autobiographical text written by a man, *Brothers and Keepers* by John Edgar Wideman. See her "Listening to the Secret Mother: Reading John Edgar Wideman's *Brothers and Keepers*," *American Women's Autobiography: Fea(s)ts of Memory*, ed. Margo Culley (Madison: University of Wisconsin Press, 1992), 295–321. For an acute assessment of the problems intrinsic to any elaboration of a poetics of difference, see also Shirley Neuman, "Autobiography: From Different Poetics to a Poetics of Differences," *Essays on Life Writing: From Genre to Critical Practice*, ed. Marlene Kadar (Toronto: University of Toronto Press, 1992), 213–30.

10. Doris Sommer, "Not Just a Personal Story: Women's *Testimonios* and the Plural Self," *Life/Lines: Theorizing Women's Autobiography*, 107–130.

11. Any examination of the rhetoricity and fictionality of autobiography, especially in its contemporary manifestations, has to deal also with issues of self-reflexivity. This matter has been broached by many

critics and writers of autobiography and is addressed here in the chapter on Juan Goytisolo.

12. Jacques Derrida, *Points . . . Interviews, 1974–1994,* ed. Elisabeth Weber, trans. Peggy Kamuf et al. (Stanford, Calif.: Stanford University Press, 1995), 219–220, 259, and 274.

13. In Richard Kearney, "Dialogue with Jacques Derrida," *Dialogues with Contemporary Continental Thinkers: The Phenomenological Heritage* (Manchester: Manchester University Press, 1984), 125. In "The Freudian Subject: From Politics to Ethics," *The Emotional Tie: Psychoanalysis, Mimesis, and Affect* (Stanford, Calif.: Stanford University Press, 1992), 15–35, Mikkel Borch-Jacobsen argues that "the intemperate use of the word *subject* by French psychoanalysts" (17), from where it spread to many variants of contemporary theory, began with Lacan. However, Louis Montrose makes a sound defense of the term on critical grounds: "*Subject,* both a grammatical and a political term, has come into widespread use not merely as a fashionable synonym for *the individual* but precisely as a means of emphasizing that individuals and the very concept of the individual are historically constituted in language and society." In "New Historicisms," *Redrawing the Boundaries,* ed. Stephen Greenblatt and Giles Gunn (New York: Modern Language Association, 1992), 412–13.

14. The quotes are Gilles Deleuze's, and they are from his explanations of Foucault's ideas in *Negotiations: 1972–1990,* trans. Martin Joughin (New York: Columbia University Press, 1995), 92, and from *Foucault,* trans. Seán Hand (Minneapolis: University of Minnesota Press, 1988), 101.

15. See Michel Foucault, "Technologies of the Self," *Technologies of the Self,* ed. Luther H. Martin et al. (Amherst: University of Massachusetts Press, 1988), 21–22; *The Care of the Self,* trans. Robert Hurley (New York: Vintage, 1988), 43–61, vol. 3 of *The History of Sexuality;* and *The Use of Pleasure,* trans. Robert Hurley (New York: Vintage, 1990), 92, vol. 2 of *The History of Sexuality.* Consequently for Foucault "ethics is a practice; ethos is a manner of being." In "Politics and Ethics: An Interview," *The Foucault Reader,* ed. Paul Rabinow (New York: Pantheon, 1984), 377.

16. "On the Genealogy of Ethics: An Overview of Work in Progress," *The Foucault Reader,* 369.

17. Michel Foucault, "Technologies of the Self," 27.

18. Both Foucault and Levinas are indebted to Blanchot's formulation of the outside, whose folding over itself originates the subject in Foucault's formulation, while Levinas sees the apparition of the subject as an overcoming of the "there is" ("*il y a*"), which he characterizes as the "nonsense," "the phenomenon of impersonal life," a rumbling that is "[n]either nothingness nor being" and that he associates with what Blanchot denominates the "neutral," the "outside," or the "disaster." See Levinas, *Ethics and Infinity: Conversations with Philippe Nemo,* trans. Richard A. Cohen (Pittsburgh: Duquesne University Press, 1985), 47–52.

19. Richard Kearney, "Dialogue with Emmanuel Levinas," *Dialogues with Contemporary Continental Thinkers: The Phenomen-ological Heritage,* 65. Morality, however, "is ultimately founded on an ethical responsibility towards the other" (65), adds Levinas. In *The Seminar of Jacques Lacan. Book 7: The Ethics of Psychoanalysis 1959– 1960,* ed. Jacques-Alain Miller, trans. Dennis Porter (New York: Norton, 1992), Lacan also posits a similar difference between what he calls "the service of goods" and true ethics, which he associates with an injunction to forget the search for self-knowledge and to act instead in conformity with one's desire.

20. "God and Philosophy," *The Levinas Reader,* ed. Seán Hand, trans. Richard A. Cohen and Alphonso Lingis (Oxford: Basil Blackwell, 1989), 179.

21. "Outside the Subject," *Outside the Subject,* trans. Michael B. Smith (London: Athlone Press, 1993), 158.

22. *Ethics and Infinity,* 60.

23. Jacques Derrida, "Violence and Metaphysics: An Essay on the Thought of Emmanuel Levinas," *Writing and Difference,* trans. Alan Bass (Chicago: University of Chicago Press, 1978), 103.

24. Emmanuel Levinas, "Signature," *Difficult Freedom: Essays on Judaism,* trans. Seán Hand (Baltimore, Md.: Johns Hopkins University Press, 1990), 293. Some, but not all, translators and critics of Levinas capitalize the word *other,* and quotations herein accurately reflect the original source.

25. *Otherwise Than Being or Beyond Essence,* trans. Alphonso Lingis (The Hague: Martinus Nijhoff, 1981). The quotes are from pages 49, 53, 43, and 50.

26. Ibid., 50.

27. "Responsibility does not come from fraternity, but fraternity denotes responsibility for another, antecedent to my freedom" ("God and Philosophy," 181). In the wake of Levinas, Derrida will obsessively return to an unremitting reconsideration of the other, responsibility, and the promise. Echoing Levinas's view of ontology and epistemology as philosophies of violence, Derrida speaks of self-identity as violence to the other, since the subject's traditional determinations as property, appropriation, and self-presence depend on an opposition to the other. In the same vein Derrida defends the affirmative nature of deconstruction as "a positive response to an alterity which necessarily calls, summons or motivates it." See Richard Kearney, "Dialogue with Jacques Derrida," 117 and 118.

28. *Otherwise Than Being,* 153.

29. "God and Philosophy," 180.

30. Levinas's ideas went through extensive reformulations during his life—in an effort to expunge them of any psychologism or any phenomenological intentionality—and reached their most elaborated expression in *Otherwise Than Being.* An extremely condensed summary of his life and thought can be found in "Signature." The bibliography on Levinas has already reached considerable proportions. For a listing of Levinas's works, consult *The Levinas Reader,* 301–6. A good bibliography on Levinas can be found in John Llewelyn, *Emmanuel Levinas: The Genealogy of Ethics* (New York: Routledge, 1995), 229–32. Besides Llewelyn's book, other useful, recent works are Simon Critchley, *The Ethics of Deconstruction: Derrida and Levinas* (Cambridge, Mass.: Blackwell, 1992), and the collective books, *Face to Face with Levinas,* ed. Richard A. Cohen (Albany, State University of New York Press, 1986); *The Provocation of Levinas: Rethinking the Other,* ed. Robert Bernasconi and David Wood (New York: Routledge, 1988); *Re-Reading Levinas,* ed. Robert Bernasconi and Simon Critchley (Bloomington: Indiana University Press, 1991); and *Ethics as First Philosophy,* ed. Adriaan T. Peperzak (New York: Routledge, 1995).

31. Jacques Derrida, "Violence and Metaphysics," 147 and 148. Two important clarifications are called for in this regard. Although for Levinas the subject originates before and beyond history, that does not imply that time, morality, and the social are irrelevant for him. While emphasizing the domain of ethics at the expense of morality, he does not ignore the latter nor consider it irrelevant. On the other hand, Derrida's work on Levinas after "Violence and Metaphysis" is more tempered in its criticism, and in any case a good part of Derrida's writings are permeated by, and respond to, Levinas's formulations. See Derrida's "At this very moment in this work here I am," *Re-Reading Levinas,* 11–48, and his funeral oration for Levinas, "Adieu," *Critical Inquiry* 23 (Autumn 1996): 1–10.

32. Richard Kearney, "Dialogue with Emmanuel Levinas," 57–58,

33. *Otherwise Than Being,* 157, 158.

34. Ibid., 159.

35. Some areas of cultural theory make frequent reference to the concept of the other. There are two important differences between those formulations of the other and Levinas's: for Levinas the other is an ethical priority that precedes any subject, and therefore for him alterity is a given in any cultural or political context; also, for him the other and the self are inextricably tied. On the other hand, the other in cultural theory is a political construct that could be replaced with the word *different.* To cite one specific case, the postcolonial other is often seen as forming a rigid dichotomy with its opposite, as happens in Gayatri Chakravorty Spivak's article "Can the Subaltern Speak?" *Marxism and the Interpretation of Culture,* ed. Cary Nelson and Lawrence Grossberg (Urbana: University of Illinois Press, 1988), 271–313. In *The Rhetoric of English India* (Chicago: University of Chicago Press, 1992), Sara Suleri offers a sound critique of authors such as Spivak, Bhabha, and JanMohamed, whose concepts of alterity are informed by what she calls a static "rhetoric of binarism" that eschews the "complicity and guilt" of the colonized. The importance of Levinas's other resides precisely in its ethical dimension. Asked if the Palestinian is the other of the Israeli, Levinas logically responds: "My definition of the other is completely different" ("Ethics and Politics," trans. Jonathan Romney, *The Levinas Reader,* 294).

36. See Mikkel Borch-Jacobsen, "The Freudian Subject: From Politics to Ethics." The quotes are from pages 16 and 34.

37. Another consequential manifestation of the triangular configuration is the well-known explanation of desire's structure proposed by René Girard, in Lacan's wake, in several works, starting with *Deceit, Desire and the Novel* (Baltimore, Md.: Johns Hopkins University Press, 1965).

38. See his *Lacan: The Absolute Master,* trans. Douglas Brick (Stanford, Calif.: Stanford University Press, 1991), especially chapter 2, "The Statue Man." In a Lacanian vein, Kaja Silverman, *Male Subjectivity at the Margins* (New York: Routledge, 1992) also begins by proposing a primary force—"fantasy and imaginary 'captation'"—through which later operate the ideological facilitations that promote our access to what she calls the "dominant fiction," which she sees as constituted by the symbolic order and the mode of production. While Lacan avoids untheorizable affection, Silverman ends up by arguing that "even the earliest and the most decisive of the subject's identifications [the Lacanian *moi*] may be ideologically determined" (22), thus implausibly giving an absolute precedence to the ideological.

39. Martin Jay, "The Ethics of Blindness and the Postmodern Sublime: Levinas and Lyotard," *Downcast Eyes: The Denigration of Vision in Twentieth-Century French Thought* (Berkeley: University of California Press, 1993), 543–86. Jay offers an excellent contextualization of Levinas's thought in reference to Jewish thought and Western philosophy, especially its contemporary French manifestations. For a useful elucidation of the increasing indebtedness of Lyotard's thought to Levinas, see 573–94.

40. Gilles Deleuze and Félix Guattari, *A Thousand Plateaus: Capitalism and Schizophrenia,* trans. Brian Massumi (Minneapolis: University of Minnesota Press, 1994). The quotes are from pages 342, 257, and 256.

41. G. Deleuze, *Negotiations,* 6.

42. Michel Foucault, "The Subject and Power," *Critical Inquiry* 8 (Summer 1982): 789.

43. Ibid., 789.

44. *A Thousand Plateaus,* 79.

45. *Negotiations,* 88.

46. See, for instance, Sylvia Molloy, *At Face Value: Autobiographical Writing in Spanish America* (Cambridge: Cambridge University Press, 1991), who studies the complex ways in which Spanish American autobiographers appropriate the European literary canon for their autobiographical narratives.

47. *Negotiations,* 95.

48. *A Thousand Plateaus,* 203.

49. See *Otherwise Than Being,* 37–51 and 153.

50. Ibid., 47 and 153.

51. "God and Philosophy," 183.

52. *Otherwise Than Being,* 48. Steven G. Crowell, "Dialogue and Text: Re-marking the Difference," *The Interpretation of Dialogue,* ed. Tullio Maranhão (Chicago: University of Chicago Press, 1990), 338–60, explains the different conceptions of dialogue maintained by Gadamer, Derrida, and Levinas. Assuming that reading follows the question-and-answer model of dialogue, Gadamer views dialogue ontologically, as a symmetrical encounter between opposing parties that are guided by the referent in their movement toward truth. Derrida, for his part, views reading not as dialogue but as a *writing* whose referential dimension is problematic, while Levinas conceives dialogue not in ontological terms, but as an ethical, asymmetrical relationship with the other.

53. *Otherwise Than Being,* 155.

54. There is still another linguistic dimension in autobiographical reference. It manifests itself as a conflict, stressed by Paul de Man, between the referential and the performative, which leads him to question the cognitive dimension of autobiography and therefore its very existence as a genre. This is taken up later.

55. "Autobiography as De-Facement," 69.

56. Darío Villanueva suggests a way out of the conflict between *referentiality* and *fictionality* in autobiography by proposing that the

genre's fundamental rhetorical figure is that of paradox. In "Realidad y ficción: la paradoja de la autobiografía," *Escritura autobiográfica: actas del II Seminario Internacional del Instituto de Semiótica Literaria y Textual,* ed. José Romera et al. (Madrid: Visor, 1993), 15–31.

57. "Autobiography as De-Facement," 80 and 81.

58. A number of critics have insisted, in different ways, on a presumedly "fictive" nature of the autobiographical self. In "Fictions of the Self: The End of Autobiography," *Autobiography: Essays Theoretical and Critical,* ed. James Olney (Princeton, N.J.: Princeton University Press, 1980), 321–42, Michael Sprinker writes about the fictive nature of the autobiographical self, which is constituted by a discourse that emanates from a changing and ungraspable unconscious that the subject never controls. Like de Man, Sprinker remains in the aporetic terrain of the cognitive. Stressing another form of linguistic disappropiation, Jeffrey Melhman tries to unveil in autobiographical texts "a persistent textual organization . . . whose coherence throws into jeopardy the apparent intentions of the author and expropriates him in an intertextual circuit of relations." In *A Structural Study of Autobiography* (Ithaca, N.Y.: Cornell University Press, 1974), 14. Arguing that an autobiographical "life" is nothing more than a narrative created with communal signs, in "'Ma Vie' comme effet de discours," *La Licorne* 14 (1988): 161–77, Herman Parret maintains that the autobiographical self is an effect, a simulacra, and its uniqueness just an illusion.

59. *A Thousand Plateaus,* 11 and 4.

60. Ernesto Laclau and Chantal Mouffe, *Hegemony and Socialist Strategy: Towards a Radical Democratic Politics* (London: Verso, 1993), 108. I would suggest that the materiality of discourses is possible due to their "affective" import. Although the affective would not find a direct "expression," its existence and effects can be inferred through the peculiar relationships—attachments, rejections, dissensions, etc.—between the subject and the discourses that make up its autobiographical writings.

61. Laclau and Mouffe argue that from the point of view of discourse as a constitutive force that does away with the dichotomy thought/reality, rhetorical figures can no longer be conceived as purely mental categories: "Synonymy, metonymy, metaphor are not forms of

thought that add a second sense to a primary, constitutive literality of social relations; instead, they are part of the primary terrain itself in which the social is constituted" (110).

62. Paul de Man, *Allegories of Reading: Figural Language in Rousseau, Nietzsche, Rilke, and Proust* (New Haven, Conn.: Yale University Press, 1979), 301 and 298.

63. For a different commentary on de Man's texts on autobiography see Gregory S. Jay, "Freud: The Death of Autobiography," *Genre* 19 (Summer 1986): 118–20.

64. Quintilian, *Institutio Oratoria*, trans. H. E. Butler, vol. 2 (Cambridge: Harvard University Press, 1986), 9. 2. 30–31.

65. See Heinrich Lausberg, *Handbuch der Literarischen Rhetorik,* 2d ed. (München: Max Hueber Verlag, 1973) 1: #820 and #826, pp. 407 and 411.

66. Quintilian, 9. 2. 58, defines "ethopoeia" as "[t]he imitation of other persons' characteristics" and adds that others prefer to call it "mimesis."

67. See Lausberg #826. This is the conception of prosopopeia that dominates in modern times through the influence of rhetoricians such as Fontanier, whose classical definition appears in *Les figures du discours* (1830), intro. Gérard Genette (Paris: Flammarion, 1977), 404: "mettre en quelque sorte en scène, les absens, les morts, les êtres surnaturels, ou même les êtres inanimés; à les faire agir, parler, répondre . . ." (to bring to the fore absent, dead, supernatural or even inanimate people; to make them act, talk, answer . . .). Following Fontanier, Riffaterre offers an even broader definition: "Prosopopeia in most cases merely lends a voice to a voiceless always, or now silent, entity by a mere convention." In Michael Riffaterre, "Prosopopeia," *The Lessons of Paul de Man,* ed. Peter Brooks et al., *Yale French Studies* 69, special issue (1985): 107–108.

68. Quintilian, 9. 2. 38, p. 397; see also Lausberg, 2: #762.

69. In "History as Gesture; or, The Scandal of History," *Consequences of Theory,* ed. Jonathan Arac and Barbara Johnson (Baltimore, Md.: Johns Hopkins University Press, 1991), Lynn Hunt makes a case for history as an ethicopolitical practice, stressing the dialogical

character of history writing and proposing a view of reference and undecidability close to the ones suggested here: "History . . . is not a repository of facts or anecdotes because it has no ontological status whatsoever. . . . History is better defined as an ongoing tension between stories that have been told and stories that might be told. In this sense, it is more useful to think of history as an ethical and political practice than as an epistemology with a clear ontological status. On the other hand, a concept of a history that is "out there" does inform most historians' work and for good reason: it stands as a constant reminder that we cannot get at the "real" truth and yet that we must always continue to try to do so" (102–3).

70. In *Apology to Apostrophe: Autobiography and the Rhetoric of Self-Understanding in Spain* (Durham, N.C.: Duke University Press, 1992), James D. Fernández views apostrophe as a determining figure in nineteenth-century Spanish autobiography. Apostrophe, he suggests, is used by some autobiographers who, choosing to stay above historical contingencies, invoke a transcendental addressee who knows the "truth."

71. In *La confesión: género literario* (Barcelona: Mondadori, 1988; originally published in 1941), María Zambrano proposes some suggestive ideas on autobiography as confession. The chapter on María Teresa León addresses Zambrano's views.

72. *The Ear of the Other,* ed. Christie McDonald, trans. Peggy Kamuf (Lincoln: University of Nebraska Press, 1988), 51. Derrida is careful to distinguish the signature from the proper name. The signature, he argues, "is not only a word or a proper name at the end of a text, but the operation as a whole, the whole of the active interpretation" (52). In another place he characterizes the proper name as a "singular set of marks, traits, appellations by means of which someone can identify him- or herself, call him- or herself, or still yet be called, without having totally chosen or determined them him- or herself. . . . It is never certain that this set gathers itself together . . ." (*Points,* 222).

73. In *The Ear of the Other* 50–51, Derrida stresses that the signature takes place when the other receives the message, hears it, and understands it. One could add that such responsibility goes permanently or partially unfulfilled, entrusting the signing of autobiography to a

permanent deferral. See Robert Smith, *Derrida and Autobiography* (Cambridge: Cambridge University Press, 1995), for an informed, although rambling and unfocused, presentation of the importance of the other in Derrida's understanding of autobiography, with attention to Levinas's imprint on Derrida's views on alterity.

74. *Confessions,* trans. R. S. Pine-Coffin (Harmondsworth, U.K.: Penguin, 1961), Book 10, no.3, p. 208. At the beginning of that book, St. Augustine ponders the function and workings of autobiography, and, in natural accordance with this inquiry, the rest of the book is devoted to an examination of the faculty of memory.

75. Philippe Lejeune, *On Autobiography,* 48.

76. Jean-Jacques Rousseau, *The Confessions,* ed. Christopher Kelly et al., trans. Christopher Kelly (Hanover, N.H.: University Press of New England, 1995), vol. 5 of *The Collected Writings of Rousseau,* 235.

77. Ibid., 147. The role of the addressees becomes complicated when Rousseau manifests, in a way similar to Augustine's, that only God can be the ultimate judge of his life.

78. *Rousseau Judge of Jean-Jacques: Dialogues,* ed. Roger D. Masters and Christopher Kelly, trans. Judith R. Bush et al. (Hanover, N.H.: University Press of New England, 1990), vol. 1 of *The Collected Writings of Rousseau,* 6.

79. From its very beginnings, then, modern autobiography shows to be a very unstable genre, contrary to Sidonie Smith's clear-cut understanding of it as one of the "West's master discourses" that, according to her, would represent an "indivisible," "unitary," "essential self." See the first chapter of her *Subjectivity, Identity, and the Body: Women's Autobiographical Practices in the Twentieth Century* (Bloomington: Indiana University Press, 1993). Undeniably certain discourses try to impose that vision of the self, but as Sidonie Smith later readily admits, autobiography is never dominated solely by any of those discourses (21), nor is it as inflexible a genre as appears in Smith's initial reification of it (61). Besides, she privileges the twentieth-century manifestations of the genre as sites of multiplicity, contestation, and rupture, but I believe that autobiography clearly shows itself to be discursively conflictual and narratively unstable already in its first modern manifestations in the eighteenth century, as evinced not only by Rousseau's

Confessions but also by an even earlier Spanish autobiographical work, Torres Villarroel's *Vida* (1743–1758).

80. In *The Facts: A Novelist's Autobiography* (New York: Farrar, Straus, 1988), one of the most lucid and fascinating autobiographical accounts of our time, Philip Roth foregrounds some of the themes being discussed in this study. Roth expresses that "the person I've intended to make myself visible to here has been myself, primarily" (4) but begins his narrative, nevertheless, with a letter directed to Zuckerman, one of his fictional characters, thus pointing to autobiography as an other-directed, dialogical act that calls for a response, which here takes the form of the letter by Zuckerman that closes the book but simultaneously leaves it open to new rejoinders. At the same time, Roth calls attention to another ethical strand, the Foucaultian care of the self, when he explains that his book originated in the need "to recover what I had lost" during a period of serious depression, which impels him to write: "Here, so as to fall back into my former life, to retrieve my vitality, to transform myself into *myself,* I began rendering experience untransformed" (5). Although one can easily be skeptical about Roth's vocabulary of self-knowledge, his attempt at re-(dis)covery is undeniably "truthful" as an ethical act. Two other essential components of *The Facts,* and of self-writing in general, that are dealt with in this book are autobiography's inbuilt ironic self-consciousness and the role of "trauma" in life writing.

81. "Circumfession," in Geoffrey Bennington and Jacques Derrida, *Jacques Derrida,* trans. Geoffrey Bennington (Chicago: University of Chicago Press, 1993), 25 and 48–49.

82. In *Imagined Communities: Reflections on the Origin and Spread of Nationalism,* 2d ed. (London: Verso, 1991), Benedict Anderson defines the nation as an "imagined political community" but warns that "imagining" is not a "fiction" or a "falsity," but a creation (6). The same distinction can be applied to autobiography, a construction that is always provisional but that should not be measured in cognitive terms of truth or falsity. Besides, its ethical dimension (autobiography's main import) is always true.

83. Ernesto Laclau, "Deconstruction, Pragmatism, Hegemony," *Deconstruction and Pragmatism,* ed. Chantal Mouffe (New York: Routledge, 1996), 52. Laclau's brilliant argument about deconstruction's

political import is accompanied, however, by a faulty understanding of Levinasian ethics, which he wrongfully takes as "a universal principle that precedes and governs any decision" (53). While the ethics proposed by Levinas is universal, the apparition of the "third," that is, of politics, opens a whole new game by introducing the freedom not to heed the ethical injunctions of the other, and therefore it is not correct to say that ethics governs any decision.

84. Graham Greene, *A Sort of Life* (New York: Simon & Schuster, 1971), 11–12.

85. Levinas, *Ethics and Infinity*, 50.

Chapter Two: Blanco White

1. Kant, "What Is Enlightenment?" *On History,* ed. and trans. Lewis White Beck (New York: Macmillan, 1963), 3; Michel Foucault, "What Is Enlightenment?" trans. Catherine Porter, *The Foucault Reader,* ed. Paul Rabinow (New York: Pantheon, 1984), 35. In coincidence with Blanco White, Kant concentrates on religious matters. Blanco will echo Kant's concept of enlightenment when he asserts that, individually and collectively, people still are children. See *The Life of the Rev. Joseph Blanco White, Written by Himself; with Portions of His Correspondence,* ed. John Hamilton Thom, 3 vols. (London: John Chapman, 1845), 3: 78.

2. Marcelino Menéndez Pelayo, *Historia de los heterodoxos españoles,* vol. 2, 4th ed. (Madrid: BAC, 1987), 791. All translations of Menéndez Pelayo are mine. For details of Blanco's life, see Martin Murphy's well-informed and balanced biography, *Blanco White: Self-Banished Spaniard* (New Haven, Conn.: Yale University Press, 1989).

3. *The Life of the Rev. Joseph Blanco White* 1: 242. A selection of his journals was included in *The Life of the Rev. Joseph Blanco White* by the editor.

4. *Letters from Spain* was published in 1822 as a series of thirteen letters in which a fictional narrator, Leucadio Doblado, a Spaniard who "has resided many years in England" (1), returns to his country to write an account of the customs, opinions, and contemporary events of Spain. Already in 1811 Robert Southey had suggested that

he write a depiction of the Seville of his youth in a series of letters, but not until 1816, when Lady Holland persuaded him to resume that project, did he write a draft that he later used for *Letters of Spain,* a work that the editor of the *New Monthly Magazine* commissioned and published serially in 1821–1822, before it appeared as a book in 1822. For the details concerning the gestation of this work, see Murphy 102, 114 and 247. References to *Letters* are from its second edition, revised and corrected by Blanco White (London: Henry Colburn, 1825). In "Letter III" (52), the narrator, Doblado, writes that he has befriended a priest from Seville who confides to him his doubts concerning Catholicism, in a narrative entitled "A Few Facts Connected with the Formation of the Intellectual and Moral Character of a Spanish Clergyman." That narrative, which takes up most of that letter (58–118), is a disguised autobiography of Blanco White, in which he emphasizes the effects that institutions such as universities and the clerical establishment have on the formation of a young mind. In the second edition Blanco added a short preface in which he confesses that "Doblado and his inseparable friend, the Spanish clergyman, are but one and the same person; whose origin, education, feelings, and early turn of thinking, have been made an introduction to the personal observations on his country" (iv). The name Leucadio Doblado is a take on "Blanco White," based on the Greek root of Leucadio ("Blanco") and the Spanish "double" (Doblado).

5. "Despedida" appeared in *Variedades ó Mensagero de Londres* 2 (October 1, 1825), 299–311. He uses the word *tyranny*—which obviously had deep resonances in Spanish America at that moment—three times (306, 307 twice) in this brief piece to characterize the church's power. In his writings in English, Blanco will continue to use the word *tyranny* in reference to religion, but he will also favor the expression *mental slavery,* a term more attuned to the British liberal drive to abolish slavery, a cause to which Blanco contributed an informed pamphlet commissioned in 1814 by the African Association, "Bosquejo del comercio de esclavos" ("A Sketch of the Slave Commerce"; Murphy 91–92). Besides being considerably shorter, "Despedida," which he wrote when he decided to leave his post as editor of *Variedades,* a magazine that he directed between 1823 and 1825, published in London and intended for the Spanish American countries, is even more general and much less personal than the priest's story in *Letters from Spain.*

6. Quoted from the U.S. edition of *Practical and Internal Evidence* (Cambridge, Mass.: Manson and Grant, 1835), which was based on the 2d English edition (1826).

7. *The Examination of Blanco by White, Concerning His Religious Notions and Other Subjects Connected with Them*, ed. Angel G. Loureiro, *Revista de Estudios Hispánicos* 33.1 (1999): 3–40. Blanco wrote *The Examination of Blanco by White* as the "best means to unravel my ideas on the subject of Religion" and to reach some peace of mind (*The Life of the Rev. Joseph Blanco White* 1: 354–55). Murphy finds *The Examination of Blanco by White* "free of the self-justificatory tone which mars the later apologias" (107).

8. Already in *Letters from Spain* he attributed the Catholic Church's influence to its mischievous manipulation of superstition and enthusiasm at the expense of reason: "no genuine persuasion exists upon unearthly subjects, without the cooperation of the imaginative faculty. Hence the powerful effects of the splendid and striking system of worship adopted by the Roman church" (*Letters* 107). His denunciation— which will reach obsessive dimensions at the end of his life—of the role of the imagination in the church's baneful influence frequently fixes upon the case of his mother, whose "sensibility beyond description" and lack "of a rational and enlightened religion and moral education" made her easy prey to the "blind zeal and enthusiasm" (*Examination* 9) that the Catholic Church both produced and supported. He usually portrays his mother as the reproducer, in the bosom of the family, of the church's ideological manipulation of the feelings.

9. His years of atheism would haunt Blanco's figure even after his death. See W. E. Gladstone, "Blanco White," *Gleanings of Past Years, 1845–76* (London: John Murray, 1879), 48.

10. Around 1835 he writes in *The Life of the Rev. Joseph Blanco White* that in *The Examination of Blanco by White* he cultivated an exaggerated humility and represented himself as "a monster of iniquity," when in reality "my deviations from the path of strict duty were neither numerous, nor uncommon" (*The Life of the Rev. Joseph Blanco White* 1: 331). At this point in his life, he makes the Catholic Church responsible as well for that excessive humility, which he calls asceticism. Also, at least since the time he wrote *Letters from Spain*, he attributes the "first taste of remorse" to the effects of confession (*Letters* 66).

11. Some of his pieces for *Variedades* dealt with Spanish American politics, mainly to warn the newly independent countries to avoid the traps of Spanish intolerance.

12. *Blanco White,* 131. Murphy also asserts that Blanco gained his place at Oxford thanks to his opposition to Catholic emancipation (138, 147).

13. *The Life of the Rev. Joseph Blanco White* 1: 493–96. For Blanco's political ideas—especially in reference to Spain, but also in relation to the fight for independence in Spanish America—see André Pons, *Blanco White et la crise du monde hispanique, 1808–1816* (Paris: Université de Paris III-Sorbonne Nouvelle, Etudes Hispano-Americaines, 1990), 4 vols. Pons characterizes Blanco's political output as editor and writer for *El Español* as honest and sincere in its handling of the facts although debatable in its opinions (see 1: 316). Blanco supported Spanish American independence, but he thought it premature and wanted independent America to respect the legitimate interests of the Spanish crown. It could also be argued that in his attempt to disseminate the ideas and institutions of English liberalism through Spain and Spanish America with his work in *El Español* he might have been acting, whether he knew it or not, as the mouthpiece of British interests. Murphy proves that Blanco actually worked for the Foreign Office between 1811 and 1814, mainly doing "translations or abstracts of the Spanish American press," and he also points out that Blanco seemed to have "forgotten" the extent of his involvement at the time he wrote *The Life of the Rev. Joseph Blanco White* (84). Overall Blanco's politics were idealistic and were presided by his faith in reason.

14. The selection culled by Thom from Blanco's journals and letters takes part of the first volume of *The Life of the Rev. Joseph Blanco White* and the entirety of the other two. The final selection is a letter, addressed to William E. Channing (1780–1842), the well-known leader of the Unitarians in the United States, in which Blanco offers an account of the evolution of religious thought that is permeated by an enlightened faith in truth's final victory (*The Life of the Rev. Joseph Blanco White* 3: 307–08). Martin Murphy rightly observes that the journal extracts and the selected correspondence concentrate above all in the last nine years of his life (the entire last two volumes are devoted to that period, 1833–1841), which would explain the predominance of

theological and Unitarian topics. Since Thom did not know Spanish, he had to exclude all of Blanco's correspondence in that language, omitting therefore the family letters—especially those to and from his brother Fernando—as well as those exchanged with close friends, many of them dealing with political and literary subjects. In general, concludes Martin, the playful and affective facets of Blanco's character have been left out, and for that reason Blanco's image appears excessively one-sided (Murphy 195). It could be argued, however, that Thom's selections are congruent with Blanco's own emphasis in the first two parts of *The Life of the Rev. Joseph Blanco White*—and, for that matter, in all his autobiographical writings—on religious topics at the expense of almost any other subject.

15. *The Life of the Rev. Joseph Blanco White* was written in English and was not intended for publication until after Blanco's death.

16. He reread, corrected, and added frequent clarifying notes to the narrative throughout the years, the last note being from January 8, 1841, just a few months before his death: "Deprived of the use of my legs, these three years, and now cruelly tormented by a most severe rheumatism, I have nevertheless made an effort to read the preceding manuscript for the last time, to assure myself that nothing in it is incorrect in point of fact, and that nothing can be painful to any of my friends" (*The Life of the Rev. Joseph Blanco White* 1: 234–35, note).

17. He began "A Sketch" in Dublin in 1834, shortly before moving to Liverpool, where he finished it in 1836. Although a heading under the title "A Sketch" indicates that it covers from 1814 to 1818, in fact it reaches until the end of 1823.

18. Blanco explains that his "sufferings" forced him to interrupt "A Sketch" in 1836, and he wrote "Letter to . . . Thom" (included in *The Life of the Rev. Joseph Blanco White* 3: 125–161) in August of 1839 as a complement to "A Sketch" (see *The Life of the Rev. Joseph Blanco White* 1: 406). In "Letter to . . . Thom," Blanco picked up the narrative of his life in 1826, right where he had left it in "Narrative of the Events of His Life," reaching until 1929, when his backing of Peel (the member of Parliament for Oxford University, who was now in favor of Catholic emancipation) began to alienate him from many of his friends at Oxford, among them Newman, and made his stay at Oriel increasingly unpleasant. The gist of this letter, however, does not bear on the facts

of his life but on his opinions, and, after only eight pages of narrative, Blanco writes: "But enough of external matters: let us come to the workings of my mind in regard to religious subjects during that period" (3: 133). Yet, the presentation of the ideas he professed at such a crucial time in his life—when his doubts about the Church of England were mounting—leads him ineluctably from a history of his ideas to an exposition of his notions at the time of writing, making this work bear more on his thinking in the late thirties than in the mid-twenties. As a matter of fact, this 1839 statement is the most sustained commentary that we have of his final ideas concerning religious and philosophical issues.

19. Benito Feijoo, *Teatro crítico universal,* ed. Agustín Millares Carlo (Madrid: Espasa-Calpe, 1968), 1: 81. For Blanco's devotion towards Feijoo see Lucienne Domergue, "Feijoo y Blanco White (Homenaje de un 'hereje' al Padre Maestro)," *II Simposio sobre el Padre Feijoo y su Siglo* (Oviedo, Spain: Universidad de Oviedo, 1983), 333–48.

20. For the "readings" of Blanco White, see James D. Fernández's perceptive analysis in *Apology to Apostrophe: Autobiography and the Rhetoric of Self-Representation in Spain* (Durham, N.C.: Duke University Press, 1992), 57–87.

21. The narrative of his "real" intellectual and moral education continues after his years of formation, and includes his influential encounters in Salamanca with the poet and "devout Deist" Meléndez Valdés (1754–1817) and Bishop Antonio Tavira, hater of "gross superstition," and "suspected of *Jansenism,* because he was . . . a reformer" (1: 127, 128).

22. All references to Blanco's description of spiritual exercises are taken from *The Life of the Rev. Joseph Blanco White* 1: 42–49.

23. Linda H. Peterson, *Victorian Autobiography: The Tradition of Self-Interpretation* (New Haven, Conn.: Yale University Press, 1986), 1–28, 49, 93–119. Like Scott, Newman rejected spiritual autobiography's enthusiastic tones, but he went still further, discarding a strict typological interpretation—a hermeneutical model that sees the figures of the Old Testament as patterns of the New, and considers both as models for future Christian lives. Blanco goes one better, showing strong displeasure for the merciless God of the Old Testament, and denying Christ's divine origins, preferring to see him instead as a human

witness and example of the true spirit of Christianity. As I will later explain, Blanco will fashion the last image of his self after the figure of Christ.

24. Peterson, 99, 98 and 16.

25. As spiritual autobiographers often do, Blanco will frequently refer to his years under Catholicism as a period of "bondage."

26. Peterson, 117–19.

27. Jonathan Loesberg, *Fictions of Consciousness: Mill, Newman, and the Reading of Victorian Prose* (New Brunswick, N.J.: Rutgers University Press, 1986), 1, 14, 3, 92.

28. For Blanco's constant "re-reading" of himself, see Fernández, *Apology to Apostrophe.*

29. Blanco justifies writing the "Sketch" because in his opinion the narrative of his life has the defect of not offering an evolution of his ideas, when, he argues, for his story to be useful to others, they have to know "the intellectual workings of a man who has loved truth above all things" (*The Life of the Rev. Joseph Blanco White* 1: 239). However, in the previous "Narrative of his Life in England" he indicates that he had dealt with the history of his mind so fully in other works that he is going to say little about it: "The workings of my mind, my struggle, my waverings. . ., have all been recorded in my private Journals" (1: 211).

30. This is how he characterizes the road that led him to challenge the theory of inspiration: "Long, morally dangerous, and intellectually laborious has been the process by which I have arrived at this conclusion" (1: 282).

31. In his view, theological thinking is a form of superstition, and emotional religious behavior is a form of enthusiasm. For him, both superstition and enthusiasm emanate from the faculty of the imagination, and their manifestation indicates the prevalence of the imagination over what he calls reason or the understanding.

32. In the "Letter to . . . Thom" he describes the "temper and constitution" of his soul as an "apparent contradiction," by pointing out "how susceptible I am of religious sympathy, and how unconquerable is my love of rational conviction. Here you see at once the fountainhead of all my sufferings through life" (3: 137).

33. Blanco considers the theory of the Bible's divine inspiration, which he sees as a form of superstition that makes the Bible into a responsive Oracle (1: 245), as analogous to Roman Catholic infallibility (1: 274).

34. In a letter dated December 15, 1940, he writes: "The Phantoms that haunted my soul have completely vanished" (3: 225). In the same year he also wrote: "As soon . . . as I gave full freedom to my judgement, and arrived at the conclusion that Christianity is not Orthodoxy . . ., my soul found itself in perfect repose" (3: 451).

35. True Christianity "lies perfect under the monstrous excrescence which now surrounds it—in Creeds, Articles, and Catechisms" (3: 156).

36. Blanco White finds in this quote from Marcus Aurelius such an exact expression of his own ideas that he not only offers two different translations of it made by other writers but, finding them wanting, proposes also his own (3: 153–54), which is the one reproduced here. For yet another translation see Marcus Aurelius, *The Meditations,* trans. G. Long, II. 13, *The Stoic and Epicurean Philosophers,* ed. Whitney J. Oates (New York: Random House, 1940), 499–500.

37. Blanco calls Marcus Aurelius a "truly inspired moral teacher" (3: 150), and he would also find confirmation of his own linkage of nature and reason in the Stoic philosopher, who wrote that "to the rational animal the same act is according to nature and according to reason" (*Meditations* VII. 11, 536).

38. In the same vein, he compares the unfolding of his views against orthodoxy to seeds kept from germination "by a superincumbent mass of earth" that, once released, expanded "with a rapid growth" (3: 139). Murphy believes that Blanco learned from Burke the preference "for the principle of organic growth" (as opposed to sudden change), and he indicates that Blanco began using organic metaphors in *El Español* (78).

39. Journal, July 19, 1939 (*The Life of the Rev. Joseph Blanco White* 3: 70). He reproduces this entry in the "Letter to . . . Thom" (*The Life of the Rev. Joseph Blanco White* 3: 142). In January 1835, just days before moving to Liverpool, he already depicted himself as a martyr in his journal: "I really feel grateful that I have been found worthy to suffer

for the CAUSE of truth and mankind. . . . I feel it my bounden duty to show, by my sufferings, to the world, how injurious to the cause of religion, of Christian charity, and of humanity itself, that Church system must be, which makes such sacrifices to *the love of truth* unavoidable to me. . . . For the sake of opening the eyes of people to the evils of this kind of Orthodoxy, I trust in Heaven I should have fortitude enough to go to the gallows, or the stake" (*The Life of the Rev. Joseph Blanco White* 2: 74–76).

40. His relentless condemnation of the imagination caused the alarm even of one of his staunchest admirers, Dr. Channing, who, in a letter dated November 20, 1839, writes: "You seem to me to make religion too exclusively a product of the Reason, and carry your jealousy of the Imagination too far" (3: 118). Channing also points to the role of the imagination in the appreciation of the divinity in the universe.

41. Peter Gay, *The Rise of Modern Paganism*, vol. 1 of *The Enlightenment: An Interpretation* (New York: Norton, 1977).

42. Michel Foucault, "On the Genealogy of Ethics: An Overview of Work in Progress," *The Foucault Reader*, ed. Paul Rabinow (New York: Vintage, 1984).

43. Blanco also finds in the Greek concept of "Logos," which he calls "the light of God in man," an exact characterization of what he calls "conscientious reason" (*The Life of the Rev. Joseph Blanco White* 1: 154). Foucault observes that while Descartes's *cogito* offers a foundation for scientific knowledge, it simultaneously opens a rift between self-knowledge and ethics; after him, therefore, philosophy faces the task of reconciling the subject of scientific knowledge with the subject of ethics, a problem that Kant tried to solve with his critiques (Foucault, "On the Genealogy of Ethics," 372). This is also the quandary faced by Blanco in his rationalism, and not coincidentally he identifies himself completely with Kant's solution, as already pointed out.

44. Gilles Deleuze, *Negotiations: 1972–1990*, trans. Martin Joughin (New York: Columbia University Press, 1995), 88.

45. Gilles Deleuze and Félix Guattari, *A Thousand Plateaus: Capitalism and Schizophrenia*, trans. Brian Massumi (Minneapolis: University of Minnesota Press, 1994), 400.

46. Referring to Foucault's formulation of ethics in the last two volumes of *History of Sexuality,* Deleuze emphasizes that the subject is not a residue but a point of resistance, a constant re-creation in the process of subjectivation of knowledge and power. In *Foucault,* trans. Seán Hand (Minneapolis: University of Minnesota Press, 1988), 105.

47. *A Thousand Plateaus,* 127.

48. His self-image as a witness pervades also his polemical works. In the preface to the second edition (1826) of *Practical and Internal Evidence against Catholicism* he writes, referring to the issue of Catholic emancipation: "Deeply impressed, as I am, with my personal insignificance, I could not doubt that Providence had, by very unusual means, placed me in a situation which loudly demanded my testimony in a trial, on the issue of which the prevalence of true religion, and the welfare of this country, might ultimately depend" (10). In *The Victorian Self: Autobiography and Biblical Narrative* (Ithaca, N.Y.: Cornell University Press, 1989), 29–31, Heather Henderson argues that the figure of the "trial" dominates Newman's *Apologia.*

49. Blanco had plans to write a second part of his memoirs, and he prepared for that project by writing a series of "Sunday Letters" to Thom, a fairly lengthy statement that Blanco punctiliously composed every Sunday from July 10 to October 16 of 1836 (*The Life of the Rev. Joseph Blanco White* 3: 366–435). Still, on January 20, 1840, he began "Plain Dialogues on Religious Subjects" (see *The Life of the Rev. Joseph Blanco White* 3: 171), another autobiographical document structured as a dialogue between a "Layman" and a "Clergyman" (Blanco White) that starts out as a self-critique of his *Poor Man's Preservative against Popery* (it appears as an appendix in *The Life of the Rev. Joseph Blanco White* 3: 436–56). There is even more. An undated document, presumably written also toward the end of his life, that bears the title "Dialogue on Religion" and presented as yet another dialogue between an "Inquirer" and an "Answerer" (obviously Blanco, as it should be expected) is one more rehashing of Blanco's religious ideas. And, finally, in 1840 Blanco wrote another dialogical essay, named "The Rationalist A-Kempis, or The Religious Sceptic in God's Presence" (*The Life of the Rev. Joseph Blanco White* 3: 231–92), a "confession" to God.

50. Once again, in *The Life of the Rev. Joseph Blanco White* Blanco did not keep the letter form for very long, although throughout the narrative

of his life he invokes Whately or, in other cases, the reader. Logically "A Sketch of His Mind in England" could not be addressed to a sympathetic Whately, since Blanco began to write it precisely at a time when, no longer willing to hide his Unitarian ideas, he had decided to leave the archbishop's house and to move to Liverpool.

51. Michel Foucault, *An Introduction*. Vol. 1 of *The History of Sexuality*. Trans. Robert Hurley (New York: Vintage, 1980), 61–62.

52. Martin Murphy refers to two dialogues on celibacy "between a Clergyman and an Arab" that Blanco published in *El Espanol* in 1813, as "an early example of his skill in elaborate literary self-disguise and mystification" (91) and points to the possible influence of Cadalso's *Cartas marruecas* and Erasmus's dialogues on celibacy. Independently of concrete influences, both the dialogical and the question-and-answer forms have to be related to Catholic confession and catechism and, even more deeply, to confession as taking responsibility before the other.

53. He also believes that the same ascetic impulses made him too severe with himself in *The Examination*.

54. Jacques Derrida, "Remarks on Deconstruction and Pragmatism," *Deconstruction and Pragmatism*, ed. Chantal Mouffe (New York: Routledge, 1996), 80.

55. Emmanuel Levinas, *Totality and Infinity: An Essay In Exteriority*, trans. Alphonso Lingis (The Hague: Martinus Nijhoff, 1978), 101.

56. Martin Murphy suggests that four out of the six of Blanco's autobiographical works (he excludes *The Examination* and *The Life of the Rev. Joseph Blanco White*) are apologias (x). One could argue, however, that all six are, provided that one expands apologia's usual, narrow meaning.

57. Levinas, *Totality and Infinity*, 110.

58. See Louis Althusser, "Ideology and Ideological State Apparatuses (Notes towards an Investigation)," *Essays on Ideology* (London: Verso, 1984), especially 45–51.

59. *A Thousand Plateaus*, 130.

60. While Althusser proposes that ideology "'transforms' the individuals into subjects"—which implies some anteriority of the

"individual," whatever that is for Althusser—he also affirms that *"individuals are always-already subjects"* ("Ideology and Ideological State Apparatuses," 48 and 50), thus positing an absolute priority of ideology. Interestingly enough, he exemplifies his thesis about ideological interpellation with the case of religious ideology and, concretely, with God's interpellation of Moses. In an exposition indebted to Hegel and Lacan—and very close to Levinas in its vocabulary although not in its explanations—he emphasizes the role of obedience in Moses' answer to God's interpellation, but he is far from explaining why such obedience should take place. As pointed out in the first chapter, Kaja Silverman's understanding of subjectivity in *Male Subjectivity at the Margins* (New York: Routledge, 1992) is also grounded on the primacy of ideology, which in her opinion shapes even the Lacanian imaginary, a stage that in Lacanian theory antecedes the impositions of the ideological symbolic.

61. Although Channing was, like Blanco, a rationalist in religious matters, he was a foe of any orthodoxy, even if it was a Unitarian one.

62. *Historia de los heterodoxos españoles,* vol.2, 790–91.

63. Juan Goytisolo, "Presentación crítica de J. M. Blanco White," *Obra inglesa de Blanco White,* 3d edition, ed. Juan Goytisolo (Barcelona: Seix Barral, 1982), 4. In *Practical and Internal Evidence,* Blanco had anticipated— and voided—Menéndez Pelayo's damming depiction by stating that "the epithets of *Apostate* and *Renegade* . . . are, I confess, pleasing to my ear; being acknowledgements of intellectual and moral qualities" (*Practical and Internal Evidence* 8). Among the numerous works by Llorens on Blanco see for in stance his "Introducción" to *Antología de obras en español* by José María Blanco White (Barcelona: Labor, 1971), 7–49, which he also edited. Llorens also wrote the introduction to the first Spanish edition of *Letters from Spain,* published as *Cartas de España,* trans. Antonio Garnica (Madrid: Alianza, 1972). Martin Murphy, *Blanco White* (194–204), and James D. Fernández, *Apology to Apostrophe* (72–86), survey some of the abundant responses that *The Life of the Rev.*

Joseph Blanco White elicited (especially throughout the nineteenth century).

Chapter Three: María Teresa León

1. In chronological order of publication, the following are some of the autobiographical writings authored by Spanish women in exile: Constancia de la Mora (1906–1950), *In Place of Splendor: The Autobiography of A Spanish Woman* (New York: Harcourt, Brace, 1939); Isabel de Palencia, *I Must Have Liberty* (New York: Longmans, Green, 1940) and *Smouldering Freedom: The Story of the Spanish Republicans in Exile* (New York: Longmans, Green, 1945; Isabel de Palencia's birth year has been given variously as 1872, 1878 and 1881; it seems she died in the sixties, but again, that date is uncertain); Victoria Kent (1897–1987), *Cuatro años en París (1940–1944)* (Buenos Aires: Sur, 1947); Federica Montseny (1905–1994), *Seis años de mi vida (1939–1945)* (Barcelona: Galba Ediciones, 1978) and *Mis primeros cuarenta años* (Barcelona: Plaza & Janés, 1987); Dolores Ibárruri (1895–1989), *Memorias de Pasionaria: 1939–1977. Me faltaba España* (Barcelona: Planeta, 1984). For a more detailed listing and an overall view of exiled women's autobiographies, see Shirley Mangini, *Memories of Resistance: Women's Voices from the Spanish Civil War* (New Haven, Conn.: Yale University Press, 1995), especially chapter 10, "Memory Texts of Exiled Women," 155–74. For an overview of autobiographical writings by Spaniards who had to leave the country in 1939, see Michael Ugarte, *Shifting Ground: Spanish Civil War Exile Literature* (Durham, N.C.: Duke University Press, 1989), especially chapter 6, "Exilic Autobiographies," 82–96.

2. Rosa Chacel, *Desde el amanecer* (Madrid: Revista de Occidente, 1972); María Zambrano, *Delirio y destino (Los veinte años de una española)* (Madrid: Mondadori, 1989)—Zambrano wrote most of her text in the early fifties; María Teresa León, *Memoria de la melancolía* (Buenos Aires: Losada, 1970). Although she belongs to an earlier generation, María Martínez Sierra (1874–1974), another exile, is the author of an autobiographical work, *Una mujer por caminos de España* (Buenos Aires: Losada, 1952), in which she narrates her travels through Spain in the early thirties, doing

propaganda for the Spanish Socialist Party (PSOE). For its innovative autobiographical technique, this book deserves to be placed along the complex autobiographical works of the three younger writers just mentioned. It has been reissued with an introduction by Alda Blanco (Madrid: Castalia, 1989). In addition to their autobiographical writings, Chacel and Zambrano also published personal reflections on the genre. See María Zambrano, *La confesión: género literario* (Barcelona: Mondadori, 1988); it was originally published in the journal *Luminar* (México) in two parts (in 1941 and 1943), and it appeared later as a book in Editorial Luminar in 1943); Rosa Chacel, *La confesión* (Barcelona: EDHASA, 1971). Rosa Chacel returned from exile in 1973 and lived permanently in Madrid from 1977 on, but León was not able to come back until 1977, because of her affiliation with the Spanish Communist Party. Although she did not face such strong impediment as León, Zambrano did not return to live in Spain until 1984. In "Three Voices of Exile," *Monographic Review* 2 (1986): 208–215, Shirley Mangini explores briefly the autobiographical works of Victoria Kent, María Teresa León, and Federica Montseny.

3. In "*Desde el amanecer:* Confesiones de una hija voluntariosa," *Journal of Interdisciplinary Literary Studies* 5.1 (special issue 1993): 61–73, Reyes Lázaro interprets Chacel's autobiography as a response to Ortega and the Generation of '98.

4. María Teresa León, *Juego limpio* (Buenos Aires: Editorial Goyanarte, 1959), reissued by Seix Barral (Barcelona, 1987). In "La obra literaria de María Teresa León (cuentos y teatro)," *Anuario de Estudios Filológicos* 7 (1984): 361–84, and in *La obra literaria de María Teresa León: autobiografía, biografía, novelas* (Cáceres, Spain: Universidad de Extremadura, 1987), Gregorio Torres Nebrera offers a good overall view of León's works. Juan Carlos Estébanez Gil, *Mᵃ Teresa León: estudio de su obra literaria* (Burgos, Spain: Editorial La Olmeda, 1995), is recommended for its biographical information but useless as an analysis of León's literary production. The collective work *María Teresa León* (Valladolid, Spain: Junta de Castilla y León, 1987) includes a variety of views on León's life and works.

5. María Teresa León, *La historia tiene la palabra: noticia sobre el Salvamento del Tesoro Artístico* (Buenos Aires: Patronato Hispano-

Argentino de Cultura, 1944). The second edition was printed in Spain much later, with a prologue and notes by Gonzalo Santonja (Madrid: Editorial Hispamerca, 1977). León included a number of pages from this booklet, with hardly any changes, in *Memoria de la melancolía*. In the 1977 edition of *La historia,* León's text takes less than forty pages (there are several appendices with documents), fifteen of which (pp. 40–54) are disseminated throughout pages 176, 183–84, and 200–205 of *Memoria de la melancolía*.

6. For biographical information about León see Estébanez Gil, *Mª Teresa León,* 29–56.

7. Sigmund Freud, "Mourning and Melancholia," *Collected Papers,* trans. Joan Riviere, vol. 4, The International Psycho-Analytical Library 10 (New York: Basic Books, 1959), 152–70.

8. Although León does not provide explicit information in this respect, some parts of *Memoria de la melancolía* date from the early forties, as has already been indicated, while other parts were written shortly before its publication date. Many episodes are recounted in almost identical fashion both in *Memoria de la melancolía* and in her 1959 novel, *Juego limpio,* which would indicate that Leon wrote them for *Memoria de la melancolía* at some point in the fifties (or at least, that her views on them did not change substantially with time). On page 281 she implicitly indicates that she is writing in 1967, and on page 221 she indicates she is writing in 1968, when she declares that León Felipe (1884–1968) "has died today." On page 278 she announces that Rivas Cherif (1898–1969) has just died in Mexico, and the 1969 writing date is also confirmed by her reference (p. 298) to a political amnesty that has just been conceded in Spain, "thirty years later." Although Franco granted some partial amnesties, León must undoubtedly be referring to the one announced on April 1, 1969 (thirty years to the day after the end of the civil war), which brought to an end any culpability for wartime activities. Besides many of *Memoria de la melancolía*'s final pages, León undoubtedly wrote at least a good part of the first forty pages of *Memoria de la melancolía,* and also some others dispersed throughout the book, after she moved to Rome in 1963.

9. *Memoria de la melancolía,* 11. All translations of *Memoria de la melancolía* are the author's.

10. Obviously Leon is using a translation in verse, although the original, an epigram, is in prose. In *The Greek Anthology,* vol. 4, The Loeb Classical Library 85 (London: Heinemman, 1926), W. R. Paton translates it as "All that belongs to mortals is mortal, and all things pass us by; or if not, we pass them by" (21). Paton's translation is accurate but too literal. He translates the verb *parerkhomai* as "pass by," which Henry George Liddell lists in his *A Greek-English Lexicon* (Oxford: Clarendon Press, 1968) as the more usual reading of that word (Liddell gives an example from Homer in which a ship passes by another). However, as Liddell illustrates, in its temporal dimension the term refers to the past, to leave behind, and thus, by extension, to transience. The Spanish verb "pasar" puts an emphasis on fleetingness that is not as evident in "pass by." A more expressive translation could be "All that belongs to mortals is mortal, and all things will vanish; or if not, we'll be the ones to perish."

11. In melancholy, Freud argues, episodes of sorrow can alternate with moments of manic exultation (164). Freud's thought here provides not a final explanation or explication of León's melancholy in "medical" terms, but simply a first step on the way to a political and an ethical reading of *Memoria de la melancolía.*

12. In a 1948 article, "Para quién escribimos nosotros," *El escritor y su siglo* (Madrid: Alianza, 1990), 197–223, Francisco Ayala scathingly urged his fellow exiles to get over their constraining nostalgias. Later discussion addresses in more detail the varied attitudes toward the exile caused by the Spanish Civil War.

13. She had arrived in the city [Rome] determined to kiss the facades. . . . Years and years living with the feeling of being expelled, rejected, hurt by the eaves and the balconies and the edges of doors and the paved streets that never were hers and everything always fleeing from her. . . . Her soul had fallen apart, she had lost it, she found it scattered in fragments. . . . Why didn't everything come to an end, why wasn't everything forgotten . . . ? The last speck of Spanish soil had fallen from her shoes. . . . Let me forget, please.

Don't leave me in front of a foreign window, looking in. . . . She was terrified thinking that they might have closed the shutters of the windows of life. . . . For many years, only her Jewish friends understood her solitude, and there was a time when she believed she could erect a world of hope, brick by brick. . . . Then. . . .

Then she felt expelled from society like an evil object. . . . On the move again? Where to? . . . For that reason, when she arrived in the city she felt like kissing its facades and its windows. . . . Please, my Lord, a homeland, a homeland small as a courtyard. . . . A homeland to replace the one they tore from my soul with a single yank.

14. A few pages before (221–25 and 258–59), she writes about the deaths of León Felipe (1884–1968) and Cipriano Rivas Cherif (1898–1969).

15. In *Juego limpio*, for instance, the Spanish Civil War is explained initially as class warfare, but ultimately as the fight of international capital against the exploited workers.

16. Their travel book *Sonríe China* (Buenos Aires: Jacobo Muchnik Editor, 1958) is also an unabashedly positive account of Communist China.

17. Lost in the dark Stalinist night. . . . When I inquired about them, I saw those questioned drop their eyes with a certain resignation of victims saved without reason. . . . The Communist Party was gathering to attempt a new life [the XXth Congress]. . . . (191)

The forgotten were to return, the disappeared and the dead to show up. The Soviet government had just risen to its feet to tell the truth, something other governments would never have dared to do. But great Russia had had the courage to kneel, to let the dead and forgotten speak again . . . (192).[17]

18. In *Juego limpio* she repeatedly illustrates the war with the figure of two rabid dogs' fighting (80), but the emphasis still falls on the elation the main group of Republican characters share as a result of being united by a common cause (and hence one of the characters, a priest, feels regret for not being fully one of the Republicans).

19. León ultimately obviates her peculiar interpretation of the political by positing that what really unites people is not a commonality of ideas but a community of feelings, which makes communication possible despite differences in language, class, nationality, or even ideology. She exemplifies this point through her accounts in *Memoria de la melancolía* of episodes in which she was able to elicit sympathetic responses in diverse audiences (Russian women, Spanish peasants, people in the United States) she faced in various political activities. Her political utopia rests ultimately upon a universality of feelings that presumably could overcome all differences and wars.

20. Ernesto Laclau and Chantal Mouffe, *Hegemony and Socialist Strategy: Towards a Radical Democratic Politics* (London: Verso, 1993), 111.

21. Laclau and Mouffe clarify that "far from being an objective relation, [antagonism] is a relation wherein the limits of every objectivity are *shown.*" Setting the impossibility of a final suture of the social, they add, antagonism "is the 'experience' of the limit of the social. Strictly speaking, antagonisms are not *internal* but *external* to society; or rather, they constitute the limits of society, the latter's impossibility of fully constituting itself" (125).

22. Slavoj Žižek, *The Sublime Object of Ideology* (London: Verso, 1989), 45.

23. Her novel *Juego limpio* expounds on her vision of war in *Memoria de la melancolía.* Although *Juego limpio* alternates the first person narratives of seven of its characters, the novel consists basically of the memoir a priest writes, full of remose, in his cell of El Escorial shortly after the end of the war. Living in an area controlled by the Republican enemies, he decides at the beginning of the novel to join their army rather than stay in hiding, undergoing an almost instant process of conversion that takes him from professing ignorance and intolerance about the workers's side to sharing in their solidarity and generosity. At any rate her account of the war in *Juego limpio,* where the rigid ideological positions on both sides are equally criticized, is more nuanced than it is in her earlier novel *Contra viento y marea* (Buenos Aires: Ediciones Aiape,

1941), in which Marielena Zelaya Kolker, *Testimonios americanos de los escritores españoles transterrados de 1939* (Madrid: Ediciones Cultura Hispánica, Instituto de Cooperación Iberoamericana, 1985), observes an excessive "polarización ideológica" (ideological polarization) that appears as a drastic contrast in the characterization of Republicans and Francoists (80).

24. Similarly León rarely dwells on the responsibility the Francoist regime has for her predicaments in exile, concentrating instead on the agony of separation and loss and on the memory of wartime fraternity. Also illustrative is her disquiet regarding the endless stream of wars and conflicts in the world, a realization that had already driven her grandmother to decide never to read a paper again, convinced there was no hope for humanity. As an answer to León's anguish regarding the perpetuity of conflict, a young granddaughter of León writes a "fable" (when they were already living in Rome), which León, most fittingly, includes in the last pages of *Memoria de la melancolía*. In that story, which renews a variant of the topos of *adynaton* (the world upside down), all antagonisms and animadversions, not only between humans but also between animals, have come to an end, showing the utopic colors of León's politically implausible dream: "Hay una jaula con muchos pájaros de colores. Un gato se los quiere comer, pero María Teresa León se lo impide. De pronto se abren las puertas del mundo a la Humanidad y se acaban las guerras y ya no hay papeles [sic] en Roma. ¡Qué bien! Las guerras [sic] del Vietnam han desaparecido, el gato ya no come al pájaro y tampoco vuelca la pecera. . . . Ya no pelean las mujeres en la plaza del mercado ni los hombres van a toda velocidad. Vivan las puertas mágicas, las que dieron felicidad a la Humanidad. Las plantas crecen flores en invierno. Las mariposas están también en invierno. El invierno es primavera . . ." (328; There is a cage with many birds of many colors. A cat wants to eat them, but María Teresa León doesn't let the cat have its way. Suddenly the world's doors open for Humanity and all wars come to an end and there are no more papers [sic] in Rome. Great! The Vietnam wars [sic] have disappeared, the cat doesn't eat the bird anymore nor upset the fish bowl. . . . The women in the market no longer fight nor do men go around in haste anymore. Long live the

magical doors that brought happiness to Humanity. Plants bloom in winter. Butterflies also live in winter. Winter is spring . . .). In *Sonríe China* she writes that destruction manifests itself in "la edad infantil de los pueblos" (75; the childhood of nations). Her portrayal of China, like that of the Spain during its civil war, offers a thoroughly positive image of that nation, one of whose principal features is precisely "la amistad entre los pueblos" (the friendship between nations), its contribution to "la convivencia pacífica, futura constructora del mundo" (44; peaceful coexistence, the future builder of the world). As she does with her representation of the civil war in *Memoria de la melancolía,* her depiction of revolutionary China glosses over any possibility of internal problems, divisions, or differences.

25. Fraternity and generosity, among other qualities, are for Levinas precisely forms in which the ethical continues to manifest itself in the midst of the political. As has been discussed, for Levinas the process of individuation that starts in the call from the other is a way to escape the realm of "the *il y a*," which shares with Lacan's Real, and with Laclau and Mouffe's *antagonism,* its nonsensical and unsettling character.

26. Julia Kristeva, *Black Sun: Depression and Melancholia,* trans. Leon S. Roudiez (New York: Columbia University Press, 1989), 19. Kristeva depicts melancholics as "prisoners of affect. The affect is their thing" (14). Kristeva uses *affect* as synonym of *feeling.* As explained previously, however, the word *affection* is used herein not to indicate the sense of *feeling,* but to designate the originary effect of the other on the self, which is thus initially constituted as a form of (self)affection upon which ideological interpellation (or whatever term we want to use for the final stage of the process of subjectivation) performs its work. Without assuming that originary affect of the other on the self, it would be impossible to explain why the self would later heed any form of interpellation and do it passionately.

27. Her anxiety before loss becomes ultimately in León's life the fear of not being seen, of not being "recognized." This aspect is more fully developed later.

28. Memory can have indulgent eyes. The noises that reach us are no longer alive but dead. Memory of forgetfulness, wrote Emilio Prados, melancholy memory, almost extinguished, memory of melancholy. I don't remember who in my family used to say: one must have memories. To live is not as important as to remember. The horrible thing was not to have anything to remember. . . . But how horrible it is that memories assail us, forcing us to look at them, biting us and wallowing in our entrails, where memory is located.

29. *All Rivers Run to the Sea* (New York: Knopf, 1995), 150.

30. *Black Sun,* 60, 61.

31. Philip Roth, *The Facts: A Novelist's Autobiography* (New York: Farrar, Straus, 1988), 8.

32. *Black Sun,* 145.

33. In *Eros in Mourning: Homer to Lacan* (Baltimore, Md.: Johns Hopkins University Press, 1995), Henry Staten theorizes that the philosophical-religious tradition that underlies Western literature is permeated by the self's anticipation of loss that results in strategies of idealization and transcendence, mastering or, at least, mitigation of mourning. That mourning would be essentially for the self's lost unity that Staten sees authors as diverse as Augustine and Lacan explicity incorporate or formulate.

34. Edward W. Said, *Representations of the Intellectual* (New York: Vintage, 1996), 49.

35. José María Naharro-Calderón, *Entre el exilio y el interior: el "entresiglo" y Juan Ramón Jiménez* (Barcelona: Anthropos, 1994), 35, 37. In a highly critical essay, "Crisis de la nostalgia," *Andalucía e Hispanoamérica: crisol de mestizajes* (Sevilla, Spain: Edisur, 1982), 105–19, which Manuel Andújar wrote in the fifties, he argues that one of the errors committed by his fellow Spanish exiles in Mexico was to install themselves in a dead past (112–13), wallowing in "añoranzas enfermizas y castradoras" (114; morbid, castrating nostalgias). As already noted, Ayala castigates the Spanish exiles along similar lines. In *Memorias de una emigración: Santo Domingo, 1939–1945* (Barcelona: Ariel, 1975), Vicente Lloréns portrays the

Spanish exiled community in the Dominican Republic, of which he was part, as moving toward accepting their situation between two worlds without belonging to either of them (Lloréns wrote his chronicle more than twenty years after the facts). He presents a similar view, now in reference to all civil war exiles, in "Entre España y América," *Literatura, historia, política* (Madrid: Revista de Occidente, 1967), 223–36.

36. Randolph Pope, "La autobiografía del exilio: el ser previamente preocupado de Rafael Alberti y María Teresa León." *El exilio de las Españas de 1939 en las Américas: "¿Adónde fue la canción?"* ed. José María Naharro-Calderón (Barcelona: Anthropos, 1991), 376. Pope also contrasts Alberti's strict narrative chronology with the much more unconventional, aleatory organization that León gives to her materials. Their dissimilar textual organizations are in agreement with the differing emphasis of their autobiographical writings. The above-mentioned interviews were published by José Miguel Velloso as *Conversaciones con Rafael Alberti* (Madrid: Ediciones Sedmay, 1977). In "Antidotes for Exile: Rafael Alberti's Struggle against a Persistent Malady," *Monographic Review* 2 (1986): 68–83, Catherine G. Bellver examines the strategies Alberti used to soothe exile.

37. "For the one truth of the matter is that exile is a metaphysical condition," writes Brodsky in "The Condition We Call 'Exile,'" *Literature in Exile,* ed. John Glad (Durham, N.C.: Duke University Press, 1990), 103.

38. María Zambrano, "El exiliado," *Los bienaventurados* (Madrid: Siruela, 1990), 31, 39.

39. *Cartas a Rosa Chacel,* ed. Ana Rodríguez-Fischer (Madrid: Versal, 1992), 39 (letter of September 4, 1941). A comparison between the conceptions of exile of León and Zambrano would require much more space. For Zambrano exile is an experience of limits through which one should go to reach lucidity; in *Memoria de la melancolía,* instead, León keeps devising strategies to avoid accepting exile, and not necessarily and simply as physical expatriation but as a "figure" of the experiences of loss, solitude,

abandonment, etc., that León, paradoxically, experiences with such intensity but refuses to interpret for what they are, choosing instead to see them as temporary setbacks on the road to restoration of plenitude.

40. "El exiliado," 42, 43.

41. Michael Rowlands, "Memory, Sacrifice and the Nation," *New Formations* 30 (Winter 1996): 10.

42. Michael Ugarte, *Shifting Ground: Spanish Civil War Exile Literature,* 60, 62.

43. León's works are *Rodrigo Díaz de Vivar, el Cid Campeador* (Buenos Aires: Ediciones Peuser, 1954); *Doña Jimena Díaz de Vivar: gran señora de todos los deberes* (Buenos Aires: Losada, 1960). *Doña Jimena* was reissued by Biblioteca Nueva (Madrid, 1968), and this is the version used for quotations. In *Doña Jimena,* writes León in *Memoria de la melancolía,* "yo regresaba a mi infancia donde el cuento del Cid aparece siempre. Y no por ser burgalesa mi madre, sino por las horas de mi infancia pasadas en la casa de mi prima Jimena" (256; I was returning to my childhood, where the story of the Cid was constantly present, and not because my mother was from Burgos, but because of the hours spent in my childhood in the company of my cousin Jimena).

44. "Reconquistemos la antigua patria española que ahora tienen los moros" (*Rodrigo,* 85; see also 164; let's reconquer the old Spanish homeland now in the hands of the moors). León puts these words in the character Rodrigo's mouth, obviating the fact the Spain did not exist as a nation until after the Moors had been expelled from the peninsula.

45. "Van los desterrados dejándose los ojos y el corazón entre las encinas y robles del camino. Parece que hasta las piedras les dicen: soy tu patria. Nada puede haber más triste para un hombre que este echarse a andar hacia lo desconocido" (*Rodrigo,* 89; see also 70; the exiles depart leaving their eyes and hearts among the oaks and chaparrals along their way. It seems that even the stones tell them: I am your homeland. There is nothing sadder for a

person than this experience of starting out toward the unknown). In *Poema de Mío Cid,* Rodrigo also experiences sadness upon leaving Castile.

46. Robert Edwards, "Exile, Self, and Society," *Exile in Literature,* ed. María-Inés Lagos-Pope (Lewisburg, Pa.: Bucknell University Press, 1988), 25, 26. Michael Ugarte suggests that the Cid is an archetype of exile, "both a literary model for later writing and the rewriting of a previous model" (*Shifting Ground,* 9).

47. *Memoria de la melancolía,* 256–57.

48. Ibid., 257.

49. *Rodrigo,* 116; see also 142 and 196. Despite this note of subservience, Jimena represents also some of the feminist preoccupations León displays in various writings. In "'Las voces perdidas': silencio y recuerdo en *Memoria de la melancolía,*" *Anthropos* 125 (October 1991): 45–49, Alda Blanco proposes a feminist interpretation of *Memoria de la melancolía.*

50. *Doña Jimena,* 31. As an exile, Rodrigo is also presented as a member of that lineage of Spaniards, embodied preeminently by the romantic writer Larra, to whom "le dolía España" (*Doña Jimena,* 38; Spain hurts).

51. In one occasion, when the friar [Cardeña's abbot] was reading to her from Idiáquez's book "What matters that you are not in your homeland? Your homeland is the place where you have found your wellbeing, and the cause of wellbeing does not reside in the location but in the heart of a human being," Doña Jimena cried out haughtily: "You are lying or you are reading a falsity!" And although the perplexed abbot attempted to calm her down while closing the book bound in good calf leather: "You are lying, who could betray her mother's bosom?," she cried. . . .

52. *Memoria de la melancolía,* 52–53. Located in an area that later became part of Old Castile, Numancia was a city whose inhabitants chose to sacrifice their lives by fire rather than to surrender to the Romans in 133 B.C. Numancia has been traditionally used as an embodiment

of an essence of Spain (that, paradoxically, would have thus existed even before Spain became a nation).

53. Ibid., 54.

54. At another moment that is also filled with emotion, she apostrophizes Spain on account of an exile's death (*Memoria de la melancolía*, 50, 51). Both episodes (the performance of *Numancia* and the recitation of *Cantata*) are given ample space in *Juego Limpio*, where two of the members of the theatrical company (an undisguised representation of the real life "Guerrillas of the Central Army Theater") to which the main characters belong are killed by Francoist planes in Sagunto. The place of death is significant because Sagunto is yet another exemplary city. As traditionally explained in Spanish history books, Sagunto was destroyed in 219 B.C. by the Carthaginians, but only after putting up a heroic resistance.

55. Carolyn Boyd, *Historia Patria: Politics, History, and National Identity in Spain, 1875–1975* (Princeton, N.J.: Princeton University Press, 1997), 184.

56. Michael Rowlands, "Memory, Sacrifice and the Nation," 13.

57. *Memoria de la melancolía,* 51.

58. We are the exiles from Spain, those who are looking for the shadow, the silhouette, the sound of the steps of silence, the lost voices. Our paradise does not consist of trees or permanently colored flowers. Leave the ruins to us. We must start from the ruins. We will return. We will return with the law, we will teach you the words buried under the excessively big buildings in cities that are no longer ours. Our paradise, the one we defended, is lying under today's facades. It is also yours. Don't you feel, young people devoid of exile and tears, that we must start from the ruins, from the flattened houses and the burning fields in order to erect our fraternal city of the new law?

59. Besides reproducing them in the epigraph, León quotes Lucian's lines twice in *Memoria de la melancolía,* the first time, as

previously mentioned, in connection with her childhood uprootedness, and the second in reference to the death of Eva Perón: "¡Qué
manera de pasar la Historia! 'Si ellas no pasan, somos nosotros los
que pasamos.' ¡Ay, cosas de este mundo!" (271; What a way history has of passing! "Or if not, we'll be the ones to perish." Ah, the
things of the world!).

60. Walter Benjamin, *The Origin of German Tragic Drama*, trans.
John Osborne (London: Verso, 1990), 224. Extolling the lucidity of
preromantic allegory in opposition to the obfuscation of romantic
symbol, Paul de Man links allegory and time in a manner very similar to Benjamin's: "the prevalence of allegory always corresponds to
the unveiling of an authentically temporal destiny," and thus "allegory designates primarily a distance in relation to its own origin
and . . . establishes its language in the void of this temporal difference" (207). In "The Rhetoric of Temporality," *Blindness and Insight,*
2d ed. (Minneapolis: University of Minnesota Press, 1983), 206, 207.

61. Kristeva, *Black Sun,* 10.

62. Max Pensky, *Melancholy Dialectics: Walter Benjamin and the
Play of Mourning* (Amherst: University of Massachusetts Press,
1993), 116.

63. Ibid., 117. On the other hand, melancholy is not exempt
from pleasure. As Benjamin writes, "the only pleasure the melancholic permits himself, and it is a powerful one, is allegory" (185).
As noted before, Kristeva argues that the sorrow involved in melancholy is also, paradoxically, another form of pleasure.

64. In *Darkness Visible: A Memoir of Madness* (New York: Vintage,
1992), William Styron's personal chronicle of the "ravages of melancholia," he sees that condition as "a simulacrum of all the evil of our
world: of our everyday discord and chaos, our irrationality, warfare
and crime, torture and violence, our impulse toward death and our
flight from it" (83–84). Styron emphasizes the link between melancholia and death, but in that flight from death one can recognize
Pensky's cognitive moment, which allows for the possibility of a figural construction (which Benjamin calls "allegory") that counterbalances melancholy's deathly impulse.

65. And in León's case that object never existed, being retro-spectively constructed by her. Besides, her evocation of the object follows the logic of nostalgia, according to which nostalgia is a fan-tasy that maintains itself alive precisely by not becoming realized. See in this respect Oliver Sacks, *An Anthropologist on Mars* (New York: Knopf, 1995), 168–69.

66. Benjamin, 183–84.

67. For instance, baroque allegorical plays, Benjamin asserts, tend to end with an apotheosis that not only brings a resolution to the plot but also establishes the absolute grounding that guarantees the validity of their allegorical meanings.

68. Benedict Anderson, *Imagined Communities: Reflections on the Origin and Spread of Nationalism,* 2d ed. (London: Verso, 1991), 11.

69. Pensky, 116–17.

70. It is as if I didn't belong to that country [Spain] whose news-papers I read. . . . I feel everything outside myself, wrenched from me. . . . It is as if I were separated, as if I were looking at myself. I can-not find the formula either to dialogue or to unite with people. . . . Many times I have felt anguish upon looking at, seated next to me, human beings who tell me they are my people [Spaniards] but I am unable to recognize them . . . , so different is everything the passage of time has left me.

71. I am afraid to look at myself in mirrors because I no longer see anything in my pupils and, if I hear anything, I don't know what they are telling me and I don't know why they insist so much on reviving my memory. But I suffer to forget and . . . I feel they are pushing me forward, towards grief, towards death. At those mo-ments I prefer to go towards the past and I speak, I speak with the meager sense of memory, with the cracks and blemishes, with the unavoidable blotches of the mirror of memory.

72. *Memoria de la melancolía, 93.*

73. Ibid., 237, 238.

74. Shoshana Felman, "Education and Crisis, or the Vicissitudes of Teaching," *Trauma: Explorations in Memory*, ed. Cathy Caruth (Baltimore, Md.: Johns Hopkins University Press, 1995), 17 and 14–15.

75. Following Barbara Harlow's ideas about autobiographies of female prisoners, Mangini argues that *Memoria de la melancolía* offers a collective testimony, "though not as consistently" as those of the women who were imprisoned for their participation in the civil war (*Memories of Resistance*, 162).

76. *La confesión: género literario*, 27.

77. *Memoria de la melancolía*, 185.

78. Especially at the beginning of *Memoria de la melancolía*, León reproduces as inner dialogues conversations that she held at several moments in her life, especially in her childhood. It is highly significant for this argument concerning personal memory and the other that she chooses to relate many of her memories as a running conversation and not as a narrative controlled by the first person.

79. The most poignant and conspicous case in this respect is her dialogue with her dead mother, which ends in the following recognition scene: "¡Si tú supieras, madre! Esta mañana al abrir un cajón . . . encontré un retrato tuyo. Hasta hoy no he sabido mirarlo. . . . ¡Cuánto te quise de pronto! Eras mía, únicamente mi madre." "La voz tuya, tan admirable, me anunciaba que yo iba a ser como tú, nada más que como tú" (112; If you knew, mother! This morning when I opened a drawer . . . I found a picture of you. Until today I hadn't known how to look at it. . . . How much I suddenly loved you! You were mine, only my mother. Your voice, so admirable, announced to me that I was going to be like you, only like you). By finding herself in her recognition of her mother, León grounds her identity on a dead other. The chapter on Semprún further explores the connections among identity, the dead other, and responsibility.

80. In his classical study *On Collective Memory,* trans. Lewis A. Coser (Chicago: University of Chicago Press, 1992), Maurice Halbwachs shows that one cannot separate individual memory from collective memory. The inclusion in social groups (and mainly those of family, religion, and social class) is what allows individuals to acquire, locate, and recollect their past.

81. In "Criticism and Its Alterity," *Borders, Boundaries, and Frames: Essays in Cultural Criticism and Cultural Studies,* ed. Mae G. Henderson (New York: Routledge, 1995), Sara Suleri advocates a type of autobiographical criticism that, participating in what she calls "the category of inbetweenness" (179), would differ from confessional criticism, in that it "takes autobiography as a strategy of dismantlement that dispenses with such dichotomies as public and private or inside and outside in order to position itself at the border of outsidedness" (175). However, all personal writing, no matter the type of genre it favors, lies always between the private and the public, the only difference being how responsive, and thus how responsible, the writer is to the voices and injunctions of alterity.

82. León's addressee is doubly imposed on her: in the first place no autobiography is conceivable without it; furthermore Kristeva emphasizes the need for the melancholic to find an addressee in order to name his/her solitude and thus to avoid being trapped by melancholy (*Black Sun,* 91).

83. This request for recognition finds a complement in her depiction of another episode, one in which she first really recognized her mother (111–112), of whom she writes, in a chilling foreboding of her own fate: "Concluyó su vida hablando sola, olvidando" (275; In her final years she ended up talking to herself, forgetting).

84. She expresses the same fear on page 16.

85. As suggested in the first chapter, following Quintilian, there are always three people involved in apostrophe, the third, unidentified one being the real addressee of the speaker.

86. Estébanez Gil, *Mª Teresa León* (55), identifies her condition as Alzheimer's, adding that her mother and grandmother had also suffered from it. In reference to the state of León's memory when she returned to Spain, see Florentino Huerga, "Una patria, señor. María Teresa León," *Quimera* 123 (1994): 32–33; and Elena Bilbao, "María Teresa León, aún exiliada," *El País* (October 19, 1997).

Chapter Four: Juan Goytisolo

1. *Coto vedado* (Barcelona: Seix Barral, 1985) was published in English as *Forbidden Territory: The Memoirs of Juan Goytisolo 1931–1956,* trans. Peter Bush (San Francisco: North Point Press, 1989), while the English translation of *En los reinos de taifa* (Barcelona: Seix Barral, 1986) is *Realms of Strife: The Memoirs of Juan Goytisolo 1957–1982,* trans. Peter Bush (San Francisco: North Point Press, 1990). In the quotes they will appear as *CV* and *RT,* and the pagination of the Spanish original and English translation are given respectively. In a few cases there are slight modifications in Peter Bush's translations, as   indicated. The translations of quoted material from other works by Goytisolo are this author's.

2. Goytisolo himself foregrounds this dilemma when he wonders whether his autobiographical work is that of an archeologist or an engineer (*CV* 193/164).

3. Paul Julian Smith, "Juan Goytisolo and Jean Baudrillard: The Mirror of Production and the Death of Symbolic Exchange," *Revista de Estudios Hispánicos* 23.2 (1989): 38.

4. The opposition between the cultivated and the rough, the mask and the (true) face, which he equates with the false and the authentic, respectively, are displayed in his autobiography in his preference for simple, rugged people (both in his social and sexual interactions), his identification with meager landscapes such as the desert or the tundra (and his consequent, and profound, dislike of luxuriant sceneries, as he asserts in the section of *En los reinos de taifa* devoted to his trip to Russia), and finally in his professed admiration for writers who flaunt their values at the expense of their images.

5. Peter Bush translates "esa etapa de pose e inautenticidad" as "this life as an insincere poseur" (*CV* 117/98), but in the context of Goytisolo's text sincerity and authenticity are not synonymous,

especially in regard to the inflections given to the latter term by Heidegger and Sartre. In *Situations,* trans. Benita Eisler (New York: G. Braziller, 1965), Sartre defines authenticity as "the real connection with others, with oneself and with death" (199). While it is not likely that Goytisolo uses authenticity in a strict philosophical sense, the term had an existentialist imprint in Goytisolo's formative period—the Spain of the fifties—and therefore should be distinguished from mere sincerity. Even in a more common sense, sincerity and authenticity, although related, have different meanings since authenticity would allude to the internal search for one's true self, while sincerity would refer to the truthful expression of what one is. As Lionel Trilling states in *Sincerity and Authenticity* (Cambridge, Mass.: Harvard University Press, 1972), sincerity "is the avoidance of being false to any man through being true to one's own self" (5), while authenticity, as Charles Taylor suggests in *The Ethics of Authenticity* (Cambridge, Mass.: Harvard University Press, 1992), 25–29, implies a struggle to get in touch or to recover contact with one's true self, a belief that, at the beginning of the modern era, also made the self into something original, different to any other self. Both sincerity and authenticity have self-knowledge as their horizon of intelligibility, but in an ethical consideration of autobiography they acquire a meaning radically different from the ones Blanco White or Goytisolo impart to them.

6. Bush translates "genio y figura hasta la sepultura" as "a genius and character right up to the grave: the more genius, the more character: the more character, the more genius" (*CV* 165/140). Although *genio* can be translated as "genius," and *figura* as "character," a literal translation does not convey the meaning of the saying, which refers to the cultivation of external appearances as a way to show that one is a genius, therefore privileging an external image at the expense of substance (or, in Goytisolo's case, authenticity). The *Simon and Schuster International Dictionary* (New York, 1973) translates *genio y figura* correctly, if unidiomatically, as "creative and personal image of a person (artist, politician, etc.)."

7. For the ratification of the imaginary national as a way of self-ratification, see Eve Kosofsky Sedgwick, "Nationalisms and Sexualities in the Age of Wilde," *Nationalisms and Sexualities,* ed. Andrew Parker, Mary Russo, Doris Sommer, and Patricia Yaeger (New York: Routledge, 1992), 236.

8. In "Cronología," *Juan Goytisolo,* ed. Manuel Ruiz Lagos (Madrid: Ediciones de Cultura Hispánica, 1991), Goytisolo writes for the year 1963: "Su personalidad de representante oficial del progresismo hispano comienza a resultarle embarazosa e interponerse entre su yo real como un doble o, en expresión de Cavafis en uno de sus más bellos poemas, 'un huésped importuno. 'Se entrega a una desgarradora labor de autocrítica—política, literaria, personal—que le aísla paulatinamente de sus amigos y le ayuda a cortar el cordón umbilical que todavía le une a España" (113; his personality as official representative of Spanish progressive views starts to become embarrassing to him, and to mask his real self with a double or, as Cavafy wrote in one of his most beautiful poems, 'an unwelcome guest.' He engages in a wrenching self-criticism—political, literary, personal—that gradually isolates him from his friends and helps   him cut the umbilical cord that still links him to Spain). This "Cronología," written by Goytisolo in the third person, has appeared in several places, but this version seems to be the most updated.

9. See also 222–23/188–89.

10. Judith Butler, *The Psychic Life of Power: Theories in Subjection* (Stanford, Calif.: Stanford University Press, 1997). The quotes are from pages 95, 96–97, 98, and 99.

11. *The Psychic Life of Power,* 102.

12. In this light one can also understand the displacement effected by the final Foucault from a consideration of the domain of power/knowledge to an exploration of the terrain of an ethics that he opposes to (Christian) self-knowledge and that he views as care of the self, as a permanent work of the self on itself. See Michel Foucault, *The Use of Pleasure,* trans. Robert Hurley, vol. 2 of *The History of Sexuality* (New York: Vintage, 1990), and *The Care of the Self,* trans. Robert Hurley, vol. 3 of *The History of Sexuality* (New York: Vintage, 1988).

13. Jacques Lacan, *The Seminar of Jacques Lacan.* Book 3: *The Psychosis 1955–1956,* ed. Jacques-Alain Miller, trans. Russell Grigg (New York: Norton, 1993), 11.

14. Judith Butler, *Bodies That Matter: On the Discursive Limits of "Sex"* (New York: Routledge, 1993), 71.

15. Jacques Lacan, *Television,* trans. Denis Hollier, Rosalind Krauss, and Annette Michelson, ed. Joan Copjec (New York: Norton, 1990), 6.

16. *The Seminar of Jacques Lacan. Book 3: The Psychosis,* 241.

17. *The Psychic Life of Power,* 94. Referring in particular to an anatomical delimitation of the body, she suggests in another place that the anatomical is only given through its signification, "and yet it is also that which exceeds and compels that signifying chain" (*Bodies That Matter,* 90). It would seem, however, that here Butler conflates the body and the anatomical, and where she writes "the anatomical" one should understand "the body."

18. Other events in his life that he highlights are his first fulfilling homosexual experience, in Paris in 1964, and two accidents in the early eighties, narrated at the beginning of *Coto vedado,* that bring him an intimation of mortality and from which arises Goytisolo's need to tell the story of his life.

19. Gilles Deleuze, *Masochism,* trans. Jean McNeil (New York: Zone Books, 1991), 126. For the ideas summarized here see especially pages 60–61, 90, and 127.

20. See, for instance, his reconstruction of his mother's "true" personality derived from her picture and the books she used to read (*CV* 51/42). In "The Construction/Deconstruction of the Self in the Autobiographies of Pablo Neruda and Juan Goytisolo," *Forum for Modern Language Studies* 26.3 (1990): 212–21, Jo Labanyi argues that "Goytisolo's rejection of the Father's voice is an attempt to give back a voice to the various women silenced by the patriarchal family order" (216), a statement that is accurate provided that one sees that Goytisolo's vindication of the familial female has the further aim of giving himself a new origin. For Goytisolo's alternative maternal lineage and obsession with origins see also Angel G. Loureiro, "Autobiografía del otro (Rousseau, Torres Villarroel, Juan Goytisolo)," *Siglo XX/20th Century* 9.1–2 (1991–1992): 71–94, and Manuel Hierro, "Por los territorios del anti-Edipo: la genealogía indeseada de Juan Goytisolo en *Coto Vedado,*" *Revista Monográfica* 9 (1993): 93–103.

21. In "Vigencia actual del mudejarismo," *Contracorrientes* (Barcelona: Montesinos, 1985), he writes, underscoring the imbrication of life,

writing, and (gay) sex, that his interest in Arab issues had a "valor seminal, espermático" (seminal, spermatic significance) that transformed his life and writings (11).

22. The idea of death and rebirth is not only present in Goytisolo's autobiography, but has a constant presence also in his mature novels, as Annie Perrin suggests in "El laberinto homotextual," *Escritos sobre Juan Goytisolo: coloquio en torno a la obra de Juan Goytisolo, Almería, 1987* (Almería, Spain: Instituto de Estudios Almerienses, 1988), 76. In *Black Sun: Depression and Melancholia,* trans. Leon S. Roudiez (New York: Columbia University Press, 1989), Julia Kristeva suggestively argues that "the manic position" that alternates with, or sheaths, depression "can be manifested through the establishment of a symbolic lineage. We may thus find a recourse to proper names linked to a subject's real or imaginary history, with that subject declaring itself their heir or equal; what they truly memorialize, beyond paternal weakness, is nostalgic dedication to the lost mother" (24). While this statement fits Goytisolo's situation perfectly, following it literally in an interpretation of Goytisolo's nostalgia for origins and new rebirths as a search for a lost mother would reduce the impetus of his autobiographical quest to a punctual cause (his mother's death in his childhood) that, for all its wrenching dramatism and its undeniable significance, would make one lose sight of the loss, and the ensuing melancholia, latent in any autobiography. This latent loss that lurks within autobiography brings melancholia into proximity with ethics. Perhaps unavoidably, Goytisolo's reconstruction of identity has been interpreted "as a search for his lost mother and for the feminine within himself," as Robert Richmond Ellis puts it in "Cutting the Gordian Knot: Homosexuality and the Autobiographies of Juan Goytisolo," *Anales de la Literatura Española contemporánea* 19.1-2 (1994): 49.

23. As could be expected, the masochistic episode has attracted the attention of the critics. Jo Labanyi interprets it as Goytisolo's "release from repression through a violent sexual encounter" ("The Construction/Deconstruction," 215). For his part, in "Cutting the Gordian Knot," Ellis argues that Goytisolo effects here "the final destruction within himself of his past identities as European, bourgeois, and heterosexual. The beating that he receives is thus an experience of catharsis which delivers him to the threshold of authenticity" (58). However, in this episode there is more than the liberation from

repression suggested by Labany, but less than the sweeping destruction argued by Ellis.

24. In "Cronología," Goytisolo stresses the importance of Eulalia's death when he writes under 1965: "Pasa el otoño en Tánger. La desaparición de Eulalia le afecta mucho más que la muerte del padre" (114; he spends the fall in Tangiers. Eulalia's death affects him much more than his father's).

25. Jacques Lacan, *The Seminar of Jacques Lacan*. Book 7: *The Ethics of Psychoanalysis 1959–1960*, ed. Jacques-Alain Miller, trans. Dennis Porter (New York: Norton, 1992), 131. One should keep in mind that Lacan distinguishes between the real and reality, which he describes as "a grimace of the real" (*Television* 6).

26. Goytisolo will later repeatedly "hallucinate" his father as an old man: "*las sucesivas encarnaciones de tu padre en zocos y callejas de Fez o Marraquech, acurrucado, digno, implorante, cruces casuales o metódicamente planeados generadores del chispazo, el arco voltaico que nunca brotó en vida : itinerante ritual, medineo evocador de la tristeza de un desencuentro que lo trae no obstante a tu memoria y cariñosamente lo resucita*" (CV 134/112; trans. modified; "the succession of incarnations of your father in the squares and alleys of Fez or Marrakesh, crouching down, dignified, begging, chance or methodically planned encounters generating the spark, the arc light that was never lit in life: itinerant ritual, rambling through the maze of the streets evoking the sadness of a non-meeting that nevertheless recalls him to your memory and affectionately brings him to life)."

27. Lacan, *The Ethics of Psychoanalysis*, 319.

28. Ibid., 321.

29. His allegiance to the Cuban cause will continue, although with some reservations, until the beginning of the seventies when he was involved with some Latin American intellectuals in the magazine *Libre*, an episode that provokes the reflections that form section 4 of *En los reinos de taifa*, "El gato negro de la rue de Bièvre" (A Black Cat on the Rue de Bièvre).

30. See Judith Butler's suggestions in *Excitable Speech: A Politics of the Performative* (New York: Routledge, 1997) in which she writes: "If the performativity of injurious speech is considered perlocutionary (speech leads to effects, but is not itself the effect), then such speech

works its injurious effect only to the extent that it produces a set of non-necessary effects. Only if other effects may follow from the utterance does appropriating, reversing, and recontextualizing such utterances become possible" (39).

31. In "Juan Goytisolo's Portable *Patria:* Staying on Home Ground Abroad," *Renaissance and Modern Studies* 34 (1991): 78–96, Abigail Lee Six discusses the idea of language as fatherland in Goytisolo.

32. John Guillory, *Cultural Capital* (Chicago: University of Chicago Press, 1993), 42.

33. In "Vigencia actual del mudejarismo," Goytisolo affirms that his novels *Reivindicación del conde don Julián* (1970), *Juan sin tierra* (1975; John the Landless), *Makbara* (1980), and *Paisajes después de la batalla* (1982; Landscape after the Battle) connect with "los textos fundacionales del castellano" (the Spanish foundational texts) because of the "Mudejarism" they share with them (12).

34. In "Hacia una lectura 'mudéjar' de *Makbara,*" *Huellas del Islam en la literatura española: de Juan Ruiz a Juan Goytisolo* (Madrid: Hiperión, 1985), 181–209, Luce López-Baralt asserts that *Reivindicación del conde don Julián* is fundamentally a fictional rewriting of Américo Castro's seminal *La realidad histórica de España.*

35. For a development of these ideas, see his article "Abandonemos de una vez el amoroso cultivo de nuestras señas de identidad," *Contracorrientes* (Barcelona: Montesinos, 1985), especially 134–36. In a 1989 conference on his work, Goytisolo refused any representational role: "cuando hablo de España, lo hago a título individual. No soy, no formo parte de este gremio de escritores que cuando van al extranjero se convierten en embajadores de su propio país y hablan en nombre de cincuenta millones de personas. . . . Yo soy incapaz de representar lo español, puesto que apenas soy capaz de representarme a mí mismo" (64; when I speak about Spain, I only speak for myself. I am not one of those writers who when they go abroad become ambassadors of their country and speak for fifty million people. . . . I am unable to represent Spain because I am barely able to represent myself). In *Juan Goytisolo,* ed. Manuel Ruiz Lagos, 64.

36. Edward W. Said, *Representations of the Intellectual* (New York: Vintage, 1996), especially 32 and 109. Besides being tied by friendship,

Goytisolo and Said have also in common a critical view of Western constructions of the Arab world. Said's *Orientalism* (New York: Pantheon, 1978) inspired Goytisolo's article "De *Don Julián* a *Makbara:* una posible lectura orientalista," *Crónicas sarracinas* (Barcelona: Seix Barral, 1989), 27–46. See also Luce López-Baralt, "Juan Goytisolo's Fictionalized Version of *Orientalism," The Review of Contemporary Fiction* 4 (Summer 1984): 138–45.

37. Ernest Renan, "What Is a Nation?" *Nation and Narration,* ed. Homi K. Bhabha (London: Routledge, 1990), 11.

38. Benedict Anderson, *Imagined Communities: Reflections on the Origin and Spread of Nationalism,* 2d ed. (London: Verso, 1991), 198.

39. In "El cuerpo del delito," *Contracorrientes* (Barcelona: Montesinos, 1985), Goytisolo acknowledges that his writings on Rojas and Blanco White have taught him "que dichos escritores eran meros, sucesivos pretextos para mi propio y obsesivo discurso: que, hablando de ellos, no cesaba un instante de hablar de mí. Al releer mis ensayos y artículos, imaginaba su sorpresa, confusión, quiza su cólera contenida ante la reconstrucción peculiar elaborada con fragmentos y materiales dispersos extraídos de sus escritos" (84; that those writers were mere, successive pretexts for my own, obsessive discourse: that, talking about them, I was always talking about myself. Upon rereading my essays and articles, I would imagine their surprise, confusion, perhaps their suppressed anger at the peculiar reconstruction that I elaborated with fragments and other scattered materials culled from their writing).

40. Gopal Balakrishnan, "The National Imagination," *Mapping the Nation,* ed. Gopal Balakrishnan (London: Verso, 1996), 209.

41. In an interview with Miguel Riera, "Retorno al origen," *Quimera* 73 (January 1988): Goytisolo establishes a conclusive link between the end of *En los reinos de taifa* and *Reivindicación del conde don Julián,* hinting in that process at the autobiographical dimension of what he calls the beginnings of "my adult work" (36).

42. For the Genetian connections of betrayal in Goytisolo, especially in *Reivindicación del conde don Julián,* see Bradley S. Epps, *Significant Violence: Oppression and Resistance in the Narratives of Juan Goytisolo, 1970–1990* (Oxford: Oxford University Press, 1996), 25 (n. 4), 81 and 92.

43. Edmund White, *Genet: A Biography* (New York: Knopf, 1993), xvii.

44. Under 1955, he writes in "Cronología" that two people, Monique and Genet, have had a deep and lasting influence in his life: "Monique es una mujer de 30 años, llena de vitalidad, generosidad, calor y simpatía, con la que podrá vencer su natural reserva por el otro sexo; Genet le ayudará más tarde a desprenderse sucesivamente de sus tabús políticos, patrióticos, sociales, sexuales. El encuentro con una y otro desempeñará en su existencia futura un papel comparable, en importancia, a la guerra civil o la muerte de su madre" (111; Monique is a thirty-year-old woman, full of vitality, generosity, warmth and sympathy, with whom he will be able to overcome his natural reservation towards the opposite sex. Genet will later help him to get rid successively of his political, patriotic, social and sexual taboos. Meeting both of them will have as important a role in his future life as the civil war or the death of his mother did).

45. Juan Goytisolo, "Presentación crítica de J. M. Blanco White," *Obra inglesa de Blanco White,* 3d edition, ed. Juan Goytisolo (Barcelona: Seix Barral, 1982), 98.

46. Lacan, *The Ethics of Psychoanalysis,* 324.

47. "The Construction/Deconstruction," 220. For his part, in "Theory and Autobiographical Writing: The Case of Juan Goytisolo," *Siglo XX/20th Century* 8.1–2 (1990–1991): 87–101, Randolph Pope argues that "the self is for Goytisolo a conscience with no stable content and no clear delimitations, joyfully assumed more than made, where History and histories overlap or contradict each other in the effort to link successive moments of existence" (98). This assertion fits the self in Goytisolo's novels, but in his autobiographical works a more stable sense of self ultimately prevails. For the contrasts and interactions between Goytisolo's novels and autobiographical works see also Cristina Moreiras Menor, "Ficción y autobiografía en Juan Goytisolo: algunos apuntes," *Anthropos* 125 (October 1991): 71–76.

48. Roland Barthes, *Roland Barthes by Roland Barthes,* trans. Richard Howard (New York: Hill and Wang, 1977), 120.

49. Brad Epps, "Thievish Subjectivity: Self-Writing in Jean Genet and Juan Goytisolo," *Revista de Estudios Hispánicos* 26 (May 1992): 174.

50. For Genet and Goytisolo see also Randolph Pope, "La herman-
dad del crimen: Genet examina a Goytisolo," *Estudios en homenaje a
Enrique Ruiz-Fornells*, ed. Juan Fernández Jiménez et al. (Erie, Pa.:
ALDEEU, 1990), 514–18.

51. Most of those textual self-reflexions appear in fourteen sections in
italics, whose goal is, according to Aline Schulman, to subvert the text's
temporality, to cast doubts on the text as autobiography and to foreground
the biographical discontinuity of the narrating subject. See "El nómada
narrador en la obra de Juan Goytisolo," *Escritos sobre Juan Goytisolo: coloquio en torno a la obra de Juan Goytisolo, Almería, 1987,* 56–57.

52. Paul Jay, *Being in the Text: Self-Representation from Wordsworth to
Roland Barthes* (Ithaca, N.Y.: Cornell University Press, 1984), 37, 167,
and 38.

53. Ibid., 180–81. Paul John Eakin, *Fictions in Autobiography:
Studies in the Art of Self-Invention* (Princeton, N.J.: Princeton University
Press, 1985), postulates a two-fold concept of referentiality similar to
Jay's. For a consideration of Eakin's ideas see the first chapter of this
book, "Before Reference."

54. James Fernández, "La novela familiar del autobiógrafo: Juan
Goytisolo," *Anthropos* 125 (October 1991): 55.

55. Notice that in his closing remarks Goytisolo never questions the
existence of a past's truth, but laments only the aesthetic hindrances that
compel the autobiographer to its unavoidable betrayal (again this crucial
concept). For a polemic concerning the "truth" of Goytisolo's text see his
brother Luis's criticisms in "Acotaciones," originally published in the
newspaper *El País* and later included in his *Investigaciones y conjeturas de
Claudio Mendoza* (Barcelona: Anagrama, 1985), 77–117. Gonzalo Díaz-
Migoyo examines their polemic in "La ajena autobiografía de los hermanos Goytisolo," *Anthropos* 125 (October 1991): 61–62.

56. Cristina Moreiras Menor, "Juan Goytisolo, F. F. B. y la fundación
fantasmal del proyecto autobiográfico contemporáneo español," *MLN*
111 (March 1996): 330. For Cristina Moreiras, accordingly, Goytisolo's
autobiographical texts would be emblematic of the Spanish political
transition to democracy, one of whose dominant traits was precisely a
flurry of autobiographical writings (342).

57. Goytisolo views Franco as a superego of whose power Spanish writers are finally free after his death. "Lo que hoy soy, a él lo debo. El me convirtió en un Judío Errante, en una especie de Juan sin Tierra, incapaz de aclimatarse y sentirse en casa en ninguna parte. El me impulsó a tomar la pluma desde mi niñez para exorcizar mi conflictiva relación con el medio y conmigo mismo por conducto de la creación literaria" (What I am today, I owe to him. He made me a Wandering Jew, a kind of John Landless, unable to adapt and feel at home anywhere. He compelled me to write since I was a child, as a way of coming to terms with my conflicting relationship with my surroundings and with myself) "In Memoriam F. F. B. (1892–1975)," *Libertad, libertad, libertad* (Barcelona: Anagrama, 1978), 17. In this document Goytisolo sees Franco as the key to understanding his life, but the critics do not necessarily have to agree with what Goytisolo wrote in 1975, just hours after Franco's death, when they interpret his autobiographical works, which were written several years later. Besides, the story he paints in his autobiography is far more complex, and in it Franco, and his death, plays a very limited role.

58. In "La hermandad del crimen: Genet examina a Goytisolo," Randolph Pope acutely condenses the idea that Genet is the privileged addressee of Goytisolo's autobiography, by referring to it as a letter that would be part of an exam Genet administers to Goytisolo: "Años más tarde, una larga carta a Genet, compuesta por tres novelas y dos volúmenes de autobiografías, . . . serán material suficiente para pasar el examen" (517–18; years later, a long letter to Genet, consisting of three novels and two autobiographical volumes . . . will be enough to pass the exam).

59. Gonzalo Navajas, however, argues that in his autobiography Goytisolo undermines any possible ethical foundation: "autobiographical memory is not able to resolve the axiological indetermination that the process of unremitting negativism brings about. Writing does not prove to be sufficient foundation on which to erect a solid ethical construction. The progressive annihilation of all established principles may produce only a vast but sterile space of freedom." In "Confession and Ethics in Juan Goytisolo's Fictive Autobiographies," *Letras Peninsulares* 3.2–3 (1990): 276. This could be true of ethics as morality, but, viewing ethics as preontological, the subject does not need to establish any foundations of ethics since they are always already a given that precedes the subject.

60. In an interview with Marie-Lise Gazarian Gautier, *Interviews with Spanish Writers* (Elmwood Park, Il.: Dalkey Archive Press, 1991), Goytisolo has declared that he wrote *Coto vedado* "for the simple and even moral reason that there was no such work in Spanish literature," and he continues, commenting on its title: "in Spain, traditionally, there has been great reluctance to speak about intimate matters. The Spanish authors of memoirs tend to engage in small talk about others, while remaining very quiet about themselves. They don't want their self-image destroyed. That's why in Spain they have always been either hypocritical, more commonly, or exhibitionistic, and I can't bear either. I have said the things I needed to say with a great deal of modesty and in a very unpretentious way" (147).

Chapter Five: Jorge Semprún

1. The dates in parenthesis in the text correspond to the French originals. *Le grand voyage,* translated into English as *The Long Voyage,* trans. Richard Seaver (New York: Schoken, 1964); *Quel beau dimanche*, English version as *What a Beautiful Sunday!* trans. Alan Sheridan (New York: Harcourt Brace Jovanovich, 1982).

2. Saul Friedlander, *Memory, History, and the Extermination of the Jews of Europe* (Bloomington: Indiana University Press, 1993), 133 and 129–130.

3. Geoffrey H. Hartman, "Introduction: Darkness Visible," *Holocaust Remembrance: The Shapes of Memory,* ed. Geoffrey H. Hartman (Cambridge, Mass.: Basil Blackwell, 1994), 5.

4. Dwight D. Eisenhower, letter to General Marshall, and telegram to General Marshall (April 19). Eisenhower visited Buchenwald on April 13, just two days after its liberation. The quotes are taken from David A. Hackett, Introduction, *The Buchenwald Report,* ed. and trans. David A. Hackett (Boulder, Colo.: Westview Press, 1995), 10 and 11.

5. Quoted by Hackett (11), who indicates that Eisenhower promptly sent Churchill photographs and descriptions of Buchenwald.

6. Lawrence Langer, *Preempting the Holocaust* (New Haven, Conn.: Yale University Press, 1998), 15; Tzvetan Todorov, *Facing the Extreme: Moral Life in the Concentration Camps,* trans. Arthur Denner and Abigail Pollak (New York: Metropolitan Books, 1996).

7. Ibid., 22, 1, 2.

8. Hayden White, "The Politics of Historical Interpretation: Discipline and De-Sublimation," *The Content of the Form: Narrative Discourse and Historical Representation* (Baltimore, Md.: Johns Hopkins University Press, 1987), 70, 81.

9. Hayden White, "Historical Emplotment and the Problem of Truth," *Probing the Limits of Representation: Nazism and the "Final Solution,"* ed. Saul Friedlander (Cambridge, Mass.: Harvard University Press, 1992), 50, 52.

10. Ibid., 51.

11. Jean-François Lyotard, *Heidegger and "the jews,"* trans. Andreas Michel and Mark S. Roberts (Minneapolis: University of Minnesota Press, 1990), 22, 21, 32.

12. Dominick LaCapra, *History and Memory after Auschwitz* (Ithaca, N.Y.: Cornell University Press, 1998), note 21, p. 33. See also pp. 33–39.

13. Alain Finkielkraut, "From the Novelistic to Memory," trans. Roger Butler-Borrault, *Auschwitz and After: Race, Culture, and "the Jewish Question" in France,* ed. Lawrence D. Kritzman (New York: Routledge, 1995), 92–93.

14. Joan Copjec, "Introduction: Evil in the Time of the Finite World," *Radical Evil,* ed. Joan Copjec (London: Verso, 1996), xiv.

15. The first page number is from *L'écriture ou la vie.* The second page number corresponds to the English translation, *Literature or Life,* trans. Linda Coverdale (New York: Viking, 1996). *Evil* is capitalized (when it means radical Evil) to keep consistency with the way Semprún writes it.

16. Copjec, xv.

17. Cathy Caruth, *Unclaimed Experience: Trauma, Narrative, and History* (Baltimore, Md.: Johns Hopkins University Press, 1996), 11, 4.

18. Friedlander, *Memory, History,* 123.

19. Lawrence Langer, *Admitting the Holocaust: Collected Essays* (New York: Oxford University Press, 1995), 3–23.

20. Primo Levi, *The Reawakening,* trans. Stuart Woolf (New York: Collier Books, 1993), 207–8. Primo Levi and other survivors often use the German word (*Lager*) for camp.

21. Langer, *Holocaust Testimonies: The Ruins of Memory* (New Haven, Conn.: Yale University Press, 1991), 95.

22. Primo Levi, *The Drowned and the Saved,* trans. Raymond Rosenthal (New York: Vintage, 1989), 112.

23. Ibid., 106.

24. Ibid., 78. See also Langer, *Preempting the Holocaust,* 33.

25. Primo Levi, *Survival in Auschwitz,* trans. Stuart Woolf (New York: Touchstone, 1996), 171–72.

26. Caruth, *Unclaimed Experience,* 62.

27. Ibid., 64.

28. Semprún's train accident and his awakening from it are at the center of *L'Évanouissement* (The Blackout), a novel in which Semprún deals, in the third person, with the tribulations involved in returning to normal life after the camp.

29. Although in a different way, Aharon Appelfeld, a Jewish refugee in Israel who grew up in Europe during the war, talks about personal reconstruction in terms of oblivion and awakening. See his "The Awakening," *Holocaust Remembrance: The Shapes of Memory,* ed. Geoffrey H. Hartman, 149–52. Semprún gives the cognitive narratives of passage between sleep and awakening still another configuration, this time in spatial terms of an impossible return to the homeland, which has been replaced by a new homeland (the "plenitude" of the camp), to which return is obviously impossible. A lost homeland/reality infects with lack/absence everything that comes after it.

30. Langer, *Admitting the Holocaust,* 15.

31. See Ludwig Wittgenstein, *Tractatus Logico-Philosophicus,* trans. D. F. Pears and B. F. McGuinness (London: Routledge & Kegan Paul, 1963), 6. 4311.

32. Wittgenstein's dictum resembles Paul de Man's scandalous pronouncement, "Death is a displaced name for a linguistic predicament."

De Man translates in linguistic terms Wittgenstein's cognitive statement, but both proclaim the same impossibility of adscribing meaning to death. Or, as Wittgenstein asserts in the *Tractatus*'s final interdiction: "Wovon man nicht sprechen kann, darüber muß man schweigen" (*Tractatus* 7; what we cannot speak about we must pass over in silence). See de Man, "Autobiography as De-Facement," *The Rhetoric of Romanticism* (New York: Columbia University Press, 1984), 81.

33. Emmanuel Levinas, *Entre Nous: On Thinking-of-the-Other,* trans. Michael B. Smith and Barbara Harshav (New York: Columbia University Press, 1998), 173, 186. Ethics can therefore be defined in terms of death: "Ethics, concern for the being of the other- than-one-self, non-indifference toward the death of the other" (202).

34. Maurice Halbwachs, also a Buchenwald inmate, had been Semprún's teacher at La Sorbonne. The German soldier he mentions was killed by Semprún and another French Resistance fighter before Semprún was caught by the Gestapo. This episode, narrated in *L'écriture ou la vie* (45–50/31–37), had already played a significant role in *L'Évanouissement.*

35. For Heidegger's "Sein zum Tode," see *Being and Time,* trans. John Macquarrie and Edward Robinson (New York: Harper & Row, 1962), 296–311. Heidegger asserts that it is impossible to reach an ontological interpretation of one's death through the death of others: "The dying of Others is not something which we experience in a genuine sense; at most we are always just 'there alongside'" (282). In an *ethical* reply to Heidegger's "being-towards-death," Levinas talks about "dying for the other" and "dying together" (*Entre Nous* 215). Semprún also confronts Heidegger, although this time without mentioning him: "Le temps a passé, Halbwachs était mort. J'avais vécu la mort de Halbwachs" (53/43; "Time had passed, Halbwachs had died. I had experienced the death of Halbwachs"). In the only reference to him in *L'écriture ou la vie,* Semprún states that Levinas's writings induced him to buy, when he was only seventeen, Heidegger's *Being and Time,* a book that, nonetheless, did not impress him very much (107/91–92). In *Adieu, vive clarté . . .* he states that he owes to Paul-Louis Landsberg his discovery (around 1940) that "Mon identité serait douteuse san cetter alterité partagé de la mort du prochain" (191; My identity would be doubtful without that shared alterity of the other's death). Be that as it

may, doubtless Semprún's formulation of the interplay between one's identity and the other's death is strikingly similar to Levinas. Precisely on the same page where he recognizes his debt to Landsberg, he also mentions Levinas, but only to reassert that it was through him that he discovered Husserl and Heidegger (Levinas is widely credited with introducing phenomenology to France).

36. Cathy Caruth, *Unclaimed Experience,* 100, 92.

37. Jacques Derrida, *Memoires for Paul de Man,* trans. Cecile Lindsay, Jonathan Culler, and Eduardo Cadava (New York: Columbia University Press, 1986), 33.

38. The translation of the French "s'oppose," which the English version of Semprún's book actually translates in two different ways: "clash" (in the epigraph), and "hang in the balance" (63/53), has been modified.

39. *Entre nous,* 94.

40. *Admitting the Holocaust,* 20.

41. Pierre Vidal-Naquet, "The Holocaust's Challenge to History," *Auschwitz and After,* ed. Kritzman, 31, 32.

42. The agreement reached in that discussion will become Semprún's program in *L'écriture ou la vie.* After stating that there will be countless testimonies, documents, and books of history on the Holocaust, one inmate sums up: "Tout y sera dit, consigné. . . . Tout y sera vrai. . . . sauf qu'il manquera l'essentiel vérité, à laquelle aucune reconstruction historique ne pourra jamais atteindre, pour parfaite et omnicompréhensive qu'elle soit" ("Everything will be said, put on record. . . . Everything in these books will be true . . . except that they won't contain the essential truth, which no historical reconstruction will ever be able to grasp, no matter how thorough and all-inclusive it may be"). And he continues: "L'autre genre de comprehénsion, la vérité essentielle de l'expérience, n'est pas transmissible. . . . Ou plutôt, elle ne l'est que par l'écriture littéraire," which for Semprún means, "[p]ar l'artifice de l'oeuvre d'art" (136/124-25; "The other kind of understanding, the essential truth of the experience, cannot be imparted. . . . Or should I say, it can be imparted only through literary writing," which means "[t]hrough the artifice of a work of art").

43. See Hackett, Introduction to *The Buchenwald Report,* 9–19. Hackett states that the text of the report was organized by Rosenberg

and Eugen Kogon. The report was apparently not intended for publication (it did not appear until 1995), but Kogon was commissioned by the military to write a book based on the information compiled, and the resulting work, *Der SS-Staat*, was published in 1946. The revised edition (1949) was translated into English as *The Theory and Practice of Hell* (1950).

44. Discussing the representation of trauma in *Hiroshima, mon amour*, Cathy Caruth reaches the exact same conclusion. In her view, by refusing to make a documentary, Resnais implies that archival footage "cannot maintain the very specificity of the event," something that is accomplished instead "through the fictional story" (*Unclaimed Experience*, 27). It does not come as a surprise to find this coincidence between Resnais and Semprún, former collaborators in *La guèrre est finie*.

45. For a view of the Final Solution's ineffability, see Richard Stamelman, "The Writing of Catastrophe: Jewish Memory and the Poetics of the Book in Edmond Jabès," *Auschwitz and After*, ed. Kritzman, 267.

46. Commenting on his arrival in Israel after the war, Appelfeld makes a similar observation: "The questions from the outside were useless. They were questions full of endless misunderstanding, questions from this world, having no contact at all with the world from which we came. As though you were catching up with information about the unfathomable abyss or, rather, eternity." See "The Awakening,," 149–50.

47. Shoshana Felman, "Education and Crisis, or the Vicissitudes of Teaching," *Trauma: Explorations in Memory*, Cathy Caruth, ed. (Baltimore, Md.: Johns Hopkins University Press, 1995), 24. For the interrelation between witness and listener and how it can affect the account, see also Susan Rubin Suleiman, "War Memories: On Autobiographical Reading," *Auschwitz and After*, ed. Kritzman, 50, and *L'écriture ou la vie*, 61–64.

48. Nelly Furman, "The Languages of Pain in *Shoah*," *Auschwitz and After*, ed. Kritzman, 299.

49. Andrés Soria Olmedo, "Vida y razones de Jorge Semprún," *Boletín de la Unidad de Estudios Biográficos* 1 (January 1996): 71.

50. Ibid., 72.

51. *The Buchenwald Report* does not mention any Lt. Walter Rosenfeld. Semprún must be referring to Second Lt. Albert G. Rosenberg (Hackett, "Introduction," *Buchenwald Report*, 2), who commanded the team that compiled the report. Perhaps Semprún has an imperfect recollection, or perhaps he created Rosenfeld based on data about Lt. Rosenberg. At any rate, the coincidences or similarities between the two are numerous. Both are Jewish, were born in Germany, and immigrated to the United States before the beginning of the War. However, Rosenfeld is from Berlin, and he left Germany in 1933, at the age of 14 (*L'écriture ou la vie,* 107/96), while Rosenberg was born in Göttingen, attended the university there, and moved to the United States in 1938 (Hackett, "Introduction, "*Buchenwald Report,* 15).

52. As Kogon explains in *The Theory and Practice of Hell: The German Concentration Camps and the System behind Them,* trans. Heinz Norden (New York: Farrar, Straus, 1950), although in every camp there were always a mixture of different categories of prisoners (Jews, political prisoners, common convicts, gay men and lesbians, Jehovah's Witnesses, and Gypsies), and their distribution shifted greatly in time. Buchenwald was predominantly a "Red" camp from the beginning (when camps were created to intern political prisoners) and right down to the end (45). Except for a brief period in 1942, when the common convicts ruled, in Buchenwald the German Communists controlled the internal organization (232). In that position, they helped many prisoners in different ways, in many cases saving lives, although in a selective way that favored their own comrades. Being a *Rotspanier* (Spanish Red) helped Semprún secure an administrative position in the Labor Record Offices (*Arbeitstatistik*), which, manned by prisoners and not exempt from "sordid intrigue" (62), controlled the utilization of workers, work assignments, and transfers to other camps: "That work was guided by the principle that anti-Fascist forces—which meant, in the main, Communists—must be kept in camp while elements likely to sabotage the common effort, as well as the physically weak, had to be smuggled into the shipments to be got rid of. Undesirables included chiefly men who had shown a lack of solidarity in camp—bread thieves, racketeers, hoarders and the like" (238). As Levi observes, "the best historians of the Lagers emerged from among the very few who had the ability and luck to attain a privileged observatory without bowing to compromises, and

the skill to tell what they saw, suffered, and did with the humility of a good chronicler, that is, taking into account the complexity of the Lager phenomenon and the variety of human destinies being played out in it." They were "almost all . . . political prisoners" because the camps were originally political, had a cultural background that allowed them to interpret the events, realized the value of testimony, had access to data, held positions in the camp, and often formed part of secret defense organizations (*The Drowned and the Saved*, 18). In "Al Filo de la Escritura. Entrevista con Jorge Semprún," *Quimera* 88 (January 1989), 20–27, Semprún describes Buchenwald and the *Arbeitstatick* in a manner very similar to Kogon's.

53. *Lettre sur le poivour d'écrire* (Paris: Seghers, 1947).

BIBLIOGRAPHY

Alberti, Rafael. *Conversaciones con Rafael Alberti*. With José Miguel Velloso. Madrid: Ediciones Sedmay, 1977.

Althusser, Louis. "Ideology and Ideological State Apparatuses (Notes towards an Investigation)." *Essays on Ideology*. London: Verso, 1984. 1–60.

Anderson, Benedict. *Imagined Communities: Reflections on the Origin and Spread of Nationalism*. 2d ed. London: Verso, 1991.

Andújar, Manuel. "Crisis de la nostalgia." *Andalucía e Hispanoamerica: crisol de Mestizajes*. Sevilla, Spain: Edisur, 1982. 105–19.

Appelfeld, Aharon. "The Awakening." *Holocaust Remembrance: The Shapes of Memory*. Ed. Geoffrey H. Hartman. Cambridge, Mass.: Basil Blackwell, 1994. 149–52.

Augustine. *Confessions*. Trans. R. S. Pine-Coffin. Harmondsworth, U.K.: Penguin, 1961.

Ayala, Francisco. "Para quién escribimos nosotros." *El escritor y su siglo*. Madrid: Alianza, 1990. 197–223. First published in 1948.

Balakrishnan, Gopal. "The National Imagination." *Mapping the Nation*. Ed. Gopal Balakrishnan. London: Verso, 1996. 198–213.

Barthes, Roland. *Roland Barthes by Roland Barthes*. Trans. Richard Howard. New York: Hill and Wang, 1977.

Bellver, Catherine G. "Antidotes for Exile: Rafael Alberti's Struggle against a Persistent Malady." *Monographic Review* 2 (1986): 68–83.

Benjamin, Walter. *The Origin of German Tragic Drama*. Trans. John Osborne. London: Verso, 1990.

Bernasconi, Robert, and Simon Critchley, ed. *Re-Reading Levinas*. Bloomington: Indiana University Press, 1991.

Bernasconi, Robert, and David Wood, ed. *The Provocation of Levinas: Rethinking the Other*. New York: Routledge, 1988.

Bilbao, Elena. "María Teresa León, aún exiliada." *El País* (October 19, 1997).

Blanco, Alda. "'Las voces perdidas': silencio y recuerdo en *Memoria de la melancolía*." *Anthropos* 125 (October 1991): 45–49.

Blanco White, Joseph. *Cartas de España*. Trans. Antonio Garnica. Madrid: Alianza, 1972.

———. "Despedida del autor de las *Variedades* a los Hispano-Americanos." *Variedades ó Mensagero de Londres* 2 (October 1, 1825): 299–311.

———. "The Examination of Blanco by White, Concerning His Religious Notions and Other Subjects Connected with Them." Ed. Angel G. Loureiro. *Revista de Estudios Hispánicos* 33.1 (1999): 3–40.

———. *Letters from Spain* (see under Leucadio Doblado).

———. *The Life of the Rev. Joseph Blanco White, Written by Himself; with Portions of His Correspondence*. Ed. John Hamilton Thom. London: John Chapman, 1845. 3 vols.

———. *The Poor Man's Preservative against Popery: Addressed to the Lower Classes of Great Britain and Ireland*. London: Rivington, 1825.

———. *Practical and Internal Evidence against Catholicism*. Cambridge, Mass.: Manson and Grant, 1835. (Based on the 2d English ed., revised, 1826; first published, 1825).

Borch-Jacobsen, Mikkel. "The Freudian Subject: From Politics to Ethics." *The Emotional Tie: Psychoanalysis, Mimesis, and Affect*. Stanford, Calif.: Stanford University Press, 1992. 15–35.

———. *Lacan: The Absolute Master*. Trans. Douglas Brick. Stanford, Calif.: Stanford University Press, 1991.

Boyd, Carolyn. *Historia Patria: Politics, History, and National Identity in Spain, 1875–1975*. Princeton, N.J.: Princeton University Press, 1997.

Brodsky, Joseph. "The Condition We Call 'Exile.'" *Literature in Exile.* Ed. John Glad. Durham, N.C.: Duke University Press, 1990. 100–109.

Brodzki, Bella. "Mothers, Displacement, and Language in the Auto-biographies of Nathalie Sarraute and Christa Wolf." *Life/Lines: Theorizing Women's Autobiography.* Ed. Brodzki and Celeste Schenck. Ithaca, N.Y.: Cornell University Press, 1988. 243–59.

Bruss, Elizabeth. *Autobiographical Acts: The Changing Situation of a Literary Genre.* Baltimore, Md.: Johns Hopkins University Press, 1976.

The Buchenwald Report. Ed. and trans. David A. Hackett. Boulder, Colo.: Westview Press, 1995.

Butler, Judith. *Bodies That Matter: On the Discursive Limits of "Sex."* New York: Routledge, 1993.

———. *Excitable Speech: A Politics of the Performative.* New York: Routledge, 1997.

———. *The Psychic Life of Power: Theories in Subjection.* Stanford, Calif.: Stanford University Press, 1997.

Caruth, Cathy. *Unclaimed Experience: Trauma, Narrative, and History.* Baltimore, Md.: Johns Hopkins University Press, 1996.

Chacel, Rosa. *La confesión.* 1971. Barcelona: EDHASA, 1980.

———. *Desde el amanecer.* Madrid: Revista de Occidente, 1972.

Cohen, Richard A., ed. *Face to Face with Levinas.* Albany: State University of New York Press, 1986.

Copjec, Joan. "Introduction: Evil in the Time of the Finite World." *Radical Evil.* Ed. Copjec. London: Verso, 1996. vii–xxviii.

Critchley, Simon. *The Ethics of Deconstruction: Derrida and Llevinas.* Cambridge, Mass.: Blackwell, 1992.

Crowell, Steven G. "Dialogue and Text: Re-marking the Difference." *The Interpretation of Dialogue.* Ed. Tullio Maranhão. Chicago: Chicago University Press, 1990. 338–60.

de la Mora, Constancia. *In Place of Splendor: The Autobiography of a Spanish Woman*. New York: Harcourt, Brace, 1939.

de Man, Paul. *Allegories of Reading: Figural Language in Rousseau, Nietzsche, Rilke, and Proust*. New Haven, Conn.: Yale University Press, 1979.

―――. "Autobiography as De-Facement." *The Rhetoric of Romanticism*. New York: Columbia University Press, 1984. 67–81.

―――. "The Rhetoric of Temporality." *Blindness and Insight*. 2d ed. Minneapolis: University of Minnesota Press, 1983. 187–228.

de Palencia, Isabel. *I Must Have Liberty*. New York: Longmans, Green, 1940.

―――. *Smouldering Freedom: The Story of the Spanish Republicans in Exile*. New York: Longmans, Green, 1945.

Deleuze, Gilles. *Foucault*. Trans. Seán Hand. Minneapolis: University of Minnesota Press, 1988.

―――. *Masoquism*. Trans. Jean McNeil. New York: Zone Books, 1991.

―――. *Negotiations: 1972–1990*. Trans. Martin Joughin. New York: Columbia University Press, 1995.

Deleuze, Gilles, and Félix Guattari. *A Thousand Plateaus: Capitalism and Schizophrenia*. Trans. Brian Massumi. Minneapolis: University of Minnesota Press, 1994.

Derrida, Jacques. "Adieu." *Critical Inquiry* 23 (Autumn 1996): 1–10.

―――. "At this very moment in this work here I am." *Re-Reading Levinas*. Ed. Robert Bernasconi and Simon Critchley. Bloomington: Indiana University Press, 1991. 11–48.

―――. "circumfession." *Jacques Derrida*. By Geoffrey Bennington and Jacques Derrida. Trans. Geoffrey Bennington. Chicago: Chicago University Press, 1993.

―――. *The Ear of the Other*. Ed. Christie McDonald. Trans. Peggy Kamuf. Lincoln: University of Nebraska Press, 1988.

―――. *Memoires for Paul de Man*. Trans. Cecile Lindsay, Jonathan Culler, and Eduardo Cadava. New York: Columbia University Press, 1986.

————. *Points . . . Interviews, 1974–1994*. Ed. Elisabeth Weber. Trans. Peggy Kamuf et al. Stanford, Calif.: Stanford University Press, 1995.

————. "Remarks on Deconstruction and Pragmatism." *Deconstruction and Pragmatism*. Ed. Chantal Mouffe. New York: Routledge, 1996. 77–88.

————. "Violence and Metaphysics: An Essay on the Thought of Emmanuel Levinas." *Writing and Difference*. Trans. Alan Bass. Chicago: Chicago University Press, 1978. 79–153.

Díaz-Migoyo, Gonzalo. "La ajena autobiografía de los hermanos Goytisolo." *Anthropos* 125 (October 1991): 61–62.

Doblado, Leucadio [Joseph Blanco White]. *Letters from Spain*. 2d ed. London: Henry Colburn, 1825.

Domergue, Lucienne. "Feijoo y Blanco White (Homenaje de un 'hereje' al Padre Maestro)." *II Simposio sobre el Padre Feijoo y su Siglo*. Oviedo, Spain: Universidad de Oviedo, 1983. 333–48.

Eakin, Paul John. *Fictions in Autobiography: Studies in the Art of Self-Invention*. Princeton, N.J.: Princeton University Press, 1985.

————. *Touching the World: Reference in Autobiography*. Princeton, N.J.: Princeton University Press, 1992.

Edwards, Robert. "Exile, Self, and Society." *Exile in Literature*. Ed. María-Inés Lagos-Pope. Lewisburg, Pa.: Bucknell University Press, 1988. 15–31.

Ellis, Robert Richmond. "Cutting the Gordian Knot: Homosexuality and the Autobiographies of Juan Goytisolo." *Anales de la Literatura Española Contemporánea* 19.1–2 (1994): 47–65.

Epps, Bradley S. *Significant Violence: Oppression and Resistance in the Narratives of Juan Goytisolo, 1970–1990*. Oxford: Oxford University Press, 1996.

Epps, Brad. "Thievish Subjectivity: Self-Writing in Jean Genet and Juan Goytisolo." *Revista de Estudios Hispánicos* 26 (May 1992): 163–81.

Estébanez Gil, Juan Carlos. *Mª Teresa León: estudio de su obra literaria.* Burgos, Spain: Editorial La Olmeda, 1995.

Feijoo, Benito. *Teatro crítico universal.* Ed. Agustín Millares Carlo. Vol. 1. Clásicos Castellanos 48. Madrid: Espasa-Calpe, 1968. 3 vols.

Felman, Shoshana. "Education and Crisis, or the Vicissitudes of Teaching." *Trauma: Explorations in Memory.* Ed. Cathy Caruth. Baltimore: Johns Hopkins University Press, 1995. 13–60.

Fernández, James D. *Apology to Apostrophe: Autobiography and the Rhetoric of Self-Representation in Spain.* Durham, N.C.: Duke University Press, 1992.

———. "La novela familiar del autobiógrafo: Juan Goytisolo." *Anthropos* 125 (October 1991): 54–60.

Finkielkraut, Alain. "From the Novelistic to Memory." *Auschwitz and After: Race, Culture, and "the Jewish Question" in France.* Trans. Roger Butler-Borraut. Ed. Lawrence D. Kritzman. New York: Routledge, 1995. 83–97.

Fontanier, Pierre. *Les figures du discours* (1830). Intro. Gérard Genette. Paris: Flammarion, 1977.

Foucault, Michel. *The Care of the Self.* Vol. 3 of *The History of Sexuality.* Trans. Robert Hurley. New York: Vintage, 1988.

———. *An Introduction.* Vol. 1 of *The History of Sexuality* Trans. Robert Hurley. New York: Vintage, 1980.

———. "On the Genealogy of Ethics: An Overview of Work in Progress." *The Foucault Reader.* Ed. Paul Rabinow. New York: Pantheon, 1984. 340–72.

———. "Politics and Ethics: An Interview." *The Foucault Reader.* Ed. Paul Rabinow. New York: Pantheon, 1984. 373–80.

———. "The Subject and Power." *Critical Inquiry* 8 (Summer 1982): 777–95.

———. "Technologies of the Self." *Technologies of the Self.* Ed. Luther H. Martin et al. Amherst: University of Massachusetts Press, 1988. 16–49.

————. *The Use of Pleasure.* Trans. Robert Hurley. Vol. 2 of *The History of Sexuality.* New York: Vintage, 1990.

————. "What Is Enlightenment?" Trans. Catherine Porter. *The Foucault Reader.* Ed. Paul Rabinow. New York: Pantheon, 1984. 32–50.

Freud, Sigmund. "Mourning and Melancholia." *Collected Papers.* Trans. Joan Riviere. Vol. 4. The International Psycho-Analytical Library 10. New York: Basic Books, 1959. 152–70. 5 vols.

Friedlander, Saul. *Memory, History, and the Extermination of the Jews of Europe.* Bloomington: Indiana University Press, 1993.

Friedman, Susan Stanford. "Women's Autobiographical Selves: Theory and Practice." *The Private Self: Theory and Practice of Women's Autobiographical Writings.* Ed. Shari Benstock. Chapel Hill: University of North Carolina Press, 1988. 34–62.

Furman, Nelly. "The Languages of Pain in *Shoah.*" *Auschwitz and After: Race, Culture, and "the Jewish Question" in France.* Ed. Lawrence D. Kritzman. New York: Routledge, 1995. 299–312.

Gay, Peter. *The Rise of Modern Paganism.* Vol. 1 of *The Enlightenment: An Interpretation.* New York: Norton, 1977. 2 vols.

Girard, René. *Deceit, Desire and the Novel.* Baltimore, Md.: Johns Hopkins University Press, 1965.

Gladstone, W. E. "Blanco White." *Gleanings of Past Years, 1845–76.* London: John Murray, 1879. 1–64.

Goytisolo, Juan. "Abandonemos de una vez el amoroso cultivo de nuestras señas de identidad." *Contracorrientes.* Barcelona: Montesinos, 1985. 134–38.

————. *Coto vedado.* Barcelona: Seix Barral, 1985.

————. "Cronología." *Juan Goytisolo.* Ed. Manuel Ruiz Lagos. Madrid: Ediciones de Cultura Hispánica, 1991. 101–22.

————. "De *Don Julián* a *Makbara*: una posible lectura orientalista." *Crónicas sarracinas.* Barcelona: Seix Barral, 1989. 27–46.

————. "El cuerpo del delito." *Contracorrientes.* Barcelona: Montesinos, 1985. 83–85.

———. *En los reinos de taifa*. Barcelona: Seix Barral, 1986.

———. *Forbidden Territory: The Memoirs of Juan Goytisolo 1931–1956*. Trans. Peter Bush. San Francisco: North Point Press, 1989.

———. "In Memoriam F.F.B. (1892–1975)." *Libertad, libertad, libertad*. Barcelona: Anagrama, 1978. 11–19.

———. Interview. *Interviews with Spanish Writers*. With Marie-Lise Gazarian Gautier. Elmwood Park, Il.: Dalkey Archive Press, 1991. 137–50.

———. "Presentación crítica de J. M. Blanco White." *Obra inglesa de Blanco White*. Ed. Juan Goytisolo. 3d ed. Barcelona: Seix Barral, 1982.

———. *Realms of Strife: The Memoirs of Juan Goytisolo 1957–1982*. Trans. Peter Bush. San Francisco: North Point Press, 1990.

———. "Retorno al origen." Interview with Miguel Riera. *Quimera* 73 (January 1988): 36–40.

———. "Vigencia actual del mudejarismo." *Contracorrientes*. Barcelona: Montesinos, 1985. 9–13.

Goytisolo, Luis. "Acotaciones." *Investigaciones y conjeturas de Claudio Mendoza*. Barcelona: Anagrama, 1985. 77–117.

The Greek Anthology. Trans. W. R. Paton. Vol. 4. The Loeb Classical Library 85. London: Heinemann, 1926. 5 vols. 1925–1927.

Greene, Graham. *A Sort of Life*. New York: Simon & Schuster, 1971.

Guillory, John. *Cultural Capital*. Chicago: Chicago University Press, 1993.

Gusdorf, George. "Conditions and Limits of Autobiography." Trans. James Olney. *Autobiography: Essays Theoretical and Critical*. Ed James Olney. Princeton, N.J.: Princeton University Press, 1980. 28–48.

Hackett, David A. Introduction. *The Buchenwald Report*. Ed. and trans. David A. Hackett. Boulder, Colo.: Westview Press, 1995.

Halbwachs, Maurice. *On Collective Memory*. Trans. Lewis A. Coser. Chicago: University of Chicago Press, 1992.

Hartman, Geoffrey H. "Introduction: Darkness Visible." *Holocaust Remembrance: The Shapes of Memory*. Ed. Hartman. Cambridge, Mass.: Basil Blackwell, 1994. 1–22.

Heidegger, Martin. *Being and Time*. Trans. John Macquarrie and Edward Robinson. New York: Harper & Row, 1962.

Henderson, Heather. *The Victorian Self: Autobiography and Biblical Narrative*. Ithaca, N.Y.: Cornell University Press, 1989.

Hennessy, C. Margot. "Listening to the Secret Mother: Reading John Edgar Wideman's *Brothers and Keepers*." *American Women's Autobiographies: Fea(s)ts of Memory*. Ed. Margo Culley. Madison: University of Wisconsin Press, 1992. 295–321.

Hierro, Manuel. "Por los territorios del anti-Edipo: la genealogía indeseada de Juan Goytisolo en *Coto Vedado*." *Revista Monográfica* 9 (1993): 93–103.

Huerga, Florentino. "Una patria, señor. María Teresa León." *Quimera* 123 (1994): 32–33.

Hunt, Lynn. "History as Gesture; or, The Scandal of History." *Consequences of Theory*. Ed. Jonathan Arac and Barbara Johnson. Baltimore, Md.: Johns Hopkins University Press, 1991. 91–107.

Ibárruri, Dolores. *Memorias de Pasionaria: 1939–1977. Me faltaba España*. Barcelona: Planeta, 1984.

Jay, Gregory S. "Freud: The Death *of* Autobiography." *Genre* 19 (Summer 1986): 103–28.

Jay, Martin. "The Ethics of Blindness and the Postmodern Sublime: Levinas and Lyotard." *Downcast Eyes: The Denigration of Vision in Twentieth-Century French Thought*. Berkeley: University of California Press, 1993. 543–86.

Jay, Paul. *Being in the Text: Self-Representation from Wordsworth to Roland Barthes*. Ithaca, N.Y.: Cornell University Press, 1984.

Kant, Immanuel. "What Is Enlightenment?" *On History*. Ed. and trans. Lewis White Beck. New York: Macmillan, 1963. 3–10.

Kearney, Richard. "Dialogue with Emmanuel Levinas." *Dialogues with Contemporary Continental Thinkers: The Phenomenological Heritage*. Manchester: Manchester University Press, 1984. 47–70.

————. "Dialogue with Jacques Derrida." *Dialogues with Contemporary Continental Thinkers: The Phenomenological Heritage*. Manchester: Manchester University Press, 1984. 105–126.

Kent, Victoria. *Cuatro años en París (1940–1944)*. Buenos Aires: Sur, 1947.

Kogon, Eugen. *The Theory and Practice of Hell: The German Concentration Camps and the System behind Them*. Trans. Heinz Norden. New York: Farrar, Straus, 1950.

Kristeva, Julia. *Black Sun: Depression and Melancholia*. Trans. Leon S. Roudiez. New York: Columbia University Press, 1989.

Labanyi, Jo. "The Construction/Deconstruction of the Self in the Autobiographies of Pablo Neruda and Juan Goytisolo." *Forum for Modern Language Studies* 26.3 (1990): 212–21.

Lacan, Jacques. *The Seminar of Jacques Lacan*. Book 3: *The Psychosis 1955–1956*. Ed. Jacques-Alain Miller. Trans. Russell Grigg. New York: Norton, 1993.

————. *The Seminar of Jacques Lacan*. Book 7: *The Ethics of Psychoanalysis 1959–1960*. Ed. Jacques-Alain Miller. Trans. Dennis Porter. New York: Norton, 1992.

————. *Television*. Trans. Denis Hollier, Rosalind Krauss, and Annette Michelson. Ed. Joan Copjec. New York: Norton, 1990.

LaCapra, Dominick. *History and Memory after Auschwitz*. Ithaca, N.Y.: Cornell University Press, 1998.

Laclau, Ernesto. "Deconstruction, Pragmatism, Hegemony." *Deconstruction and Pragmatism*. Ed. Chantal Mouffe. New York: Routledge, 1996. 47–67.

————. *Emancipation(s)*. London: Verso, 1996.

Laclau, Ernesto, and Chantal Mouffe. *Hegemony and Socialist Strategy: Towards a Radical Democratic Politics*. London: Verso, 1993.

Langer, Laurence. *Admitting the Holocaust: Collected Essays*. New York: Oxford University Press, 1995.

————. *Holocaust Testimonies: The Ruins of Memory*. New Haven, Conn.: Yale University Press, 1991.

————. *Preempting the Holocaust.* New Haven, Conn.: Yale University Press, 1998.

Lausberg, Heinrich. *Handbuch der Literarischen Rhetorik.* 2d ed. 2 vols. München: Max Hueber Verlag, 1973.

Lázaro, Reyes. "*Desde el amanecer.* Confesiones de una hija voluntariosa." *Journal of Interdisciplinary Literary Studies* 5.1 (special issue 1993): 61–73.

Lejeune, Philippe. *On Autobiography.* Ed. Paul John Eakin. Trans. Katherine Leary. Minneapolis: University of Minnesota Press, 1989.

León, María Teresa. *Contra viento y marea.* Buenos Aires: Ediciones Aiape, 1941.

————. *La historia tiene la palabra: noticia sobre el salvamento del tesoro artístico de España.* Buenos Aires: Patronato Hispano-Argentino de Cultura, 1944. 2d edition. Madrid: Hispamerca, 1977.

————. *Rodrigo Díaz de Vivar, el Cid Campeador.* Buenos Aires: Ediciones Peuser, 1954.

————. *Doña Jimena Díaz de Vivar: gran señora de todos los deberes.* Buenos Aires: Losada, 1960. Madrid: Biblioteca Nueva, 1968.

————. *Juego limpio.* Buenos Aires: Editorial Goyanarte, 1959. Barcelona: Seix Barral, 1987.

————. *Memoria de la melancolía.* Buenos Aires: Losada, 1970.

León, María Teresa, and Rafael Alberti. *Sonríe China.* Buenos Aires: Jacobo Muchnik Editor, 1958.

Levi, Primo. *The Drowned and the Saved.* Trans. Raymond Rosenthal. New York: Vintage, 1989.

————. *The Reawakening.* Trans. Stuart Woolf. New York: Collier Books, 1993.

————. *Survival in Auschwitz.* Trans. Stuart Woolf. New York: Touchstone, 1996.

Levinas, Emmanuel. *Entre Nous: On Thinking-of-the-Other.* Trans. Michael B. Smith and Barbara Harshav. New York: Columbia University Press, 1998.

――――. *Ethics and Infinity: Conversations with Philippe Nemo.* Trans. Richard A. Cohen. Pittsburgh: Duquesne University Press, 1985.

――――. "Ethics and Politics." Trans. Jonathan Romney. *The Levinas Reader.* Ed. Seán Hand. Oxford: Basil Blackwell, 1989. 289–97.

――――. "Ethics as First Philosophy." Trans. Seán Hand and Michael Temple. *The Levinas Reader.* Ed. Seán Hand. Oxford: Basil Blackwell, 1989. 75–87.

――――. "God and Philosophy." Trans. Richard A. Cohen and Alphonso Lingis. *The Levinas Reader.* Ed. Seán Hand. Oxford: Basil Blackwell, 1989. 166–89.

――――. *The Levinas Reader.* Ed. Seán Hand. Trans. André Orianne et al. Oxford: Basil Blackwell, 1989.

――――. *Otherwise Than Being or Beyond Essence.* Trans. Alphonso Lingis. The Hague: Martinus Nijhoff, 1981.

――――. "Outside the Subject." *Outside the Subject.* Trans. Michael B. Smith. London: Athlone Press, 1993. 151–58.

――――. "Signature." *Difficult Freedom: Essays on Judaism.* Trans. Seán Hand. Baltimore, Md.: Johns Hopkins University Press, 1990. 291–95.

――――. *Totality and Infinity: An Essay in Exteriority.* Trans. Alphonso Lingis. The Hague: Martinus Nijhoff, 1978.

Liddell, Henry George. *A Greek-English Lexicon.* Oxford: Clarendon Press, 1968.

Llewelyn, John. *Emmanuel Levinas: The Genealogy of Ethics.* New York, Routledge, 1995.

Lloréns, Vicente. "Entre España y América." *Literatura, historia, política.* Madrid: Revista de Occidente, 1967. 223–36.

――――. Introducción. *Antología de obras en español.* By José María Blanco White. Ed. Vicente Llorens. Barcelona: Labor 1971. 7–49.

————. *Memorias de una emigración: Santo Domingo, 1939–1945.* Barcelona: Ariel, 1975.

Loesberg, Jonathan. *Fictions of Consciousness: Mill, Newman, and the Reading of Victorian Prose.* New Brunswick, N.J.: Rutgers University Press, 1986.

López-Baralt, Luce. "Hacia una lectura 'mudéjar' de *Makbara.*" *Huellas del Islam en la literatura española: de Juan Ruiz a Juan Goytisolo.* Madrid: Hiperión, 1985. 181–209.

————. "Juan Goytisolo's Fictionalized Version of *Orientalism,*" *Review of Contemporary Fiction* 4 (Summer 1984): 138–45.

Loureiro, Angel G. "Autobiografía del otro (Rousseau, Torres Villarroel, Juan Goytisolo)." *Siglo XX/20th Century* 9.1–2 (1991–1992): 71–94.

Lyotard, Jean-François. *Heidegger and "the jews."* Trans. Andreas Michel and Mark Roberts. Minneapolis: University of Minnesota Press, 1990.

Magny, Claude-Edmonde. *Lettre sur le poivour d'écrire.* Paris: Seghers, 1947.

Mandel, Barrett J. "Full of Life Now." *Autobiography: Essays Theoretical and Critical.* Ed. James Olney. Princeton, N.J.: Princeton University Press, 1980. 49–72.

Mangini, Shirley. *Memories of Resistance: Women's Voices from the Spanish Civil War.* New Haven, Conn.: Yale University Press, 1995.

————. "Three Voices of Exile." *Monographic Review* 2 (1986): 208–15.

Marcus Aurelius. *The Meditations.* Trans. G. Long. *The Stoic and Epicurean Philosophers.* Ed. Whitney J. Oates. New York: Random House, 1940. 491–587.

María Teresa León. Valladolid, Spain: Junta de Castilla León, 1987.

Martin, Biddy. "Lesbian Identity and Autobiographical Difference[s]." *Life/Lines: Theorizing Women's Autobiography.* Ed. Bella Brodzki and Celeste Schenck. Ithaca, N.Y.: Cornell University Press, 1988. 177–103.

Martínez Sierra, María. *Una mujer por caminos de España.* Buenos Aires: Losada, 1952. Madrid: Castalia, 1989.

Mehlman, Jeffrey. *A Structural Study of Autobiography.* Ithaca, N.Y.: Cornell University Press, 1974.

Menéndez Pelayo, Marcelino. *Historia de los heterodoxos españoles.* Vol. 2. 4th ed. Madrid: BAC, 1987. 2 vols.

Molloy, Sylvia. *At Face Value: Autobiographical Writing in Spanish America.* Cambridge: Cambridge University Press, 1991.

Montrose, Louis. "New Historicisms." *Redrawing the Boundaries.* Ed. Stephen Greenblatt and Giles Gunn. New York: Modern Language Association, 1992. 392–418.

Montseny, Federica. *Mis primeros cuarenta años.* Barcelona: Plaza & Janés, 1987.

———. *Seis años de mi vida (1939–1945).* Barcelona: Galba Ediciones, 1978.

Moreiras Menor, Cristina. "Juan Goytisolo, F. F. B. y la fundación fantasmal del proyecto autobiográfico contemporáneo español." *MLN* 111 (March 1996): 327–45.

———. "Ficción y autobiografía en Juan Goytisolo: algunos apuntes." *Anthropos* 125 (October 1991): 71–76

Murphy, Martin. *Blanco White: Self-Banished Spaniard.* New Haven, Conn.: Yale University Press, 1989.

Naharro-Calderón, José María. *Entre el exilio y el interior: el "entresiglo" y Juan Ramón Jiménez.* Barcelona: Anthropos, 1994.

Navajas, Gonzalo. "Confession and Ethics in Juan Goytisolo's Fictive Autobiographies." *Letras Peninsulares* 3.2–3 (1990): 259–78.

Neuman, Shirley. "Autobiography: From Different Poetics to a Poetics of Differences." *Essays on Life Writing: From Genre to Critical Practice.* Ed. Marlene Kadar. Toronto: University of Toronto Press, 1992. 213–30.

Nussbaum, Felicity A. "Eighteenth-Century Women's Autobiographical Commonplaces." *The Private Self: Theory and Practice of Women's Autobiographical Writings.* Ed. Shari Benstock. Chapel Hill: University of North Carolina Press, 1988. 147–76.

Olney, James. "Autobiography and the Cultural Moment: A Thematic, Historical, and Bibliographical Introduction." *Autobiography: Essays Theoretical and Critical.* Ed. James Olney. Princeton, N.J.: Princeton University Press, 1980. 3–27.

———. *Metaphors of Self.* Princeton, N.J.: Princeton University Press, 1972.

———. "Some Versions of Memory/Some Versions of *Bios*: The Ontology of Autobiography." *Autobiography: Essays Theoretical and Critical.* Ed. James Olney. Princeton, N.J.: Princeton University Press, 1980. 236–67.

Parret, Herman. "'Ma Vie' comme effet de discours." *La Licorne* 14 (1988): 161–77.

Pensky, Max. *Melancholy Dialectics: Walter Benjamin and the Play of Mourning.* Amherst: University of Massachusetts Press, 1993.

Peperzak, Adriaan T. *Ethics as First Philosophy.* New York: Routledge, 1995.

Perrin, Annie. "El laberinto homotextual." *Escritos sobre Juan Goytisolo: coloquio en torno a la obra de Juan Goytisolo, Almería, 1987.* Almería, Spain: Instituto de Estudios Almerienses, 1988. 73–81.

Peterson, Linda H. *Victorian Autobiography: The Tradition of Self-Interpretation.* New Haven, Conn.: Yale University Press, 1986.

Pons, André. *Blanco White et la crise du monde hispanique, 1808–1816.* Paris: Université de Paris III-Sorbonne Nouvelle, Etudes Hispano-Americaines, 1990. 4 vols.

Pope, Randolph. "La autobiografía del exilio: el ser previamente pre-ocupado de Rafael Alberti y María Teresa León." *El exilio de las Españas de 1939 en las Américas: "¿Adónde fue la canción?"* Ed. José María Naharro-Calderón. Barcelona: Anthropos, 1991. 369–78.

———. "La hermandad del crimen: Genet examina a Goytisolo." *Estudios en homenaje a Enrique Ruiz-Fornells.* Ed. Juan Fernández Jiménez et al. Erie, Pa.: ALDEEU, 1990. 514–18.

———. "Theory and Autobiographical Writing: The Case of Juan Goytisolo." *Siglo XX/20th Century* 8.1–2 (1990–1991): 87–101.

Quintilian. *Institutio Oratoria.* Trans. H. E. Butler. Vol. 2. Cambridge: Harvard University Press, 1986. 4 vols. 1980–1989.

Renan, Ernest. "What Is a Nation?" *Nation and Narration.* Ed. Homi K. Bhabha. London: Routledge, 1990. 8–22.

Riffaterre, Michael. "Prosopopeia." *The Lessons of Paul de Man.* Ed. Peter Brooks et al. *Yale French Studies* 69, special issue (1985): 107–23.

Rodríguez-Fischer, Ana, ed. and intro. *Cartas a Rosa Chacel.* Madrid: Versal, 1992.

Roth, Philip. *The Facts: A Novelist's Autobiography.* New York: Farrar, Straus, 1988.

Rousseau, Jean-Jacques. *The Confessions.* Ed. Christopher Kelly et al. Trans. Chistopher Kelly. Vol. 5 of *The Collected Writings of Rousseau.* 6 vols. 1990–1997. Hanover, N.H.: University Press of New England, 1995.

———. *Rousseau Judge of Jean-Jacques: Dialogues.* Ed. Roger D. Masters and Christopher Kelly. Trans. Judith R. Bush et al. Vol. 1 of *The Collected Writings of Rousseau.* 6 vols. 1990–1997. Hanover, N.H.: University Press of New England, 1990.

Rousset, David. *The Other Kingdom.* Trans. and Intro. Ramon Guthrie. New York: Howard Fertig, 1982.

Rowlands, Michael. "Memory, Sacrifice and the Nation." *New Formations* 30 (Winter 1996): 8–17.

Ruiz Lagos, Manuel, ed. *Juan Goytisolo*. Madrid: Ediciones de Cultura Hispánica, 1991.

Sacks, Oliver. *An Anthropologist on Mars*. New York: Knopf, 1995.

Said, Edward W. *Orientalism*. New York: Pantheon, 1978.

———. *Representations of the Intellectual*. New York: Vintage, 1996.

Sartre, Jean-Paul. *Situations*. Trans. Benita Eisler. New York: G. Braziller, 1965.

Schulman, Aline. "El nómada narrador en la obra de Juan Goytisolo." *Escritos sobre Juan Goytisolo*. Almería, Spain: Instituto de Estudios Almerienses, 1988. 45–58.

Sedgwick, Eve Kosofsky. "Nationalisms and Sexualities in the Age of Wilde." *Nationalisms and Sexualities*. Ed. Andrew Parker, Mary Russo, Doris Sommer, and Patricia Yaeger. New York: Routledge, 1992. 235–45.

Semprún, Jorge. *Adieu, vive clarté...* Paris: Gallimard, 1998.

———. *Autobiografía de Federico Sánchez*. Barcelona: Planeta, 1977.

———. *L'écriture ou la vie*. Paris: Gallimard, 1994.

———. *L'Évanouissement*. Paris: Gallimard, 1967.

———. *Federico Sánchez se despide de* ustedes. Barcelona: Tusquests, 1993.

———. *Le grand voyage*. Paris: Gallimard, 1963.

———. *Literature or Life*. Trans. Linda Coverdale. New York: Viking, 1997. Trans. of *L'écriture ou la vie*. Paris. 1994.

———. *La montagne blanche*. Paris: Gallimard, 1986.

———. *Netchaïev est de retour...* Paris: J. C. Lattès, 1987.

———. *Quel beau dimanche*. Paris: B. Grasset, 1980.

———, with Miguel Riera. "Al filo de la escritura. Entrevista con Jorge Semprún." *Quimera* 88 (January 1989): 20–27.

Silverman, Kaja. *Male Subjectivity at the Margins*. New York: Routledge, 1992.

Six, Abigail Lee. "Juan Goytisolo's Portable *Patria:* Staying on Home Ground Abroad." *Renaissance and Modern Studies* 34 (1991): 78–96.

Smith, Paul Julian. "Juan Goytisolo and Jean Baudrillard: The Mirror of Production and the Death of Symbolic Exchange." *Revista de Estudios Hispánicos* 23.2 (1989): 37–61.

Smith, Robert. *Derrida and Autobiography*. Cambridge: Cambridge University Press, 1995.

Smith, Sidonie. "The [Female] Subject in Critical Venues: Poetics, Politics, Autobiographical Practices." *a/b: Auto/Biography Studies* 6.1 (1991): 109–30.

———. *A Poetics of Women's Autobiography: Marginality and the Fiction of Self-Representation*. Bloomington: Indiana University Press, 1987.

———. *Subjectivity, Identity, and the Body: Women's Autobiographical Practices in the Twentieth Century*. Bloomington: Indiana University Press, 1993.

Sommer, Doris. "Not Just a Personal Story: Women's *Testimonios* and the Plural Self." *Life/Lines: Theorizing Women's Autobiography*. Ed. Bella Brodzki and Celeste Schenck. Ithaca, N.Y.: Cornell University Press, 1988. 107–130.

Soria Olmedo, Andrés. "Vida y razones de Jorge Semprún," *Boletín de la Unidad de Estudios Biográficos* 1 (January 1996): 69–76.

Spivak, Gayatri Chakravorty. "Can the Subaltern Speak?" *Marxism and the Interpretation of Culture*. Ed. Cary Nelson and Lawrence Grossberg. Urbana: University of Illinois Press, 1988. 271–313.

Sprinker, Michael. "Fictions of the Self: The End of Autobiography." *Autobiography: Essays Theoretical and Critical*. Ed. James Olney. Princeton, N.J.: Princeton University Press, 1980. 321–42.

Stamelman, Richard. "The Writing of Catastrophe: Jewish Memory and the Poetics of the Book in Edmond Jabès." *Auschwitz and After:*

Race, Culture, and "the Jewish Question" in France. Ed. Lawrence D. Kritzman. New York: Routledge, 1995. 264–79.

Staten, Henry. *Eros in Mourning: Homer to Lacan*. Baltimore, Md.: Johns Hopkins University Press, 1995.

Styron, William. *Darkness Visible: A Memoir of Madness*. New York: Vintage, 1992.

Suleiman, Susan Rubin. "War Memories: On Autobiographical Reading." *Auschwitz and After: Race, Culture, and "the Jewish Question" in France*. Ed. Lawrence D. Kritzman. New York: Routledge, 1995. 47–62.

Suleri, Sara. "Criticism and Its Alterity." *Borders, Boundaries, and Frames: Essays in Cultural Criticism and Cultural Studies*. Ed. Mae G. Henderson. New York: Routledge, 1995. 171–82.

———. *The Rhetoric of English India*. Chicago: Chicago University Press, 1992.

Taylor, Charles. *The Ethics of Authenticity*. Cambridge, Mass.: Harvard University Press, 1992.

Todorov, Tzvetan. *Facing the Extreme: Moral Life in the Concentration Camps*. Trans. Arthur Denner and Abigail Pollak. New York: Metropolitan Books, 1996.

Torres Nebrera, Gregorio. "La obra literaria de María Teresa León (cuentos y teatro)." *Anuario de Estudios Filológicos* 7 (1984): 361–84.

———. *La obra literaria de María Teresa León: autobiografía, biografía, novelas*. Cáceres: Universidad de Extremadura, 1987.

Trilling, Lionel. *Sincerity and Authenticity*. Cambridge, Mass.: Harvard University Press, 1972.

Ugarte, Michael. *Shifting Ground: Spanish Civil War Exile Literature*. Durham: Duke University Press, 1989.

Vidal-Naquet, Pierre. "The Holocaust's Challenge to History." *Auschwitz and After: Race, Culture, and "the Jewish Question" in France*. Ed. Lawrence D. Kritzman. New York: Routledge, 1995. 25–34.

Villanueva, Darío. "Realidad y ficción: la paradoja de la autobiografía." *Escritura autobiográfica: actas del II Seminario Internacional del Instituto de Semiótica Literaria y Textual.* Ed. José Romera et al. Madrid: Visor, 1993. 15–31.

White, Edmund. *Genet: A Biography.* New York: Knopf, 1993.

White, Hayden. "Historical Emplotment and the Problem of Truth." *Probing the Limits of Representation: Nazism and the "Final Solution."* Ed. Saul Friedlander. Cambridge, Mass.: Harvard University Press, 1992. 37–53.

————. "The Politics of Historical Interpretation: Discipline and De-Sublimation." *The Content of the Form: Narrative Discourse and Historical Representation.* Baltimore, Md.: Johns Hopkins University Press, 1987. 58–82.

Wiesel, Elie. *All Rivers Run to the Sea.* New York: Knopf, 1995.

Wittgenstein, Ludwig. *Tractatus Logico-Philosophicus.* Trans. D. F. Pears and B. F. McGuinness. London: Routledge & Kegan Paul, 1963.

Zambrano, María. *La confesión: género literario.* First book publication, 1943. Barcelona: Mondadori, 1988. Originally published in *Luminar* (Mexico) 5.3 (1941): 292–323; 6.1 (1943): 20–51.

————. *Delirio y destino (Los veinte años de una española).* Madrid: Mondadori, 1989.

————. "El exiliado." *Los bienaventurados.* Madrid: Siruela, 1990. 29–44.

Zelaya Kolker, Marielena. *Testimonios americanos de los escritores españoles transterrados de 1939.* Madrid: Ediciones Cultura Hispánica, Instituto de Cooperación Iberoamericana, 1985.

Žižek, Slavoj. *The Sublime Object of Ideology.* London: Verso, 1989.

INDEX

Born in Spain, Angel G. Loureiro is professor of Spanish at the University of Massachusetts–Amherst. He is the author of a book on Torrente Ballester and the editor of a collection of feminist studies of autobiography, both published in Spain.